THE KINGS OF ALBA, *c.*1000–*c.*1130

THE KINGS OF ALBA, *c*.1000–*c*.1130

Alasdair Ross

First published in Great Britain in 2011 by
John Donald, an imprint of Birlinn Ltd

West Newington House
10 Newington Road
Edinburgh
EH9 1QS

www.birlinn.co.uk

ISBN: 978 1 906566 15 9

The publishers gratefully acknowledge the support of The Strathmartine Trust
towards the publication of this book

British Library Cataloguing-in-Publication Data
A catalogue record for this book is available on request
from the British Library

Typeset by IDSUK (DataConnection) Ltd
Printed and bound in Britain by Bell and Bain Ltd, Glasgow

Contents

Tables

Acknowledgements

This book is the product of many fruitful discussions amongst my peers and it will be immediately obvious that I owe a great many debts to a great many people. Thanks are also due to my colleagues at Stirling who read the book in draft format and I owe a number of suggestions to their insights, even though they continue to profess dismay about my peculiar obsession (their words) with units of land assessment. Any mistakes that remain are mine alone.

Thanks are also due to the Strathmartine Trust whose financial support paid for the illustrations in this book.

Finally, thanks are also due to my extended family: Moira and Alastair, Fiona and Roisin, and Doris and Heinrich. The latter two always offer a pleasant escape and Altbier in Düsseldorf and they never complain that I always seem to appear on their doorstep accompanied by a portable computer (and their daughter). Lastly, special thanks and love to Sonja.

Abbreviations

Aberdeen-Banff Illustrations [*A.B. Ill.*]	*Illustrations of the Topography and Antiquities of the Shires of Aberdeen and Banff* (Spalding Club, 1847–69)
Anderson, *Early Sources* [*ES*]	*Early Sources of Scottish History 500–1286*, ed. A. O. Anderson (Edinburgh, 1922)
Anderson, *Scottish Annals* [*SAEC*]	*Scottish Annals from English Chroniclers 500–1286*, ed. A. O. Anderson (London, 1908)
Ann. Ulster	*The Annals of Ulster* (To AD 1131), eds S. Mac Airt and G. Mac Niocaill (Dublin, 1983)
Ann. Tig.	*The Annals of Tigernach*, ed. Whitley Stokes (Llanerch, reprint 1993)
Barrow, *Chrs. David I*	G. W. S. Barrow, *The Charters of King David I: The Written Acts of David I King of Scots, 1124–53 and of his Son Henry Earl of Northumberland* (Woodbridge, 1999)
Buchanan, *History*	G. Buchanan, *The History of Scotland*, translated J. Aikman (Glasgow and Edinburgh, 1827–9)
Chron. Bower (Watt)	Walter Bower, *Scotichronicon*, gen. ed. D. E. R. Watt (Aberdeen, 1993–8)
Chron. Fordun	Johannis de Fordun, *Chronica Gentis Scotorum*, ed. W. F. Skene (Edinburgh, 1871–2)
Chron. Melrose	*The Chronicle of Melrose (Facsimile Edition)*, eds A. O. Anderson and others (London, 1936)

Chron. Wyntoun	The Original Chronicle of Andrew of Wyntoun (STS, 1903–14)
Dalrymple, Historie	The Historie of Scotland, wrytten first in Latin by the most reverend and worthy Jhone Leslie, Bishop of Rosse, and translated in Scottish by Father James Dalrymple 1596 (STS, 1888–95)
Dunfermline Registrum [Dunf. Reg.]	Registrum de Dunfermelyn (Bannatyne Club, 1842)
Cowan and Easson, Religious Houses [MRHS]	Ian B. Cowan and D. E. Easson, Medieval Religious Houses Scotland, 2nd edn (London, 1976)
Innes Review [IR]	The Innes Review (1950–)
Inverness Gaelic Trans. [TGSI]	Transactions of the Gaelic Society of Inverness (1871–)
Lawrie, Charters [ESC]	Early Scottish Charters prior to 1153, ed. A. C. Lawrie (Glasgow, 1905)
Major, History	J. Major, A History of Greater Britain (SHS, 1892)
Moray Registrum [Moray Reg.]	Registrum Episcopatus Moraviensis (Bannatyne Club, 1837)
NAS	National Archives of Scotland, Edinburgh
NLS	National Library of Scotland, Edinburgh
Proc. Soc. Antiq. Scot. [PSAS]	Proceedings of the Society of Antiquaries of Scotland (1851–)
Regesta Regum Scottorum [RRS]	Regesta Regum Scottorum, eds G. W. S. Barrow and others (Edinburgh, 1960–)
Scot. Gaelic Stud. [SGS]	Scottish Gaelic Studies (1926–)
Scot. Hist. Rev. [SHR]	The Scottish Historical Review (1903–28, 1947–)
Scot. Stud.	Scottish Studies (1957–)
SHS Misc.	The Miscellany of the Scottish History Society (SHS, 1893–)
Theiner, Monumenta [Vet. Mon.]	Vetera Monumenta Hibernorum et Scotorum Historiam Illustrantia, ed. A. Theiner (Rome, 1864)

Watson, *CPNS*   W. J. Watson, *The History of the Celtic Placenames of Scotland* (Edinburgh, 1926).

I have wherever possible followed the guidelines as supplied for Scottish sources in the 'List of Abbreviated Titles of the Printed Sources of Scottish History to 1560', supplement to the *Scottish Historical Review*, October 1963.

In accordance with current historical practice the names of the kings of Scotia before the reign of King David I (1124–1153) have been Gaelicised.

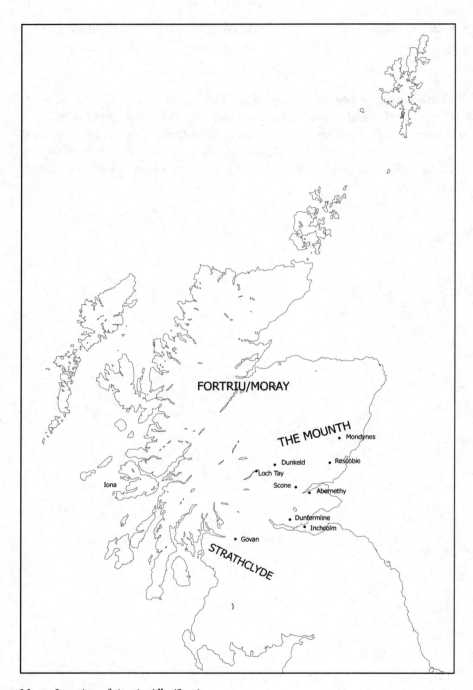

FORTRIU/MORAY

THE MOUNTH

• Mondynes

• Dunkeld

• Rescobie

•Loch Tay

Scone •

• Abernethy

Iona

• Dunfermline

• Inchcolm

• Govan

STRATHCLYDE

Map 1. Location of sites in Alba/Scotia

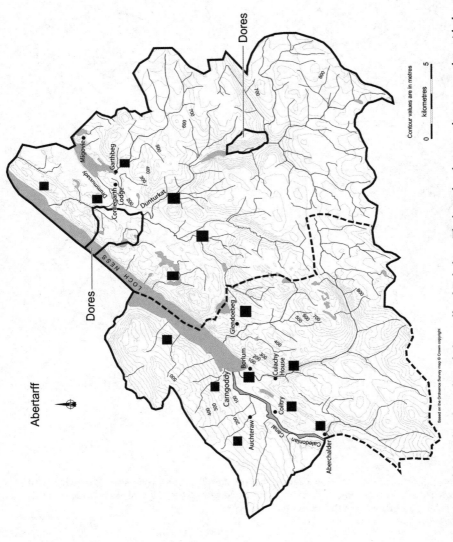

Map 2. A reconstruction of the medieval parishes of Abertarff and Boleskine. The boundary between the two, together with the conjectural S-W boundary of Abertarff, is represented by the hashed lines. Black squares indicate davochs and on this map we can see two detached portions of two different davochs belonging to the parish of Dores.

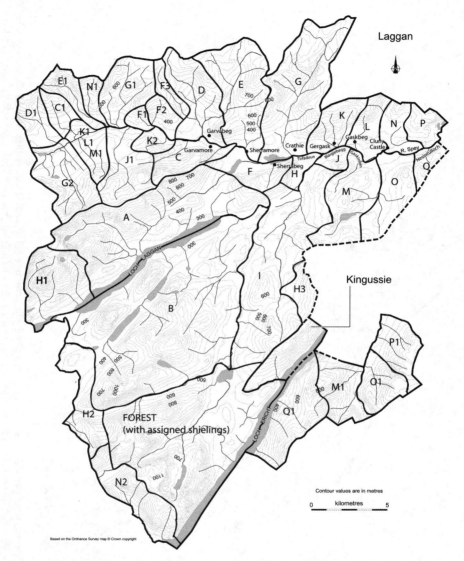

Map 3. The medieval parish of Laggan, with its davochs listed from A to Q, together with detached portions of some of those davochs, listed from C1 to Q1. Only two davochs in this parish (A and B) were of the 'self-contained' type.

Kirkmichael

Map 4. The medieval parish of Kirkmichael with its eight 'scattered' davochs (A to H) and one 'self-contained' unit (I).

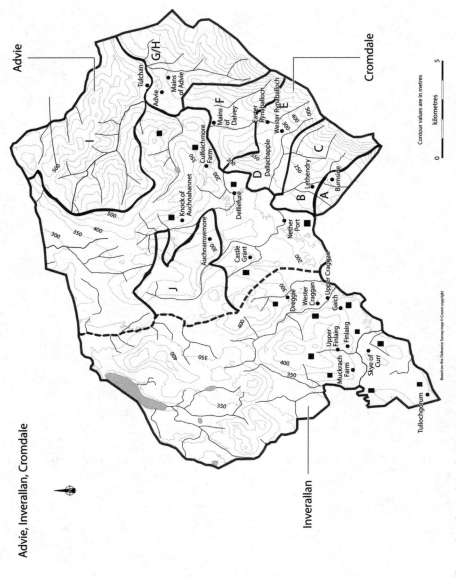

Advie, Inverallan, Cromdale

Advie

Cromdale

Inverallan

Tulchan
Advie
Mains of Advie
G/H
Mains of Dalvey
F
Easter Rynaballoch
Wester Rynaballoch
E
Culfoichmore Farm
Dallachapple
D
C
Lethendry
Burnside
A
B
Knock of Auchnahannet
Delliefure
Nether Port
Auchnarrowmore
Castle Grant
Upper Craggan
Dreggie
Wester Craggan
Gaich
Upper Finlairg
Finlairg
Muckrach Farm
Skye of Curr
Tullochgorum

300
350
400
500
500
600
350
350
400
400
400
200
250
350
300
350
250
300
550
550
350
400
500
500
600

Contour values are in metres

0   kilometres   5

Based on the Ordnance Survey map © Crown copyright

Map 5. The medieval parishes of Cromdale, Advie and Inverallan. The thanage and parish of Cromdale comprised six davochs (A to F) and the boundary between Advie and Inverallan is represented by the dashed line.

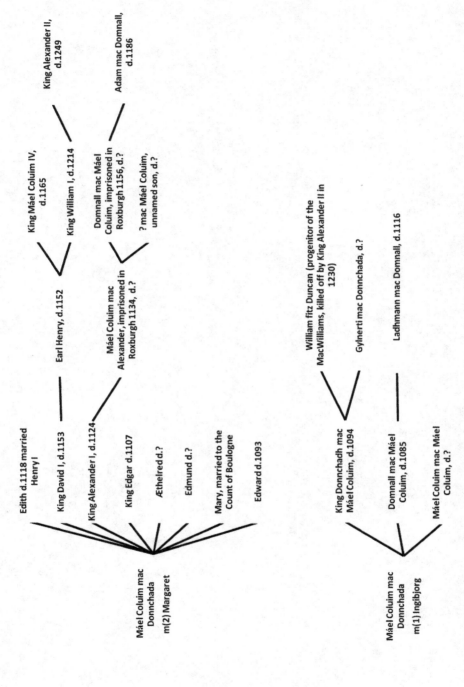

The offspring of the two marriages made by King Máel Coluim mac Donnchada to Ingibjorg and Margaret

Introduction

The period c.1000 to the 1120s may be one of the most crucial and one of the most interesting in 'Scottish' history yet it is also the least known about and researched. This is not the fault of historians but rather due to the paucity of the written sources that have been bequeathed to us in relation to the kingdom that emerged to dominate north Britain, known as *Alba* in Gaelic sources, *Scotia* in Latin. To place this paucity in context, historians of medieval Scotland only have a handful of fully authenticated charters that survive for the pre-1124 period and not all of these pertain to lands north of the River Tweed.[1] In comparison, historians who work in the field of medieval English history have over 1000 charters surviving for the pre-1066 period.[2] Yet the 'Scottish' material that does survive tells us enough to be able to make informed guesses about many of the political developments that occurred in north Britain during this c.120-year period and they shed some light on the shadowy personal relationships between many of the main actors in the political and cultural dramas that eventually led to the emergence of the medieval kingdom of the Scots.

Indeed, on one level it seems quite remarkable that a seemingly unified and unitary kingdom of the Scots emerged at all out of the four or five smaller kingdoms that once occupied north Britain before c.1100, and it should never be assumed that this was an inevitable outcome – just look at what happened in and to medieval Ireland and Wales. If trying to understand the processes that led to the emergence of the kingdom of the Scots was not complicated enough, it is equally difficult for a historian of medieval Scotland to pick a date and say, 'this is when the kingdom of the Scots emerged', or at least a version of Scotia acceptable to all living in that

---

1   Lawrie, *Charters* [*ESC*]; A. A. M. Duncan, 'Yes, the earliest Scottish charters', *SHR*, 78:1 (April, 1999), 1–38.
2   http://www.trin.cam.ac.uk/chartwww/eSawyer.99/eSawyer2.html Accessed 10 January 2010.

part of north Britain. This book will refer to this kingdom as 'Alba' until the time of the 1090s. After that time some of the earliest surviving charters indicate that the rulers of this emerging kingdom in north Britain regarded themselves as *Rex Scottorum*, even though this may just have been an intellectual concept that only existed in the minds of the upper tiers of society and government: one king reigning over a unified people who possessed a common identity. Unfortunately, there is still not a clear answer to the question of when the various peoples of seemingly different ethnic backgrounds that lived in north Britain decided that they actually were all 'Scots' and could happily live together ever after.

Was it, for example, following March 1058 when King Lulach mac Gilla Comgáin was killed by Máel Coluim mac Donnchada; or following 1130 when Oengus of Moray was killed at Stracathro; or was it the 1170s when the different 'peoples addresses' disappear from royal Scottish charters;[3] or following 1230 when the last representative of the MacWilliam claimants of the throne was brutally murdered in Forfar; or after 1266 when the Treaty of Perth was agreed? It could just as easily have been after the 1315 Statute of Cambuskenneth, which redefined what it meant to be a land-holding Scot, or the wars of independence that fully shaped the identity of the medieval kingdom and the peoples who lived in it, the latter providing 'Scots' with engagement in prolonged conflict against a common enemy? Or is it just too uncomfortable for modern post-Braveheart Scots to accept King Edward I as the midwife of a medieval Scottish 'nation'? Yet these are all secular political events. It could just as easily have been *Cum universi*, by which in 1189 the entire Scottish Church (except the see of Galloway) evaded the claims of primacy made by Canterbury and York, that laid the foundations of a medieval Scottish 'nation'. In fact, the role of the Church in shaping a medieval nation of 'Scots' is probably greater than the contribution made by King Robert I.

We cannot, however, just talk about the political or ecclesiastic events that resulted in the merging of kingdoms to form the kingdom of the Scots, since that process might also have have entailed the combining of four or five different law codes, methods of taxation, cultures, trading mechanisms, and languages. There are additional conundrums: if the kingdom of the Picts covered a greater territory than any other kingdom in

---

3 Kenji Nishioka, 'Scots and Galwegians in the "peoples address" of Scottish royal charters', *SHR*, 87, 2008, 206–32. Nishioka preferred 'peoples address' over 'racial address' because the latter has strong biological overtones.

north Britain before *c.*900 why did their P-Celtic language fail to become the language of government? Equally, since Pictish failed to become the language of government, why did a Pictish system of land assessment and local taxation (the davoch) survive in use and across over 50 per cent of modern-day Scotland, and still appear in estate rentals as late as the 1930s? What were the processes by which we think Gaelic emerged as the dominant cultural language in north Britain given that the kingdom of Dál Riata virtually disappears from the primary sources in the late eighth century? Finally, when and why did people living in Strathclyde in the 1060s stop speaking a P-Celtic language likely to have been Cumbric, lose their 'Welsh' or 'British' identity, and become Scots?

But perhaps one of the most crucial political questions associated with this period is: when did the various peoples living in north Britain accept that the kingship of Alba should shift from being shared by the royal sub-branches within Clann Custantín meic Cináeda, and become the sole property of one sub-branch of that kindred, within which kingship was decided by primogeniture? Was there a dynastic key to this shift in policy or was it just fate that the other sub-branches of Clann Custantín meic Cináeda could not produce a suitably mature candidate for inauguration at those times when the kingship became vacant? How often can historians use the excuse 'a lack of suitably mature candidates' before the long-term inability of a royal segment to achieve inauguration suggests something more sinister?

This book is not going to answer all of these questions – there are just too many extensive gaps in our evidence base. The first chapter will lay the groundwork for the remainder of the book by describing the environment and other related factors in the period of 130 years or so after 1000, which will be followed by a section on historical geography. While our historical records range from non-existent to awful for this period, landscape studies in combination with palynology and the use of proxy-climate data represent other means of obtaining information through evaluating topics like land assessment and taxation, and looking at pollen records to determine what people were growing on the land even if we cannot yet tell who those people were and exactly when the various medieval agricultural revolutions reached Scotia. Within both this and the following chapter there are fairly extensive literature reviews. These have been deliberately included to demonstrate how currently popular historical theories, particularly those in relation to land assessment and Moray, have developed across time, and are useful exercises for highlighting flaws in those theories.

The second chapter will define Alba to the best of our current knowledge and this will provide a starting point for Chapter 3 that concentrates upon the expansion of Alba/Scotia between *c*.1000 and 1130. This third chapter also attempts to assess the scale of the new resources, both natural and human, that would have become available to the kings of Alba as their overlordship expanded across north Britain, and pays particular attention to the absorption of Moray and Strathclyde into Alba.

The following three chapters then chart the gradual domination of the kingship of Alba by just one branch of the royal kindred of Clann Custantín meic Cináeda, those fortunate enough to be descended from the second marriage of King Máel Coluim mac Donnchada to Queen Margaret. Other key themes examined in these chapters include the Church and foreign policy, both of which played a key part in the emergence of the twelfth-century kingdom of Scotia. This emergence, however, was not a quick or easy process and the question of the succession and its domination by just one branch of the royal kindred was not satisfactorily resolved until 1230 during the reign of King Alexander II.

CHAPTER ONE

The Rising Sun: Environment and Landscape, c.1000–c.1130

Because of concerns about global warming, sustainability, and other environmental issues modern-day Scots are being forced to engage with a lively energy debate. Can we, for example, afford to continue utilising nuclear power or should we be moving more quickly towards renewables, in the forms of onshore and offshore wind turbines and the development of machinery that can harness tidal power? How do we (or can we) balance the disposal of nuclear waste against the fundamental alterations of land use and landscape appreciation that wind turbines force? Can renewables alone supply enough power for future generations or will we be ultimately forced to build a new generation of nuclear plants?

A thousand years ago sourcing the energy requirements to survive must have seemed more straightforward, but life would have been infinitely more brutal if the main source of that power ever faltered. Like other medieval populations across Europe and elsewhere, the various peoples living in north Britain were wholly reliant upon solar energy and water power for their livelihoods and upon wood and (increasingly) peat for fuel. Unlike today's society, however, our ancestors could not flick a switch to access power, so reliance upon the sun to ripen crops would have been much more crucial to the continued well-being of all communities from year to year. Whereas we could fly in food supplies for British supermarkets around the ash trail generated by the Icelandic volcanic eruption in spring 2010, historically such events in the northern hemisphere have frequently had quite devastating consequences for pre-industrial communities across Scotland that were dependent upon the sun, often resulting in widespread crop failure, a lowering of mean temperatures, a reduction in the length of the growing season, acid rains that killed crops, starvation, and ultimately death.[1]

1 Alastair Dawson, *So Foul and Fair a Day* (Glasgow, 2009), 74, 94–95 [hereafter: Dawson, *Foul and Fair*].

Assessing the environment and economy of north Britain

Unfortunately, we have no contemporary historic climate data for north Britain between 1000 and 1130, but entries in the Irish Gaelic Annals for the same period provide a good indication of the wide range of hardships suffered by communities bordering the Atlantic Ocean. In these records are found extremes of climate, plagues, and livestock diseases (see Table 1.1).

Table 1.1 **Entries in the Irish Gaelic Annals for the period between 1000 and 1130 indicate the wide range of hardships suffered by communities bordering the Atlantic Ocean.**

1008	Severe frosts and snow from 8 January to 28 March
1012	An affliction of colic in Ard Macha and a great number died from it
1037	Very wet stormy weather this year
1047	A great snowfall this year from 8 December to 17 March the like of which was never experienced before, and it caused the death of many people and cattle and sea-birds and beasts
1052	A violent wind arose on 21 December and it broke down houses and woods
1057	A murrain of cattle and pigs
1077	In the above year *sinech* (cow pox?) viz. Many lumps afflicted the cattle vastly and even human beings used to contract them; A violent wind in the autumn of the above year and it greatly damaged the corn-crop.
1092	Very heavy frost, and snow, at the end of this and the beginning of the following year.
1093	A violent wind in the above year which sundered the grain from the corn and blew down numerous trees; A great pestilence i.e. a febrile in the above year which caused death to a large number of people
1094	Extremely bad weather throughout Ireland which gave rise to want
1095	Great snow fell after the first of January and killed men and birds and beasts; A great sickness in Ireland that killed many people, from the first of August until the following May
1099	A great epidemic throughout all Ireland

1105	Heavy snow this year and a great loss of cows, sheep, and pigs
1107	Much wet and bad weather this year, and it ruined the corn
1109	Heavy rain and bad weather in the summer and autumn
1111	Very bad weather in the form of frost and snow, and it inflicted slaughter on domestic and wild beasts
1113	And a great mortality in this year
1115	Extremely bad weather in the form of frost and snow from 28 December to 15 February, or a little longer, and it inflicted slaughter on birds and beasts and men, and from this great want arose throughout all Ireland, and particularly in Laigin
1121	A great wind came on 5 December . . . and wrought great destruction on woods throughout all Ireland
1129	A hot summer this year and the waters of Ireland dried up, and there was a great mortality of beasts and cattle.[2]

Given the prevailing weather patterns and regular contact between Ireland and the British mainland, some of the extreme weather events and plagues listed above may also have affected north Britain. A little closer to Scotland, the chronicler Walter Bower recorded an earthquake that rocked all of England on 11 August 1089 and this event was subsequently linked to a scarcity of produce. That same year, on 17 October, he recorded a gale in London that destroyed 600 houses. In England, between 1093 and 1095, he also recorded great floods and frozen rivers that resulted in the destruction of bridges, followed by a complete failure of agriculture, famine, and rapid loss of life.[3] The extent to which these climatic events might have affected Alba is currently unknown so it is difficult to prove that they could have been a factor in the convoluted political intrigues that followed the death of King Máel Coluim mac Donnchada in 1093.

Growing awareness about historical north Atlantic weather patterns and information gained from proxy environmental data can also be used to supplement the kind of information that is derived from annals and chronicles. Greenland ice core data (GISP2) has been used to reconstruct relative changes in both air (the oxygen isotope record) and sea surface temperature across the north Atlantic. For example, the sea salt concentrations in

---

2 *Ann. Ulster*, 1008.4, 1012.1, 1037.7, 1047.1, 1094.8, 1095.1, 1095.8, 1099.1, 1107.6, 1111.1, 1115.1, 1118.7, 1121.9; S. Mac Airt (ed.), *The Annals of Inisfallen (MS. Rawlinson B. 503)* (Dublin, 1988), 1052.4, 1057.6, 1077.6, 1077.7, 1092.11, 1093.9, 1093.10, 1105.2, 1109.3, 1113.10, 1129.9.

3 *Chron. Bower* (Watt), iv, 89.

the ice derive principally from north Atlantic sea salt that has been uplifted in moisture and transported to Greenland before being deposited in snowfall. Accordingly, temporal variations in sea salt concentrations in the ice represent a proxy record for past changes in north Atlantic storminess: essentially, increased storminess leads to more salt being deposited on the ice sheets. Plotted graphically, this data shows that while the 1090s, for example, were a period of increased storminess, in general there was a downward trend in north Atlantic storms until 1425 when the North Atlantic Oscillation dramatically changed and this latter date is a marker for the onset of the so-called 'Little Ice Age'. Quantities of sea ice in the north Atlantic can also affect the climate and ecology of other areas because increased ice formation inhibits the evaporation of moisture and is often associated with the development of areas of sustained high pressure between Greenland and Scandinavia. It has been argued, for instance, that increased sea ice between AD 975 and AD 1040 at GISP2 and the associated high pressure later resulted in increased ground disturbance (more agriculture) with an associated decrease in grasses and the organic content of soils in the Faroe Islands.[4]

We must also not forget that the seeming blandness of the chronicle entries could conceal some real horror stories. The entry for 1105, for example, is probably related to the Plinian eruption of Hekla on Iceland in 1104; a similar eruption in 1693 resulted in sulphurous fogs appearing across Scotland that withered crops. Just as the Greenland ice cores preserve a sulphate peak record of the eruption of Mount Vesuvius in AD 87 so traces of ash deposits from many Icelandic eruptions are preserved in Scottish peat bogs.[5] On a slightly different tack, the chronicle entry under 1111 seems to indicate a heavy mortality among domestic beasts. If, for the sake of argument, this included horses and oxen, how did that year's ploughing impact on other activities if it took ten fit men to undertake the same amount of labour as one ox? To this catalogue of disasters can be added non-contemporary snippets of information that do directly relate to

---

4 A. G. Dawson, K. Hickey, P. A. Mayewski and A. Nesje, 'Greenland (GISP2) ice core and historical indicators of complex North Atlantic climate changes during the fourteenth century', *The Holocene*, 17, 2007, 427–34; Andrew J. Dugmore, Douglas M. Borthwick, Mike J. Church, Alastair Dawson, Kevin J. Edwards, Christian Keller, Paul Mayewski, Thomas H. McGovern, Kerry-Anne Mairs, and Guðrún Sveinbjarnardóttir, 'The role of climate in settlement and landscape change in the north Atlantic islands: an assessment of cumulative deviations in high-resolution proxy climate records', *Human Ecology*, 35, 2007, 169–78.

5 Dawson, *Foul and Fair*, 74.

Alba. For example, under the year date 1099 the fifteenth-century chronicler Walter Bower noted that on 3 November of that year the sea invaded the Scottish shore, drowning many villages, people, and innumerable oxen and sheep.[6] This description might relate to a tsunami that also affected both England and the Netherlands, but with what particular event it is connected and where Bower sourced this information is unknown. Historically, other such similar events are known to have previously impacted upon north Britain.[7]

However, gloomy information of the type found in chronicles should not affect too greatly the fact that the time-frame under discussion in this book sits within a period of general climatic upturn across northern Europe, commonly known as the Medieval Warm Epoch (MWE), which ran from approximately 950 to 1250. Of course, as detailed in the above table of material extracted from the Irish Gaelic Annals, the MWE was more complex than its name would suggest and there were clearly blips in the overall trend. Nevertheless, across northern Europe the MWE allowed for the colonisation of Iceland and Greenland and a massive expansion in arable on the British mainland with ever higher lands being brought into cultivation and the intensification of cereal production. Surviving traces of this arable expansion are probably found across the Lammermuir Hills and elsewhere in southern Scotland, up to around 450m, and these remains are often held up as a prime example of the agricultural expansion during the MWE, even if all of this rig cannot yet be dated accurately.[8] In contrast, however, palaeoenvironmental work in Glen Affric has also produced some interesting results at two sites, perhaps demonstrating that agricultural expansion during the MWE was not uniform. At Camban the pollen record demonstrates a re-establishment of woods and grassland with reduced grazing during the Pictish period at AD 700 until cultivation and

6 *Chron. Bower* (Watt), iii, 101.

7 A. G. Dawson, D. Long, D. E. Smith, 'The Storegga Slides: evidence from eastern Scotland for a possible tsunami', *Marine Geology*, 82, 1988, 271–76; Stein Bondevik, John Inge Svendsen, and Jan Mangerud, 'Distinction between the Storegga tsunami and the holocene marine transgression in coastal basin deposits of western Norway', *Journal of Quaternary Science*, 13:6, 1998, 529–37; Alastair G. Dawson, Sue Dawson, and Stein Bondevik, 'A late holocene tsunami at Basta Voe, Yell, Shetland Isles', *Scottish Geographical Journal*, 122:2, 2006, 100–8.

8 S. Carter, R. Tipping, D. Davidson, D. Lang, and A. Tyler, 'A multiproxy approach to the function of postmedieval ridge-and-furrow cultivation in upland north Britain', *The Holocene*, 7, 1997, 447–56; Richard Tipping, 'Climatic variability and "marginal" settlement in upland British landscapes: a re-evaluation', *Landscapes*, 3(2), 2002, 10–29.

grazing resumed once again *c.*1300. What the science cannot tell us in this instance, however, is whether this was a complete agricultural and human abandonment of the site or the deliberate establishment, protection, and management of a woodland resource by excluding agriculture and live-stock. At another site in the glen, Carnach Mor, the pollen record instead indicates increased cultivation between AD 350 and AD 800, with a new phase of agricultural expansion occurring in the mid-fourteenth century.[9]

In general, though, it is thought that one of the more important impacts of the MWE was that it would have allowed an expansion of the biomass produced each year, making it easier to ensure that livestock accu-mulated fat reserves, and consequently making it less difficult to feed and retain livestock during the winter months. What we do not yet know is where the extra labour came from to underpin and sustain this agricultural expansion. It may just be that it forced up the wages of agricultural labourers, but it is noticeable that some eleventh-century English sources complain about the numbers of English men and women who had been enslaved by Scottish raiders led by King Máel Coluim mac Donnchada (1058–1093) and taken northwards.[10] These unfortunates may well have formed the labour pool that was required to sustain the rate of agricultural expansion across north Britain during the eleventh century. If they did form an unpaid workforce in Alba, this would have contrasted against what was happening in England where, according to Dyer, slavery had virtually died out by 1100.[11]

The massive expansion in arable after 1000 was aided by technological advances in farming like the introduction of the mould board plough. This device alone brought three further benefits: it stifled weeds because they were buried under a turned sod, it enabled the ploughing of heavier soils, and it ploughed deeper into the soil, so releasing more nutrients into the agricultural system. An equally important invention at this time was the development of a collar that enabled horses to pull heavy equipment without choking themselves. For example, it is known that horses gradu-ally replaced oxen in northern France *c.*1000 and their use in Flanders for this purpose was widespread by 1100, yet we have no idea when this

---

9 Althea Davies, 'Upland agriculture and environmental risk: a new model of upland land-use based on high spatial-resolution palynological data from West Affric, NW Scotland', *The Journal of Archaeological Science*, 34, 2007, 2053–63.

10 *SAEC*, 92, and at 100.

11 Christopher Dyer, *Making a Living in the Middle Ages* (London, 2002), 36.

innovation first appeared in north Britain and how quickly it may have spread.[12]

What is currently unquantifiable is the degree to which the climatic upturn in combination with these new technological developments for efficiently expanding arable production was the driver behind the expansion of Alba southwards into Northumberland and Strathclyde. A lot more palaeoenvironmental sampling is going to have to be completed before we can even begin to answer that crucial question though it is interesting to note that the palynological evidence from around both Yetholm Loch and the Cheviot plateau indicates a sharp and major restructuring of farming practices that involved greater amounts of land being turned over to arable c.1100 and perhaps specialisation in winter-grown cereals. This restructuring also involved the introduction of a new crop in that sampling area, *Cannabis sativa* (hemp).[13]

Yet, despite such research, and in contrast to many other European countries, next to nothing is known about the rural economy of Alba before c.1100, what crops people grew in the fields, how much surplus was produced, which animals were nurtured, and the extent to which Alba was plugged into a European trading network. While archaeology and palaeoecology can sometimes indicate which animals were slaughtered and eaten or which types of crop were cultivated, this information tends to be site-specific, making it difficult to build up a complete picture and leaving a set of (probably) unanswerable questions. For example, Alba was clearly a Christian country during the eleventh century yet we have no idea of the quantities in which wine was imported, we do not know where it was imported from, and we do not know how it was paid for.

Equally, we have little idea about the quantities in which industrial crops like hemp or flax were grown or even the extent to which legumes were cropped, the latter being a tremendously valuable crop both for human consumption and for nitrogen fixing. Yet another interesting question is whether land was set aside for orchards and the growing of fruits like apples, plums and cherries. Nor do we know which plants, if any, were grown on an industrial scale to produce dyes or whether dyes were just

12 Georges Comet, 'Technology and Agricultural Expansion in the Middle Ages: the Example of France north of the Loire', in Greville Astill and John Langdon (eds), *Medieval Farming and Technology: the Impact of Agricultural Change in Northwest Europe* (Leiden, 1997),12–39, at 21.

13 Richard Tipping, *Bowmont: An Environmental History of the Bowmont Valley and the Northern Cheviot Hills, 10000 BC–AD 2000* (Malta, 2010), 192–94 [hereafter: Tipping, *Bowmont Valley*].

imported into north Britain from elsewhere. An equally important question concerns exports: had Alba achieved a level of agricultural self-sufficiency or were surpluses generated in both crops and animal products?

There is, however, little doubt that there must have already been an infrastructure capable of processing all the grain harvested from the massive expansion in arable lands and it is possible that tide mills played an important role in this process. Little is know about the remains of these constructions in a Scottish context and, according to Shaw, our earliest written record relating to them dates to 1526.[14] In a wider context it was thought they were a technological advance of the eleventh and twelfth centuries, even though there are also references to them in the tenth century in Iraq and a possible reference to one in an Anglo-Saxon charter dated to 949.[15] However, excavations in Ireland have now demonstrated that both horizontal and vertical tide mills were certainly operating there during the seventh century AD. The earliest such site now discovered is at the monastic site at Nendrum on the east coast of Northern Ireland where dendrochronology has dated the timber revetting in the mill dam to 619–21.[16]

It would take special pleading to argue that it would have taken 900 years for tide mill technology to reach north Britain from Northern Ireland, particularly as both the Gaelic kingdom of Dál Riata and Christianity bridged the Irish Sea between Ireland and north Britain. Fortunately, recent archaeological investigations at the Pictish monastic site at Portmahomack found two stone-lined culverts and a dam and perhaps the traces of a wheel-house for a horizontal water mill (but no actual mill), datable to between the end of the seventh and the beginning of the eighth century, so this evidence surely now indicates that this type of technology was also available at a reasonably early date in north Britain.[17]

All of which implies that in north Britain by 1000 there must have been some degree of agricultural organisation across the landscape even if those patterns would now seem alien to modern Scots. While we know there were already small towns during the eleventh century, some of which

---

14 John Shaw, *Water Power in Scotland, 1550–1870* (Edinburgh, 1984) 14.
15 Adam Lucas, *Wind, Water, Work: Ancient and Medieval Milling Technology* (Leiden, 2006), 89–90.
16 Ibid., 91.
17 Martin Carver, *Portmahomack: Monastery of the Picts* (Bodmin, 2008), 64, 118 [hereafter: Carver, *Portmahomack*].

would eventually become burghs,[18] most of the population would have lived in a rural landscape that had already been massively moulded and influenced by thousands of years of anthropogenic activity. For example, Mesolithic people first seem to have arrived in north Britain around 9,500 years ago and it appears they had an immediate effect upon the landscape and environment in terms of woodland clearance and burning.[19] Moving rapidly forward in time, while there may have been field systems in some areas of north Britain around AD 1000, these would not have formed a nice square or rectangular patchwork effect that is so familiar today. The latter is a product of agricultural improvements of the last 300 years or so. Instead, medieval rig systems would have been irregular in shape and likely formed open fields, interspersed by irregular areas in which humans could access other resources such as peat, fishings, meadows, grazings, and woodland (see Plate 1).

Within this rural landscape it is likely that vernacular structures were largely, if not wholly, built from wood and turf and this presents a problem for excavators as such structures are virtually indistinguishable in the archaeological record. It is also likely that these structures were earth-fast-post buildings because this architectural form was not superseded in Scotland until the thirteenth or fourteenth century when cruck-built structures are first thought to have appeared.[20] If the recent claim that the Balbridie-type Neolithic structures in north Britain were also built out of wood and turf is correct, this building tradition was already 5,000 years old by AD 1000 and must have been resource-intensive.[21]

It is another matter altogether to try and estimate the life-span of such structures and so quantify the amounts of raw materials and management systems required to maintain such buildings across time. Currently, the earliest surviving historical evidence relating to the vernacular building tradition in wood and turf in Scotland dates to the sixteenth century and pertains to cruck-built structures in the eastern Highlands. There, sixteen townships in one parish required an approximate 1.3km² managed

---

18 Derek Hall, personal communication.
19 T. C. Smout, Alan R. MacDonald and Fiona Watson, *A History of the Native Woodlands of Scotland, 1500–1920* (Trowbridge, 2005), 28.
20 Piers Dixon, 'The Medieval Peasant Building in Scotland: the Beginning and End of Crucks', in Jan Klápště (ed.), *The Rural House from the Migration Period to the Oldest Still Standing Buildings* (Prague, 2002), 187–200.
21 Roy Loveday, 'Where have all the Neolithic houses gone? Turf – an invisible component', *Scottish Archaeological Journal*, 28:2, 2006, 81–104.

reservoir of turf and 774,864 'trees' (probably coppiced trees) every seven years to maintain a total of 369 structures and an agricultural infrastructure. Thereafter, these components were recycled to create anthrosoils.[22] Of course, this data pertains to a different architectural style (crucks rather than earthfast posts) and is probably highly regionalised, but it gives a superb glimpse into the quantities of raw materials that were required to maintain just one small area of agricultural settlement across thirty-seven years in late medieval Scotland. It is probably safe to say that despite the large chronological gap in the evidence base, vernacular structures in the eleventh and twelfth centuries in north Britain would also have required access to large quantities of wood and turf for their maintenance on an annual basis.

In the Highlands of the sixteenth century such vast quantities of turf and timber would have required intensive management to sustain the two different resources and it is interesting to note that there are signs in the palynological record of tree management in the Bowmont valley in the Borders from a much earlier period. Tipping, in his new environmental history of that area, has argued that by the eighth century AD there are clear indications of forward planning and forest management in the pollen record because new single-generation forests appear that were sited on the land of least use to agriculturalists.[23] If this interpretation is correct, this is again indicative of a highly organised landscape at a relatively early date.

Landscape division and assessment

Understanding the organisation of the medieval landscape within the bounds of modern-day Scotland has exercised many historians and geographers since the nineteenth century. This topic is crucially important because understanding how such systems operated provides insights into the economic and human resources that a lord or king could command, including the available numbers of fighting men. Part of the problem in understanding this organisation of the landscape in north Britain is that each of the kingdoms that together eventually became the kingdom of the Scots possessed its own named units of land division. Later kings of Scots never attempted to standardise these different units, unlike the Carolingian emperors in Europe who, in order to achieve their goal of surveying and

22 NAS, Seafield Papers, GD248/13/6/9; GD248/13/6/10x.
23 Tipping, *Bowmont Valley*, 187.

controlling their new lands as their empire expanded, introduced a standardised system of land organisation called the *mansus* as a means of tax-levying and warrior-recruitment from *c*.AD 780.[24]

Scottish historical records list a wide number of different terms in relation to land division and assessment, depending on which part of the country is being researched. These include descriptors like merkland, unciate/ounceland, pennyland, husbandland, carucate, (Scottish) carucate/ploughgate, soum, oxgang, arachor, and davoch, and it is currently impossible to state with any conviction that these differently named units were created to perform similar functions in each individual kingdom, since many of these units have never been investigated in any detail. Nevertheless, since there is little doubt that some of the medieval kings of Scots also must have possessed the requisite authority to introduce a similar common country-wide system or to impose conformity of nomenclature, we might assume that in Scotland all of the different earlier established systems of land assessment worked well in practice for the whole of society from the Crown down to the level of the cottar.

During the last three decades only davochs, merklands, and pennylands have really been studied in any depth, but these studies have largely been undertaken either to try to determine the date of introduction of a particular unit of assessment or to compare different methods of assessment.[25] Of these units it has been the davoch that has attracted most attention. Partly this is because it was thought to have been Pictish in origin: with the exception of one small problematic cluster in south-west Scotland, it is only found in those areas once controlled by the Picts. Since the kingdom of the Picts is thought to have formed the core of the successor kingdom of Alba, a short digression to discuss the davoch becomes important to interpreting how Alba worked as a political and cultural entity.

The davoch has been a source of debate among antiquarians and historians since the eighteenth century, mainly because this word had different meanings in Gaelic Ireland and in Gaelic Scotland. Much of the debate concerning the davoch in Scotland has focused upon a couple of puzzles:

24 Christoph Sonnlechner, 'The establishment of new units of production in Carolingian times: making early medieval sources relevant for environmental history', *Viator*, 35, 2004, 21–48.

25 A. R. Easson, 'Systems of Land Assessment in Scotland before 1400', unpublished PhD thesis, University of Edinburgh, 1986 [hereafter: Easson, 'Systems of Land Assessment']; D. E. G. Williams, 'Land Assessments and Military Organisation in the Norse Settlements in Scotland, c.900–1266 AD', unpublished PhD thesis, University of St Andrews, 1996 [hereafter: Williams, 'Land Assessments'].

firstly, the etymology of the word, and secondly, the 'extent', or annual value, of this unit of land. There were basically two theoretical etymologies for this word in Scotland. The first of these argued that davoch was a compounded word that had been derived from the Gaelic words *damh* (ox) and *achadh* (field) and that it was supposed to signify either the amount of land on which oxen could be pastured (an oxgang/bovate), or an area of land in respect of which a number of oxen were given as render for the pasture.[26] The first person to advance an alternative to this theory was Cosmo Innes, writing in 1872. He suggested that the davoch could have been a liquid measure by which the produce of the field or the lord's proportion of produce was measured.[27] This appears to have been the first occasion on which a Scottish davoch was tentatively linked to a crop of some kind. Then, in 1880, W. F. Skene demonstrated that the supposed derivation of davoch from *damh* and *achadh* was wrong. Using evidence from the Gaelic *notitiae* in the *Book of Deer*, which had been thought to contain the earliest surviving Scottish form (*c.*1130) of the word davoch, Skene showed that the last syllable of the plural form of the word, *dabeg*, was inflected. This would not have happened if part of the word had originally been derived from *achadh*.[28]

Skene did not venture a replacement etymology for the word davoch in Scotland. This may have been because he knew that in Gaelic Ireland one of the meanings of davoch was the largest measure of liquid capacity.[29] In medieval Ireland, a davoch seems to have been a two-handled vessel for mead, which had a capacity of one *ól-meda* (*ól*-measure of mead), possibly 43.2 pints.[30] In Scotland, however, it was clear that a davoch was either originally a unit of land, or something that had quickly come to mean a unit of

26 For example: John Grant and William Leslie, *A Survey of the Province of Moray; Historical, Geographical, and Political* (Aberdeen, 1798), 67 [hereafter: Grant and Leslie, *Survey of the Province of Moray*]; E. William Robertson, *Scotland under her Early Kings*, 2 vols (Edinburgh, 1862), ii, 271 [hereafter: Robertson, *Early Kings*]. McKerral, writing in the 1940s [cf. A. McKerral, 'Ancient denominations of agricultural land in Scotland. A summary of recorded opinions, with some notes, observations and references', *PSAS*, 78, 1943–44, 39–80, at 50] seems to have been the last scholar to accept this definition.

27 Cosmo Innes, *Lectures on Scotch Legal Antiquities* (Edinburgh, 1872), 272, hereafter: Innes, *Scotch Legal Antiquities*].

28 W. F. Skene, *Celtic Scotland: A History of Ancient Alban*, 3 vols (Edinburgh, 1876–80), iii, 224 [hereafter: Skene: *Celtic Scotland*].

29 Royal Irish Academy, *Dictionary of the Irish Language based mainly on Old and Middle Irish Materials*, 4 vols (Dublin, 1913–75), D.4.42 [hereafter: RIA, *DIL*].

30 Fergus Kelly, *Early Irish Farming* (Dublin, 1988), 358 and at 578–79.

land, and Skene argued that in eastern Scotland each davoch was the equivalent of four ploughgates, or thirty-two oxgangs, whereas in the west of the
country it was the equivalent of one *Tirung*, or ounceland, which was in
turn comprised of twenty pennylands.[31] One further claim made by Skene
was that the davoch also appeared to be the equivalent of the twenty house
group found in the Gaelic kingdom of Dál Riata.[32]

Skene's dismissal of the etymology of the word davoch was not universally
accepted. In 1886, for example, F. W. L. Thomas argued that the word 'davoch'
would be represented in modern Gaelic by *damhach*, a compound of *damh*
(ox) and the augmentative particle *ach*, giving a sense of 'abounding in'.
According to him, *davach, damhach* and *davoch* simply meant a full team of
oxen.[33] In two wide-ranging articles that focused mainly on the Northern
Isles, Thomas also argued that the ounceland of the Northern Isles was a new
Scandinavian name for the davoch and that the davoch was a unit for the
assessment of tax rather than a piece of land of a fixed size.[34]

In 1887, Donald MacKinnon, first Professor of Celtic at the University
of Edinburgh, published a series of articles in the *Scotsman* concerning
the place-names and personal names of Argyll. In one of these articles
MacKinnon explained that although the word 'davoch' properly denoted a
liquid measure, in Scotland an old West Highland farmer of his acquain-
tance had frequently described his farm not as containing so many acres of
land, but as the sowing of a certain number of bolls of oats. Therefore,
according to MacKinnon, in Gaelic Scotland, where the staple industry was
agriculture, a davoch did not mean a measure of liquid but was a measure
of land surface, even though the old farmer did not specifically mention
the word davoch.[35] Seven years after this article was published, Sir Herbert
Maxwell described a davoch as follows: '. . . a measure of land, is originally,
as Professor MacKinnon has shown, a measure of capacity, and was applied
to denote the extent of land which required a davoch of corn to sow it'.[36] As
a result, the idea that a 'Scottish davoch' could be equated with a tub of

---

31 Skene, *Celtic Scotland*, iii, 224.
32 Ibid., 226.
33 F. W. L. Thomas, 'Ancient valuation of land in the west of Scotland: continuation of "What is
    a pennyland?" ', *PSAS*, 20, 1885–86, 200–13.
34 His earlier article was, F. W. L. Thomas, 'What is a pennyland? Or ancient valuation of land in
    the Scottish isles', *PSAS*, 18, 1883–84, 253–85.
35 Donald MacKinnon, 'Place-names and personal names in Argyll, xiii – The land: its divisions',
    The Scotsman, Wednesday 28 December 1887, page 7, columns 3 and 4.
36 Herbert Maxwell, *Scottish Land-Names, their Origin and Meaning* (Edinburgh, 1894), 165.

seed, and by inference arable, seems to have been readily accepted by the
end of the nineteenth century.

This association between the davoch and agriculture was not challenged
until 1926 when the Scottish place-name scholar W. J. Watson argued that
the davoch was not a measure of land but instead a definition of souming
capacity, which can be defined as the maximum number of animals a given
area of land can support during the course of a year.[37] His evidence for this
theory appears to have been derived from a statement made by Thomas
Pennant during his tour of Scotland in the eighteenth century that linked
a certain number of cows with the mountain and moor ground that formed
part of a half-davoch near Loch Broom in Wester Ross:

> Land here is set by the 'davoch' or 'half davoch'; the last consists of
> ninety-six Scotch acres of arable land, such as it is, with a competent
> quantity of mountain and grazing ground. This maintains sixty cows
> and their followers; and is rented for fifty-two pounds a year . . .[38]

These debates rumbled on through the twentieth century and it was the
1960s before historians working in Scottish landscape history reached an
uneasy truce about the davoch. In an article that first appeared in *Scottish
Studies*, but which has dominated discussion of davochs since it was
published, Barrow gently admonished earlier writers for suggesting that
the davoch may have been an administrative or fiscal unit of land. He was
of the firm opinion that each davoch was a unit of arable:

> It may be a noteworthy contrast that the English preferred to estimate
> their cultivated land in terms of the instrument which went into the soil
> at the start of the crop-growing process, while the Scots reckoned in
> terms of the amount of corn which emerged at the other end. Even so, I
> believe there is little doubt that the davoch, whenever it began to be used
> of land, was a strictly agricultural unit, a measure of arable capacity.[39]

In an important codicil to this statement Barrow added that he was unsure
whether a davoch was a measure of either seed-corn or of corn-yield.

---

37 Watson, *CPNS*, 235.
38 Thomas Pennant, *A Tour in Scotland and Voyage to the Hebrides 1772* (Edinburgh, 1998), 316
   [hereafter: Pennant, *A Tour in Scotland*].
39 G. W. S. Barrow, 'Rural settlement in central and eastern Scotland: the medieval evidence',
   Scottish Studies, 6, 1962, 123–44, at 133.

However, he argued that by the twelfth century the term davoch had come to denote an area of land, and had lost its direct connection with a measurement of volume.[40] In utilising this type of argument, Barrow fortuitously placed an important development in relation to davochs in an early time-frame for which there is no surviving evidence, making it impossible to disprove his theory. Barrow then continued to make a number of further points about the davoch. First, that each arable davoch would have carried pasture with it as people of the medieval period were incapable of thinking of arable in separation from the pasture and grazing that accompanied it. Second, that no clear relationship had ever been established between a davoch and a social unit like a township or village. Third, that since davochs were commonly named, and since many had fixed boundaries, each davoch must have possessed a physical unity centred upon a single stretch of arable land.[41] Fourth, that since there were no records of davochs in Argyll, Lennox, Menteith, the Northern Isles, Caithness, and parts of the Hebrides, there was, despite the Gaelic origin of the word, 'something inescapably Pictish about the use of the davoch of land'.[42] Fifth, that davochs were frequently divisible into fractions and that one of these fractions, the half-davoch, frequently possessed its own parish church. He further noted that this was similar to the carucate of 104 acres, south of the Forth, which also could be frequently found with its own parish church.[43] Sixth, that the use of the word *fortyris* (uplands, perhaps related to the Welsh word *gorthir*, higher land) in various davoch-related charters from Strathearn, Angus, and Ross, demonstrated careful distinction between the principal arable lands of the davoch and those lands which were either never or not regularly under the plough.[44] Finally, Barrow noted that there was a substantial body of evidence relating to davochs that contradicted his theories, particularly those units whose place-names indicated activities other than arable farming: he chose, however, to ignore this evidence since it 'did not really contradict his general thesis that the davoch was in origin and essence an agricultural unit'.[45]

---

40 Ibid., 142, fn. 35.
41 Ibid., 133.
42 Ibid., 135.
43 Ibid.
44 Ibid.
45 Ibid., 135–36. Barrow has continued to publicise these theories and they have appeared most recently in: G. W. S. Barrow, *The Kingdom of the Scots*, 2nd edn (Edinburgh, 2003), 233–49 [hereafter: Barrow, *Kingdom of the Scots*].

Duncan agreed with Barrow that the davoch was essentially either a measurement or a unit of arable land, largely because an early grant from Moray mentioned the corn teinds from the two davochs of Boharm and Adthelnachorth.[46] In effect, a general consensus had been achieved amongst the leading historians of that day, so that by 1972 Kenneth Jackson, in his discussion of the evidence relating to davochs in the *Book of Deer*, was able to state that:

The original meaning of the term is 'a large vat'; the application to land is not found at all in Ireland, however, but only in Scotland. Just how a word meaning a vat should come to be used of land is not quite clear, but this could have arisen if the term was applied to that amount of land necessary to produce, or to require for sowing it, a fixed amount of grain, enough to fill a large vat of fixed size; this being perhaps not the total yield of grain but only the proportion of it due as a fixed render of tax. This would explain the fact that when it can be checked, in later times, the actual acreage is seen to vary considerably in various parts of the country, exactly as in the case of the mediaeval bovate and ploughgate, and for the same reason. If it was originally purely a measure of arable land, it had ceased to mean this later, and applied to pastoral land and rough mountain grazing as well ... possibly it is, once again, an aspect of the Pictish socio-economic system adopted by the incoming Gaels?[47]

Recent commentators on the davoch have tended to follow the latter author and explain the davoch as an area of land that returned a tub of grain due as render.[48]

In 1986, Easson produced the first doctoral thesis on land assessments in Scotland before 1400. In this, she unequivocally stated that all davochs were located on low-lying fertile ground below 800 feet, particularly in river valleys, and that coastal situations were rare. According to her, davochs were strictly arable units of land and their location on the best soils proved her point.[49] In a series of distribution maps Easson also demonstrated that

---

46 A. A. M. Duncan, *Scotland: The Making of the Kingdom* (Edinburgh, 1975), 317 [hereafter: Duncan, *Kingdom*].
47 Kenneth Jackson, *The Gaelic Notes in the Book of Deer* (Cambridge, 1972), 116–17 [hereafter: Jackson, *Deer*].
48 For example: Robert A. Dodgshon, *Land and Society in Early Scotland* (Oxford, 1981), 76.
49 Easson, 'Systems of Land Assessment', 51–2.

the davoch was mostly found to the north of the Forth–Clyde line and that it was not present in Menteith, Strathearn, Argyll, or Caithness (the last only before 1400). Easson also attempted to prove that the davoch operated, at one and the same time, as both an agricultural and fiscal unit wherever it appeared in Scotland. Accordingly, while accepting that the davoch was an area of land which paid a vat of grain as render, she also argued, like Barrow, that every davoch was the nominal equivalent of two ploughgates of arable land.[50]

However, unlike Barrow, who suggested that the davoch could have been Pictish in origin, Easson followed Skene and argued that its origin instead lay in the Gaelic kingdom of Dál Riata. According to her, since the davoch was frequently divisible into halves (*leth-*), quarters (*ceathramh-*) and fifths (*cóigeamh-*), and because each davoch in the west of Scotland was the equivalent of twenty pennylands, these 'facts' indicated that the davoch must have originated out of the twenty-*tech* (house) unit, which was also capable of sub-division into tenths and fifths, as found in the early tax-assessment of Dál Riata, *Senchus Fer nAlban*.[51] To support this argument she claimed to have found evidence relating to a davoch in the north-east of Scotland — the davoch of Shevin in Strathdearn (to the south of Inverness) — where she argued that the four *cóigeamhan* (fifths) of Shevin were equivalent to the four quarters of the davoch. According to Easson, this meant that the sub-divisions of this davoch in the north-east were also originally based upon a five-*tech* (house) unit of Dál Riata. Therefore, she thought the davoch must have originated as a land measure with the *Scotti* of Dál Riata between c.AD 650 and c.AD 850 and was probably taken eastwards by the *Scotti* into Pictland. For her, this would also explain why davoch was originally a Gaelic word, not Pictish.[52]

This theory seems to have gained some acceptance although there were obviously worries concerning the fact that there was no direct place-name or documentary evidence for davochs within the boundaries of the old Gaelic kingdom of Dál Riata. In 1987 a highly creative and convoluted way was found around this by Oram who argued that the Scandinavian domination of western Scotland between c.842 and 1266 eliminated all

---

50 Ibid., 58–60.
51 John Bannerman, *Studies in the History of Dalriada* (Edinburgh, 1974), 42, and at 140–41 [hereafter: Bannerman, *Dalriada*]; D. N. Dumville, 'Ireland and North Britain in the Earlier Middle Ages: Contexts for *Míniugud Senchusa Fher nAlban*', in Colm Ó Baoill and Nancy R. McGuire (eds), *Rannsachadh na Gàidhlig 2000* (Aberdeen, 2002), pp. 185–212.
52 Easson, 'Systems of Land Assessment', 98.

trace of the fiscal davoch because the Norse replaced it with their own term, 'ounceland'. He further argued that in eastern Scotland post-c.842, the newly introduced davoch metamorphosed from being a Dál Riatan fiscal unit based upon notional groupings of households into something that fitted into a Pictish rural society organised in a system based on major arable units of up to thirty-two carucates in extent, and which was completely different from the Dál Riatan fiscal unit. According to him, in eastern Scotland the davoch could in this manner assume a dual character, being both a unit of fixed extent and an expression of render from that unit.[53]

Such a theory was also not without problems. While Oram noted (following Easson) that the davochs in south-western Scotland seemed to have been structured on the western (fiscal) model, there was evidence that these same davochs had also occasionally been measured according to their arable capacity. Therefore, according to Oram, the davochs in south-western Scotland must also have been a blend between the two davoch 'systems', fiscal and arable. He then suggested that the originally arable south-western davochs had been adapted in the mid-ninth century by incoming Gaels, who took their notion of fiscal davochs with them as they escaped from Norse pressure. As a result, the western fiscal system of assessment was adapted to fit new circumstances in south-west Scotland until it was displaced by the merkland in the thirteenth century.[54] Oram has more recently returned to this subject to reiterate and refine his earlier arguments. He noted that the greater concentration of davoch place-names occurred in the south-east of the Stewartry of Galloway, with a smaller concentration in Carrick. According to Oram, the locations of these place-names are proof that the davoch was closely associated with arable cultivation.[55] All of this has placed researchers in an unenviable position since it means that the davoch could be either arable, fiscal, or both, depending on which part of the country was being looked at and on which theory seemed to best fit the evidence.

The strongest challenge to the theory that the davoch originated in Dál Riata came from Williams in 1996. He argued that Easson's theory was

---

53 Richard Oram, 'Davachs and Pennylands in South-west Scotland: a Review of the Evidence', in L. J. Macgregor and B. E. Crawford (eds), *Ouncelands and Pennylands* (St Andrews, 1987), 46–59, at 48.
54 Ibid., 50–53.
55 Richard Oram, *The Lordship of Galloway* (Edinburgh, 2000), 234–38.

unreliable, partly because, like McKerral, he knew the davoch was not found either in *Senchus Fer nAlban* or in Dál Riata.[56] Williams pointed out that originally the davoch was wholly Pictish in geographical distribution and so he argued that either the davoch represented the imposition of a Gaelic assessment on to an older Pictish unit of land, or it was something new imposed on Pictland by the Scots after the Gaelicisation of Pictland and the destruction of Dál Riata by the Norse.[57] He did, however, agree with Easson's argument that davochs were only found on the best low-lying arable land.[58] Williams then suggested that, since the earliest references to this unit of land date to the reign of King Máel Coluim mac Cináeda (1005–1034), the davoch originated sometime during the tenth or early eleventh century in the course of the Gaelicisation of Pictland.[59]

Essentially, Williams argued that the rulers of the new kingdom of Alba (post-*c.*900) decided to establish a system of dues and services in their kingdom, including military service, to strengthen their authority. This, according to Williams, would account for both the Gaelic name and the Pictish distribution of the davoch. It would also help to explain why the davoch is not found either in *Senchus Fer nAlban* or in Dál Riata.[60] Finally, Williams explained the appearance of a cluster of davoch place-names in the south-west of Scotland as a result of the expansion of royal power post-1266.[61]

Perhaps wisely, since the davoch was not the main focus of his thesis, Williams dodged the issues surrounding the number of ploughgates in each davoch as well as the 'tub of grain' debate. While this did not lessen the impact of his davoch-related arguments, his treatment of the source evidence is problematic as it displays inconsistency. An example of this can be found in his discussions about the age of various units of land assessment. He argued that davochs were probably introduced into Sutherland in the thirteenth century by the De Moravia family, since there is no evidence for them before that date, and implied the same for the western Highlands and Islands by highlighting that there is no direct evidence for davochs there before the Treaty of Perth in 1266.[62] Yet, when discussing a similar

---

56 Williams, 'Land Assessments', 74.
57 Ibid., 73.
58 Ibid., 71.
59 Ibid., 73–76.
60 Ibid., 73–76.
61 Ibid., 49.
62 Ibid., 42 and 69.

lack of evidence relating to ouncelands in both the Northern Isles and Caithness before the late thirteenth century, he stated that this latter lack of evidence did not argue against the absence of ouncelands in those places before that date.[63]

Perhaps a greater flaw in this chain of reasoning concerns his assertion that there is no direct evidence for davochs in the western Highlands and Islands before the Treaty of Perth. If, by implication, davochs were imposed upon these areas by King Alexander III after 1266, why is there still no trace of them in the areas covered by the older Gaelic kingdom of Dál Riata? It seems very odd that the king of Scots, if he was going to impose davochs as a means of assessment upon the western Highlands and Islands that had previously belonged to the kings of Norway, would only do so over a portion of those lands.

Williams returned to the subject of the davoch in a paper published in *Northern Studies* in 2003, his thinking now clearly influenced by new theories relating to the early history of both Moray and Alba. In this article Williams argued that it was unlikely that Moray had been under the direct rule of the kings of Alba before 1130. Since davochs occur in both Alba and Moray, this commonality may therefore represent either a borrowing of that unit by a king of Moray from the kingdom of Alba before that date, or vice versa. Alternatively, Williams suggested, the davoch could have been extended to Moray when both Alba and Moray were ruled by King Macbethad mac Findláich (1040–1058). One final possibility suggested by Williams may have been that the davoch was only gradually introduced from Alba into Moray before the first Moravian charter attestations of the word in the final years of the twelfth century.[64]

Until 2003 no straightforward solution or common denominator in relation to land assessment in Scotland had been found and so this maze of different terms and theories continued to frustrate and baffle modern-day scholars who were looking for order in the medieval and early-modern landscapes of Scotia. In that year a new investigation was completed and this uncovered some surprising results in relation to land assessment.[65]

63 Ibid., 36.
64 Williams, 'The Davoch Reconsidered', *Northern Studies*, 2003, at 26–28.
65 Alasdair Ross, 'The Province of Moray, 1000–1230', 2 vols, unpublished PhD thesis, University of Aberdeen, 2003.

Redefining the davoch: the building blocks of Pictland and Alba?

The 2003 thesis demonstrated that the entire landscape of the province of Moray, an amalgam of the earldom and the bishopric stretching from Huntly in the east to Glenelg in the west, was completely divided into davochs, except for about 30 per cent of the Cairngorm plateau set aside for the purposes of transhumance for those people who lived closer to the coast and who normally had no direct access to mountain grazings. In Moray, davochs can be found at every height and across all types of terrain, including coastlands. This data completely contradicted Easson, who argued previously that all davochs were located below 800 feet on the best agricultural land along river valleys and that coastal locations were rare.[66] Perhaps the most damning fact in relation to Easson's thesis is that the summit cairn of Britain's highest mountain, Ben Nevis, is bisected by a davoch boundry, the northern edge of the davoch of Glen Nevis. Possibly more importantly, while Easson identified a total of fifty-five davochs in Moray, the 2003 thesis increased this number by over 600 per cent.

In addition, the 2003 thesis uncovered some further surprising information. The first of these was that there were two different types of davoch present in the landscape of Moray. The first of these types of davoch has been labelled as the 'self-contained' unit of assessment because it was located within one continuous boundary. In contrast, the second type of davoch, which has been labelled 'scattered', was divided into a number of economic units which were physically separated from each other across the landscape, essentially detached portions of land. Most davochs appear to have contained the resources and raw materials required to support communities of people and their livestock throughout the year: fishing, peat, wood, grazings, meadows, and arable.

It is also quite remarkable that in all of the records relating to Moray consulted for this doctoral research there was not a single instance of a new davoch being created pre-1940. More recent detailed research undertaken in relation to Ross, Sutherland, and Caithness has also failed to produce any examples of new davochs being created during the same time-frame and the evidence from these areas also points to a division of the entire landscape. Logically, this all means that no matter at what date a particular davoch first appears in the documentary record for Scotland north of the Mounth, it clearly refers to a unit of land that had already been in existence

---

66 Easson, 'Systems of Land Assessment', 52.

for a long period of time. In fact, in some parts of Moray and northern Scotland it is likely that some davochs were already being broken up into their constituent parts by the middle of the thirteenth century when the first baronies were created in those areas.

Nor does it appear that the boundaries of davochs changed between the high-medieval period and the nineteenth century. Between c.1100 and c.1800, not one instance has been found of a davoch boundary being altered by perambulation. Where verifiable, the boundaries of individual davochs that remained in use as viable units of land seem to have remained wholly unchanged between c.1100 and c.1800. For example, the perambulated southern boundary of the davoch of Grange in the parish of Keith (Aberdeenshire) was first recorded before 1225 and the same davoch boundary was still in use for the same purpose in 1763, giving it a lifespan of over 540 years.[67]

A large part of the reason for this stability in davoch boundaries was undoubtedly the nature of the boundaries themselves, which tended to utilise either permanent or semi-permanent landscape features. Typically, these consisted of a combination of ridges (described as 'where wind and weather shears') with named rock outcrop features and water courses. One problem with the two types of natural boundaries, ridges and streams or rivers, is that they could be changed by an extreme weather event. But across Moray only two such examples have been found between c.1100 and c.1900, both connected to extreme flooding events which shifted the course of rivers.

Yet another important point was that every medieval parish in Moray was wholly subdivided by an exact number of davochs and every detached portion of those parishes either comprised a fraction, a single unit, or multiples of davochs. This may seem surprising, but it does help explain some comments in later Scottish sources about parishes in Moray and the rest of northern Scotland. For example, in the First Statistical Account of 1791 it was remarked that the parish of Kirkmichael in Banffshire (excluding the forest of Strathavon) comprised ten davochs.[68] Similarly, the early-seventeenth-century Sutherland rentals state that the parishes of Creich and Lairg were respectively composed of twenty-four and fourteen davochs.[69] In the sixteenth and seventeenth centuries it was frequently

---

67 *Moray Registrum*, Carte Originales, 5 [hereafter: *Moray Reg.*]; NAS, RHP94427.
68 http://stat-acc-scot.edina.ac.uk/link/1791-99/Banff/Kirkmichael/ Accessed 1 November 2006.
69 NAS, GD128/47/8.

stated that the parish of Latheron in Caithness comprised six davochs.[70] Much the same case has recently been made in relation to parishes in Ireland. In the native Gaelic parts of the country the *túath* has been identified as the building block that underpinned parish formation, whereas in those areas settled by Anglo-Normans it was the new land grants themselves that formed parishes.[71]

In Scotland, research demonstrates that all of the medieval parishes in Moray, Ross, Sutherland, and Caithness were superimposed onto a pre-existing davoch pattern of secular land division and assessment. In fact, it is probably correct to state that the only reason why some medieval parishes in Moray and elsewhere in north Scotland had detached portions was because some of the davochs in those newly created parishes already possessed detached portions (see Map 2). Accordingly, rather than break up pre-existing units of land during the period of parish formation, most commonly thought to have been during the early twelfth century, the detached portions of any davochs in a particular parish were also included in that parish. The pattern of medieval parishes in Moray reflects an older system of land division and it also helps to explain why davochs remained in use as viable units of land for so long. What is still unknown about this process, however, is the decision-making process by which it was determined to group specific davochs together to form a parish. It is unlikely to have been an arbitary decision in such an organised landscape (see Maps 3–5).

But what is really important about all of this is that if Scottish parishes were really *de novo* creations of the early twelfth century (and this is not certain) it pushes the dating of the davoch back at least to the eleventh century. In this respect, it is noticeable that the first dated piece of historical evidence relating to davochs occurs in the *Book of Deer* (written c.1130) which records that King Máel Coluim mac Cináeda (1005–1034) had granted two davochs to the monks of Deer.[72] If this is a genuine record of the eleventh century, it allows us to push the davoch back in time to the kingdom of Alba c.1000 at least.

In fact, davochs may have been created at an even earlier date than that, as recent research undertaken by Taylor on the longer version of the St Andrews foundation legend shows. According to him, there is a very old

70 NAS, GD112/58/8/27; GD112/9/4/3.
71 Sinéad Ní Ghabhláin, 'The Origin of Medieval Parishes in Gaelic Ireland: The Evidence from Kilfenora', *The Journal of the Royal Society of Antiquaries of Ireland*, 126, 1996, 37–61.
72 Jackson, *Deer*, 34.

stratum within this text that goes back to Pictish times, pre-*c*.AD 900. In fact, several of the place-names mentioned in the text are given two names: what looks like the Pictish name is followed by the Gaelic version. One such place-name is *Doldocha* or *Kindrochit* (now Braemar in Deeside). In this latter example Taylor is fairly confident that *Dol-* (field or water meadow) was the Pictish form of the element borrowed from either Pictish or Brittonic into Scottish Gaelic as *Dail-*. He also argued that the second element of this Pictish place-name, *-docha*, stands for davoch. If this theory is correct, it looks as though the term davoch was in use in relation to land assessment during the Pictish historic period.[73] Since there are next to no historical sources for eleventh-century Scotia, understanding how the davoch worked may provide insights into how the kingdom operated.

Services and goods imposed upon the davoch

It is quite remarkable that across the literature relating to hundreds of davochs in north Britain there is not the slightest hint relating to renders paid in tubs of grain. In fact, some davochs seem to have contained either little or no arable land. This suggests that the 'tub of grain' theory should be regarded with suspicion, and that the other taxations levied upon each of these units should be examined in detail to try to assess the thinking behind the creation of these units.

In a European context, units of land assessment are very common and some can be dated back to the seventh century AD. In England, for example, it has been argued that although Saxons took over the existing boundaries of Roman villas and Romano-British farmsteads, they carefully developed these patterns to ensure that every community possessed an equitable share of the natural resources stretching from rivers in the valley bases to downland grazing. Where access to a particular economic resource was problematic or non-existent, care was taken to ensure such access for the community in question even though it was a considerable distance away, because access to a range of natural resources was fundamental to the continuing viability of that community of people. According to Hooke, such patterns of resource allocation are still visible in the English landscape from Wiltshire to Yorkshire.[74]

---

73 Personal correspondence with Dr Simon Taylor, 9 June 2005.
74 Joseph Betty, 'Downlands', in Joan Thirsk (ed.), *The English Rural Landscape* (Oxford, 2000), 27–49, at 35–36; Della Hooke, *The Landscape of Anglo-Saxon England* (Wiltshire, 1998), 74 [hereafter: Hooke, *Landscape of Anglo-Saxon England*].

One of the most important taxes placed upon such units of land assessment was military service. For example, the basis of Carolingian military service assessment was the *mansus* which is commonly found in west-Frankish sources from *c.*650, in Burgundy from *c.*750, and in both Italy and Provençe in the ninth century.[75] As Hollister has pointed out, although the acreages of the Carolingian *mansi* could be radically different in size, the military obligation of one foot soldier from every four *mansi* (plus bridge service and watch duty) was generally applied irrespective of the differences in acreage between *mansi*. In addition, the inhabitants of *mansi* were expected to support the fighting men with wages and provisions.[76] More recently, Brooks has dated the general Carolingian rule that one man from every four *mansi* was required for military service in Charlemagne's empire to after AD 808. Occasionally, though, more men were demanded and, in the event of invasion, the whole population was called out.[77] In this instance military service was a tax imposed upon a pre-existing unit of land assessment.

Something similar can be found in Anglo-Saxon England. In 1961, Hollister argued that his contemporaries had been wrong to question the earlier assumption that every five-hide group in Anglo-Saxon England owed the service of one warrior. After reviewing the evidence of the Domesday Book in detail, he concluded that the five-hide rule was more widespread in England than had previously been thought.[78] The Anglo-Saxon law codes of the tenth and eleventh centuries also stipulated that all free men could be required to serve in the host, to build bridges, and perform fortress-work. However, despite the lateness of this evidence, Brooks has suggested that the hide was used as a means of rental, taxation, and service assessment from at least the second half of the seventh century and so would also have been convenient to define military obligations.[79] Just like the Carolingian *mansus*, the three services of hosting, bridge building, and fortress-work were obligatory on the whole *folc* (people) of

---

75 D. Herlihy, 'The Carolingian Mansus', *The Economic History Review*, new ser. 13, i, 1960, 79–89.

76 C. Warren Hollister, 'The Five-hide Unit and the Old English Military Obligation', *Speculum*, 36, i, 1961, 61–74 at 63–64 [hereafter: Hollister, 'Five-hide unit'].

77 Nicholas Brooks, 'The Development of Military Obligations in Eighth- and Ninth-century England', in Peter Clemoes and Kathleen Hughes (eds), *England before the Conquest: Studies in Primary Sources Presented to Dorothy Whitelock* (Cambridge, 1971), 69–84 at 70–71 [hereafter: Brooks, 'Military Obligations'].

78 Hollister, 'Five-hide Unit', 61–74.

79 Brooks, 'Military Obligations', 70.

each hide who had to support the nominated fighters/workers.[80] Thanks
to these commonalities between the military services demanded from
both the *mansus* and the hide, it has been argued by some commentators
that they shared a common Germanic past.[81] Similar services are also
found in the Irish law texts where the *céile gíallnae* (base client) was
required to pay food rent, perform manual labour, and undertake the
military duties of *fubae* (hunting of pirates, horse-thieves, and wolves) and
rubae (patrolling borders and strategic military points). In addition, if the
lord organised a *slógad* (hosting), the base clients could be required to
provide maintenance for the men gathered for military service.[82]

Broadly comparable services were imposed on each davoch: military
service, castle service, and road service. In the case of the davoch the
evidence suggests that four men were levied from each unit for both fighting
and hunting service and, while these men were away on duty, the remaining
inhabitants of the davochs they had come from would look after and
support their familes and other interests. Unfortunately, this evidence is
post-medieval in date, but, even so, it is exactly the same pattern of community provision as that found in relation to the fighting men levied from
Carolingian *mansi* and Anglo-Saxon hides.

The crucial point is that the davoch was both a unit of resource exploitation and an easy way of collecting taxation in both goods and services.
They seem to have comprised an equitable division of the landscape and
the resources contained within. Since davochs could be further subdivided
into halves, quarters, thirds, fifths and eights, they also allowed for extensive micro-management of those same natural resources, like grazings and
meadows. They also provided a highly stratified system by which everyone
knew exactly what they might be expected to render in taxes from year to
year at a local level and where each lord or king could quickly estimate
what they might receive in taxes and services on an annual basis.

For example, a thirteenth-century lord of Badenoch, which comprised
sixty davochs, would know that he could levy 240 men for either local army
or hunting service (the latter included the building of temporary hunting
lodges) for a set number of days; he knew that he could demand carriage
service of up to 60 miles distance from the tenants of each davoch in his
lordship; he knew that he could demand foot service (document/message

80 Ann Williams and G. H. Martin (eds), *Domesday Book* (St Ives, 2003), 136.
81 Hollister, 'Five-hide Unit', 73; Brooks, 'Military Obligations', 69.
82 Fergus Kelly, *A Guide to Early Irish Law* (Dublin, 1988), 29–31.

carrying) from each davoch; he knew that he could demand three days' ploughing and harvesting service from each person in every davoch, and he also knew exactly how much foodstuff and fuel from a mixed bag of grain, cheese, peat, geese, hens, eggs, fish, goats, cattle, and sheep he could expect to receive each year in rent and other taxes levied upon his sixty davochs. While no such details have survived from the eleventh century, it is doubtful whether the goods and services levied upon each davoch back then would have been significantly different.

So far, all of this evidence relating to davochs has largely come from lands and territories north of the Mounth, essentially Aberdeenshire, Buchan, Banffshire, Moray, Ross, Sutherland, and Caithness. This is not problematic because a number of other sources record the presence of davochs south of the Mounth to the Forth, and one of our main sources for Alba during the eleventh century, the Gaelic property records in the *Book of Deer*, seems to combine records relating to davochs with references to the whole kingdom of Alba.[83] It is noticeable, though, that later medieval and early-modern charters and rentals for Scotland south of the Mounth contain far fewer references to davochs than the north of the country and most of the records that do survive relate to upland areas. This clear dichotomy north and south of the Mounth may just be associated with a lack of primary source research, but this is slowly changing and the gaps that remain in the evidence record are sufficiently worrying to raise a new set of research questions about the davoch. At the very least it should be questioned why its survival is virtually complete in the written record north of the Mounth and not elsewhere.

South of the Mounth to the Forth the davoch is commonly interspersed with other units of land assessment that are variously later referred to as 'officiaries', 'carucates', and 'Scottish carucates'. In lands that were absorbed by Alba during the tenth and eleventh centuries, we find two other major units of land assessment: the arachor in the Lennox and the husbandland south of the Forth. The shire should also be added to this list.

Evidence relating to these latter entities has already been examined in detail by Barrow, who noted that evidence for shires was present in 'Scottish Northumbria' before AD 1100 and reconstructed the boundaries of a number of shires across southern Scotland. Much of

---

83 Katherine Forsyth, Dauvit Broun and Thomas Clancy, 'The Property Records: Text and Translation', in Katherine Forsyth (ed.), *Studies on the Book of Deer* (Bodmin, 2008), 141 [hereafter: Forsyth, Broun and Clancy, 'The Property Records'].

his argument was based upon evidence from England where Barrow noted that:

> From Kent to Northumbria, without a break, some system of exten-
> sive royal lordship, based upon a unit known variously as lathe, soke,
> shire or *manerium cum appendiciis*, had survived long enough for its
> main features to be traceable in record of the eleventh and twelfth
> centuries. Associated with the soke or shire, indispensible for its
> management, was a class of ministerial freemen [called] free men,
> gavelkinders, sokemen, radmen, radknights, drengs, and thegns.[84]

Barrow traced shires in Scotland northwards up to the Ochils and eastwards into Fife, exactly where we might expect to find some evidence for them in areas of earlier Anglo-Saxon overlordship. He then argued (wrongly) that there was also evidence for shires in both Strathspey and Badenoch and, additionally, that Scottish thanages and their thanes traditionally rendered the same mix of goods and services as their English counterparts, the thegns, drengs, and sokemen provided in north England.[85]

While Barrow admitted that it would be impossible to prove that Scotland was once divided up into thanages, he did suggest that they had determined the patterns of lordship and land distribution over a long period pre-AD 1200. He further added that since most of the known thanages were located in the east of the country on the most fertile and populous land (that he thought generated more records), the fact that the Highlands had once had a different system of land management and assessment could not be dismissed.[86]

Of course, thanks to research into the davoch it is now known that there was no east/west split in land division and assessment across most of the Highland area and that it was the davoch that was the basic building block from which most other secular lordships and parishes (including thanages were constructed. This, however, does not invalidate Barrow's research into shires in Scotia south of the Forth and a deeper investigation into their relationship to husbandlands, hundreds and wapentakes is urgently needed. His work also clearly demonstrates that the gradual expansion of Scottish overlordship southwards across Lothian would have

84 Barrow, *Kingdom of the Scots*, 22.
85 Ibid., 38.
86 Ibid., 44.

been moving into a landscape whose natural resources had already been divided up and parcelled out by earlier kings of Northumbria.[87] Just like the inhabitants of davochs, the inhabitants of shires (and probably husband-lands) would have known exactly how much tax and what services they had to render and to whom.

However, like the husbandland, none of the other small units of land assessment in Scotland have yet been investigated in the same detail as the davoch, though preliminary studies suggest that multiples of arachors also form parishes and the officiary in Perthshire has some relationship to the medieval parish too.[88] The sooner detailed research on these units is undertaken, the quicker a much clearer picture will be formed of the extent of the resources available to a king of Alba and how these resources increased as Alba expanded. Even at this stage of research, however, this pattern of land division into davochs provides clear evidence that both Pictland and Alba must have been highly organised realms with an effi-cient system of tax assessment and collection, even if no exchequer or estate records specifically relating to this have survived. There is perhaps one clue about who might have collected these taxes and organised the services due at a local level. Some seventeenth- and eighteenth-century documents from upland Moray occasionally refer to men known as 'dochassers' (davoch assessors) and it is clear that this is an alternative (and probably earlier) name for a functionary who performed the same duties as those men later referred to as tacksmen.[89]

87 D. M. Hadley, *The Vikings in England: Settlement, Society and Culture* (Manchester, 2006), 84–89.
88 M. J. H. Robson, 'Territorial Continuity and the Administrative Division of Lochtayside, 1769', *Scottish Geographical Magazine*, 106:3, 1990, 174–85.
89 NAS, GD44/27/4/53/1.

CHAPTER TWO

Defining Alba and the Albanaig, Post-c.900

Historiography

The Irish Gaelic Annals remain major historic sources for north Britain in the post-900 period. They contain snippets of information relating to people and events associated with Alba like kings, mormaír, important events (usually battles), and obits. The most important of these annalistic sources are the *Annals of Ulster* and the *Annals of Tigernach*. Unfortunately, of these two only the *Annals of Ulster* have been edited to modern standards (up to 1131), so some care must be taken when utilising information from the *Annals of Tigernach*. In addition, both sets of Annals contain interpolated material, some of which has been dated to the sixteenth century.[1] Alba, of course, was originally a Gaelic word that denoted the whole of Britain and only in the tenth century came to be used to refer to one kingdom in north Britain. There is also some evidence relating to the use of the noun *Scotia*, which appears in a late-tenth century text of the Life of St Cathroe written at Metz, where the author clearly had access to good information concerning north Britain, although this text also has not been edited to modern standards. Does this make the *Scotti* people who lived in a place called Alba, which was in turn referred to in Latin texts as *Scotia*, derived from either Old Norse *Skottar* or Old English *Scottas*?[2]

Fortunately, as we progress through time these sources can be supplemented by other material, some of which is north British in origin. For the tenth and eleventh centuries this material essentially consists of four different Scottish sources: *The Chronicle of the Kings of Alba, De Situ Albanie, Míniugud Senchasa fher nAlban* (Explanation of the History of the People of Alba), and the Gaelic interpolations into the *Book of Deer*, written c.1130. Towards the end of the eleventh and into the twelfth century, the information in these sources is increasingly complemented by the earliest surviving Scottish charter material.

---

1 *Ann. Ulster*, viii–ix.
2 David N. Dumville, 'The Chronicle of the Kings of Alba', in Simon Taylor (ed.), *Kings, Clerics and Chronicles in Scotland, 500–1297* (Bodmin, 2000), 73–86 [hereafter: Dumville, 'Chronicle of the Kings of Alba'].

There are three further Scottish sources that can be added to this list: Fordun's *Chronica Gentis Scotorum* (based upon a thirteenth-century work by Richard Vairement), Wynton's *Orygynale Chronicle*, and Abbot Bower's *Scotichronicon*. None of these are contemporary, but they contain snippets of information that, if used properly, can supplement any discussion of Alba. To these three works we can add a southern British source, the *Anglo-Saxon Chronicle*, and Scandinavian sagas, particularly the *Orkneyinga Saga*. This latter work was probably written in Iceland between 1192 and 1200 and is a complicated source for a historian to use.[3] The author relied on both poetry and oral tradition for information, and the picture is further complicated by the fact that the original *Orkneyinga Saga* was used as a source for a work called *Heimskringla*, compiled *c*.1230. When the *Orkneyinga Saga* was then revised at a later date, *Heimskringla* was used as a source for that revision.[4]

In secondary literature, detailed discussion of the kingdom of Alba first appeared in W. F. Skene's trilogy *Celtic Scotland*, written between 1876 and 1880.[5] In this classic book Skene recognised that sometime during the reign of Domnall mac Causantín between 889 and 900, the kings of the Picts descended from Cináed mac Ailpín changed the way in which they, their kingdom, and the people over whom they exercised overlordship, were described. Domnall was the first king in north Britain to be described as king of Alba in his obit. According to Skene, this change in nomenclature from Pictland to Alba was shortly followed by the Pictish and Scottish Churches uniting and the bishops of St Andrews becoming known as bishops of Alba. Scone became the secular heart of this kingdom.[6] Skene also defined the borders of Alba as the area between the Forth and the River Spey. To the west of Druim Alban was the kingdom of Argyll, and Moray, Ross and Caithness had been overrun by Thorstein the Red and Earl Siguard of Orkney.[7]

In this account of Alba each province (or petty kingdom) contained a number of tribes. Several tribes formed a *Mortuath* (great tribe) and two or more great tribes formed a province, ruled over by a *rí* (king). In this kingdom the Pictish law of succession through females had been

3 Hermann Pálsson and Paul Edwards (trans.), *Orkneyinga Saga* (London, 1978), 9–10 [hereafter: Pálsson and Edwards, *Orkneyinga Saga*].
4 Ibid., 11.
5 Skene, *Celtic Scotland*, i, 335–83.
6 Ibid., 339–40.
7 Ibid., 340–43.

retained.[8] At the head of each tribe was the *toisech* and at the head of each *Mortuath* was the mormaer. Above them all was the *Ardrí* (great king). The general population consisted of Picts and Scots who became amalgamated, though the Scots were clearly the dominant race. According to Skene's scheme of the history of Alba, the first king of that country who attempted to project his power north of the River Spey was Máel Coluim mac Domnaill (*c.*942–954) who invaded Moray and killed someone called Cellach. Skene was also quite clear that the last king of Alba was Cináed mac Duibh who was killed in 1005 by Máel Coluim mac Cináeda (1005–1034), the first king of Scotia.[9] This exposition by Skene has been very influential in Scottish history, particularly as he established a societal hierarchy for the inhabitants of Alba, based upon Irish Gaelic models. The same scheme was accepted and followed by Macintosh in 1892 and, as late as 1974, Skene's version of the transition from Pictland to Alba continued to pass with little comment among historians.[10] Others even ignored the apparently sudden appearance of Alba completely and suggested that Pictland should be called Scotia after 850.[11]

There also seems to be general agreement that the kings of Alba expanded southwards into the Lothian plain and fully established their overlordship there during the tenth century. However, this cannot be precisely dated. The lands north of the River Tweed that belonged to St Cuthbert (like Melrose) seem to have been lost to the Cuthbertine community around this time and, perhaps more importantly, there is a record dated to between 954 and 960 that Edinburgh had been lost to the ruler of Alba even though it does not tell us who abandoned the fortress.[12]

During the last two and a half decades, the Skenesian profile of Alba has come under sustained attack from Dauvit Broun. In 1993, he began to question the origins of Scottish identity and pointed out that while Scotia and Alba were the respective Latin and Gaelic names for the same kingdom, originally Alba had been the Gaelic noun for the entire island of Britain. At that time Broun declared that such a fundamental change in definition surely signified an attempt to articulate not only a new identity but also a

8 Ibid., 343–44.
9 Ibid., 384.
10 John Macintosh, *The History of Civilisation in Scotland*, 4 vols, new edn (Paisley, 1892), i, 120–21; Gordon Donaldson, *Scotland: The Shaping of the Nation* (Newton Abbot, 1974), 16–17.
11 Duncan, *Kingdom*, 90.
12 Anderson, *Early Sources*, i, 468 [hereafter: *ES*].

new primarily territorial idea of kingship.[13] Furthermore, he suggested that this change in identity could be explained as the work of a contemporary 'Scottish' annalist working in *c*.900. Like Skene, Broun noted that Alba did not include either Dál Riata or the Lennox, and that in its most restricted sense it meant the lands between the Rivers Forth and Spey, stretching as far west as the mountain range of Druim Alban, before the kingdom expanded southwards in the tenth century to include Edinburgh and later northwards to include Moray.[14]

That same year, Broun published his second article on this topic, this time suggesting that Scandinavian pressure in north Britain, just like in Europe, could have provided a ruling elite with the opportunity to build new political structures centred around Alba as a focus as the Pictish language declined. According to Broun, the geographic location of the kingdom of Alba in the fertile east lowlands of north Britain also meant that its kings would have been able to harness key economic resources, thus allowing the nascent kingdom to extend its power and territory over the rest of north Britain.[15]

An important foray into this field was made by Patrick Wormald in 1996 when he examined the emergence of the kingdom of the Scots in a European context. In this, he pointed out that the changeover from Pictland to Alba may also have been linked to a new ecclesiastic dispensation and he questioned Broun's theory that Scandinavian pressure could have resulted in the decline of Pictish but not Gaelic. In the end, Wormald concluded that the Picts were conquered by the Scots in the ninth century and the Pictish aristocracy were marginalised as a result.[16]

Two years later Broun returned to this topic in print, drawing in later medieval evidence to demonstrate that before the thirteenth century, Scotia could be understood as the equivalent of Alba. This explained why a contemporary source described King William I as returning from Moray to Scotia in 1214 and why, for the period before the wars of independence, there were two 'Scotlands': lesser (the area defined by the Rivers Forth and Spey and Druim Alban) and greater (most of mainland Scotland north of

13 Dauvit Broun, 'The Origin of Scottish Identity', in C. Bjorn, A. Grant and K. Stringer (eds), *Nations, Nationalism and Patriotism in the European Past* (Copenhagen, 1994), 35–55, at 39–40, 48.

14 Ibid., 42–47.

15 Dauvit Broun, 'The Origin of Scottish Identity in its European Context', in Barbara E. Crawford (ed.), *Scotland in Dark Age Europe* (St Andrews, 1994), 21–32.

16 Patrick Wormald, 'The Emergence of the *Regnum Scottorum*: a Carolingian hegemony?', in Barbara E. Crawford (ed.), *Scotland in Dark Age Britain* (St Andrews, 1996), 131–60.

the Forth–Clyde line). In this article Broun argued that Alba could have been a recasting of Pictish kingship without a Pictish ethnic label.[17]

By 2000 it was obvious that Broun's various writings on Alba-related topics had piqued the interest of other scholars and, in that year, Máire Herbert tackled the emergence of Alba using an Irish Gaelic context.[18] Here, she stated that the late ninth century was a crucial period in the development of kingship in an insular context. In Ireland, the larger provincial kingships had been gathering power to the exclusion of smaller political units since the late eighth century and, by 858, the phrase *co feraib Érenn* (with the men of Ireland) had emerged in historical accounts as a common cultural identifier. Crucial to this was the emergence of the southern Uí Néill king, Máel Sechnaill mac Maíl Ruanaid, who took the Uí Néill overkingship in 846 and subsequently became *rí hÉrenn uile* (king of all Ireland).[19]

Herbert linked these developments in Gaelic Ireland to Pictland by following the marriage career of the Pictish princess Máel Muire, daughter of Cináed mac Ailpín, in Ireland. Máel Muire firstly married the northern Uí Néill king and incumbent holder of the Uí Néill overkingship, Áed Finnlaith. Following his death in 862, Máel Muire was subsequently taken in marriage by Flann, the ruler of the southern Uí Néill. Thus Máel Muire was married to two successive Uí Néill overkings and closely related to two later holders of the title *rí Érenn*. Perhaps rightly, Herbert was suspicious of the fact that the title *rí Alban* appeared in Gaelic Annals referring to north Britain at the same time as the two ruling dynasties were closely linked by marriage. Finally, Herbert also pointed out that the alternating northern and southern Uí Néill succession in Ireland could have been adopted by the descendants of Cináed mac Ailpín, represented by Clann Áeda meic Cináeda and Clann Custantín meic Cináeda.[20]

The year 2000 also saw the publication of an edited collection of essays entitled, *Alba, Celtic Scotland in the Middle Ages*, produced to celebrate the centenary of the death of W. F. Skene. In his contribution to this volume

---

17 Dauvit Broun, 'Defining Scotland and the Scots before the Wars of Independence', in Dauvit Broun, R. J. Finlay and Michael Lynch (eds), *Image and Identity, The Making and Re-making of Scotland Through the Ages* Edinburgh, 1998), 4–17.

18 Máire Herbert, 'Rí Éirenn, Rí Alban: Kingship and Identity in the Ninth and Tenth Centuries', in Simon Taylor (ed.), *Kings, Clerics and Chronicles in Scotland, 500–1297* (Bodmin, 2000), 62–72 [hereafter: Herbert, 'Rí Éirenn'].

19 Ibid., 63–64.

20 Ibid., 68–70.

Dauvit Broun deconstructed the text known as *De situ Albanie* (*De situ Albanie que in se figuram hominis habet quomodo fuit primitus in septem regionibus diuisa quibusque nominibus antiquitus sit uocata et a quibus inhabitata* – Concerning the geography of Alba which takes the shape of a man; in what way it was originally divided into seven kingdoms, and by what names it may have been called of old and by whom inhabited).

This is one of seven short texts relating to the Picts, Alba, and Scotia that have been preserved in a manuscript labelled the Poppleton manuscript, so called because it was compiled and preserved at York by a Carmelite friar called Robert of Poppleton around 1360. These seven short texts also include *Cronica de origine antiquorum Pictorum* and an account of the St Andrews foundation legend. The manuscript is now preserved in the Bibliothèque Nationale, Paris.

Broun argued that *De situ Albanie*, dated to 1202 x 14, was a problematic text, not least because it has been used by historians to reconstruct the political geography of the kingdom of the Picts while ignoring the fact that it was composed 300 years after the disappearance of Pictland from the historical record.[21] In addition, Broun demonstrated that while the two versions of the sevenfold division of Alba (which he referred to as DSa and DSb) in *De situ Albanie* had been central to earlier reconstructions of Pictish political geography, they were in fact confusing, misleading and inaccurate, and perhaps produced by the last generation of scholars who viewed Alba as a country of varying extent shortly before the wars of independence.[22]

DSa states the following:

Hec uero terra a septem fratribus diuisa fuit antiquitus in septem partes quarum pars principalis est Enegus cum Moerne ab Enegus primogenito fratrum sic nominata. Secunda autem pars est Adtheodle et Gouerin. Pars enim tertia est Sradeern cun Meneted. Quarta pars partium est | Fif cum Foth[r]eue. Quinta uero pars est Marr cum Buchen. Sexta autem est Muref et Ros. Septima enim pars est Cathanesia citra montem et ultra montem; quia mons Mound diuidit Katanesiam per medium.[23]

---

21 Dauvit Broun, 'The Seven Kingdoms in De Situ Albanie: A Record of Pictish Political Geography or Imaginary Map of Ancient Alba?', in Edward J. Cowan and R. Andrew McDonald (eds), *Alba* (East Linton, 2000), 24–42, at 27 [hereafter: Broun, 'The Seven Kingdoms'].

22 Ibid., 42.

23 M. O. Anderson, *Kings and Kingship in Early Scotland*, revised edn (Edinburgh, 1980), 242 [hereafter: Anderson, *Kings and Kingship*].

This land, in truth, was divided in antiquity into seven parts by seven brothers, of which the principal part is Angus with the Mearns, so named from Angus, the first-born of the brothers. The second part, however, is Atholl with Gowrie. The third part, then, is Strathearn with Menteith. The fourth part of the parts is Fife with Fothriff. The fifth part, in truth, is Mar with Buchan. The sixth, however, is Moray and Ross. The seventh part, then, is Caithness on this side of the mounth and beyond the mounth; because the mountain called the Mounth divides Caithness through the middle.

In DSa the pairing of provinces, with one apparently subordinate to the other, is a rather curious feature and Broun described it as 'suspiciously artificial'. He then suggested that DSa was an ingenious attempt to list all the mormaerdoms of Alba in a sevenfold division that would complement a Gaelic tract on Pictish origins found in *Lebor Bretnach* and in *Lebor Gabála Érenn*, and which related the division of Alba among the seven sons of Cruithne.[24]

In contrast, the second version, DSb, provides a little more geographic detail by mentioning the River Spey, but it also further confuses the issues. It states:

Quelibet igitur istarum partium regio tunc uocabatur et erat quia unaqueque earum subregionem in se habebat. Inde est ut hii septem fratres predicti p<ro> septem regibus habebantur septem regulos sub se habentes. Iste septem fratres regnum Albanie in septem regna diuiserunt et unusquisque in tempore suo in suo regno regnauit. Primum regnum fuit sicut mihi uerus relator retulit Andreas uidelicet et uir uenerabilis Katanensis episcopus natione Scottus et Dunfermelis monachus ab illa aqua optima que Scottice uocata est Froch Britannice Werid Romane uero Scottewatre id est aqua Scottorum q[uia] regna Scottorum et Anglorum diuidit et currit iuxta oppidum de Striuelin usque ad flumen aliud nobile quod uocatum est Tae. S[e]c[un]d[u]m reg[nu]m ad Hilef sicut mare circuit usque ad montem aquilonali plaga de Striuelin qui uocatur Athran. Tertium regnum ab Hilef usque ad De. Quartum regnum ex De usque ad magnum et mirabile flumen quod uocatur Spe maiorem et meliorem totius Scotie. Quintum regnum de Spe usque ad montem Bru[m]alban. Sextum regnum fuit Mure<f> et Ros. Septimum regnum erat A[r]rega[i]thel.[25]

24 Broun, 'The Seven Kingdoms', 40.
25 Anderson, *Kings and Kingship*, 242–43.

Each of these parts, therefore, was called a region, and that was because each one of them had within itself a sub-region. Thence it is that these seven foresaid brothers were held to be seven kings, having under themselves seven sub-kings. These seven brothers divided the realm of Albany into seven realms, and each one reigned in his own time in his own realm. The first realm was, just as a true relator related to me, Andrew, that is, and a venerable man, Bishop of Caithness, a Scot by nation and a monk of Dunfermline, from that excellent water which is called in Scottish Froch, in British the Werid, in Romance, in truth, Scot Water, that is Water of the Scots, because it divides the realms of the Scots and the English, and it runs alongside the town of Stirling as far as that other noble river that is called Tay. The second realm is to the River Isla, just as the sea goes about as far as the mountain in the northern territory of Stirling which is called Athran. The third realm from Isla as far as the Dee. The fourth realm from the Dee as far as the great and wonderful river which is called the Spey, the greatest and best of the whole of Scotland. The fifth realm from the Spey as far as the mountain Druimm nAlban. The sixth realm was Moray and Ross. The seventh realm was Argyll.

Unfortunately, mention of the River Spey in DSb does not greatly aid any attempt to reconstruct boundaries, mainly because the Spey was associated with a fifth (unnamed) realm that stretched across Scotland, rather than Moray and Ross (the sixth realm). There are a few options. The author of DSb may have been correct to state that there was a fifth realm between the Spey and the mountain called Druimm nAlban at the beginning of the thirteenth century. In fact, it has recently been argued that this fifth realm in DSb was intended to represent the territorial equivalent of the lordships of Lochaber and Badenoch.[26] Although this suggestion seems perfectly logical, it would mean that between 1202 and 1214 the lands that comprised Lochaber and Badenoch, while remaining within the diocese of Moray, were not regarded as being in the secular province of Moray by the author of *De situ Albanie*.[27] This contradicts all later evidence about the history of these two lordships.

---

26 A. Grant, 'The Province of Ross and the Kingdom of Alba', in Edward J. Cowan and R. Andrew McDonald (eds), *Alba* (East Linton, 2000), 88–126, at 96 [hereafter: Grant, 'Ross'].

27 *Moray Reg.*, no. 76.

There is a further problem. If the suggestion that the fifth realm of DSb was meant to describe the lordships of Lochaber and Badenoch is correct, it would mean that the existence of the territories of Lochaber and Badenoch must pre-date their first appearance in the charter record by some thirty years.[28] While this may not be an insurmountable problem, the lordships of Lochaber and Badenoch also never seem to have encompassed more than approximately one-third of western Strathspey. Therefore, if the theory that the fifth realm in DSb was equivalent to Lochaber and Badenoch is going to be accepted, then it must also be acknowledged that the stated geography of the fifth realm in DSb is wildly inaccurate and misleading.

The second option is that DSb was wrong to state that there was a fifth realm between the Spey and the mountain called Druimm nAlban. There is no proof for this allegation other than the suggestion, made on the strength of the frequency of Bishop Andrew's attestation of royal charters between *c.*1147 and 1184, that he had never actually visited his diocese of Caithness during his lifetime.[29] If he did not, then the whole of DSb, or at least that part of it which concerned Scotia north of the Mounth, must be regarded with a high degree of scepticism.

The third and final option is that both DSa and DSb are unconvincing and confused geographical descriptions of Alba. DSb, for example, does not contain an equivalent entry for DSa's 'Atholl and Gowrie'. Similarly, DSa has no equivalent for DSb's fifth realm. In addition, while DSa includes Caithness and omits Argyll, DSb omits Caithness and includes Argyll.[30] The omission of Atholl in DSb is particularly trouble-some since there is no indication that this province was ever separated from Pictland, Alba, or Scotia. As far as Caithness is concerned, this province had been part of Scotia since 1098.[31] If DSb can be demonstrated to be so inaccurate with respect to the earldoms of Atholl and Caithness, it really must be questioned whether DSb's inclusion and description of a fifth realm between the River Spey and the mountain called Druimm nAlban is also just another horrible geographic error. In this respect, it may well be wise to accept Isabel Henderson's description of DSa and DSb as careless and unreliable geographic accounts, and reject the

28 *Moray Reg.*, no. 86.
29 Broun, 'The Seven Kingdoms', 28.
30 Ibid., 29.
31 Barbara Crawford, 'The Earldom of Caithness and the Kingdom of Scotland, 1150–1266', *Northern Scotland*, 2, 1974–75, 97–118, at 97.

geographic information contained within them as evidence in any attempt to define Alba.[32]

A rather different approach to the development of Alba as a single unified kingship was also published in 2000. Here, Grant argued that the early Scottish state was neither as centralised nor as wealthy as other European countries before Anglo-Norman settlers and their ideas arrived in the twelfth century, bringing with them sheriffdoms, burghs, and coinage.[33] Such contentious statements appear to be predicated upon a mistaken belief that Celtic countries required an Anglo-Norman veneer before they could be counted as 'developed' and capable of generating serious wealth.

In this article Grant also paid particular attention to the 'multiple estate' or 'local territorial unit' he thought underpinned the kingdom of Alba. He further imagined that these 'local territorial units' were each equivalent in size to one or two parishes and that each township/fermtoun in these 'local territorial units' was either a half, a whole, or a double davoch, though nowhere did he discuss the evidence or his reasoning behind these deductions.[34] As the previous chapter has already shown, this cannot have been the case. Within this network of 'local territorial units' Grant envisaged (like Skene) a hierarchy of officials below the king with toiseachs and their kindreds controlling the 'local territorial units' and mormaír (sing. mormaer) controlling provinces. For Grant, mormaír were the foreunners of the later earls and the twin pillars of continuity and evolution were keys to the development of Alba, running from Pictland through to the high medieval kingdom of the Scots.[35]

Writing in 2002, Duncan drew many of these diverse threads together in *The Kingship of the Scots, 842-1292*, when he devoted the first chapter to discussing the subject of the kings of Alba. In this, Duncan argued that the establishment of the kingship of Alba saw the abandonment of Forteviot as a royal centre and the establishment of Scone as the new regnal centre for a new kingdom formed by an amalgamation of Picts and Scots.[36] Duncan accepted Herbert's suggestion that the alternating kingship of Alba could

32 Isabel Henderson, *The Picts* (Nijmegen, 1967), 36.

33 Alexander Grant, 'The Construction of the Early Scottish State', in J. R. Maddicott and D. M. Palliser (eds), *The Medieval State: Essays Presented to James Campbell* (London, 2000), 47-72 [hereafter: Grant, 'Early Scottish State'].

34 Ibid., 51-52.

35 Ibid., 55.

36 A. A. M. Duncan, *The Kingship of the Scots, 842-1292* (Edinburgh, 2002), 13-15 [hereafter: Duncan, *Kingship*].

be best explained by reference to the alternating Uí Néill overkingship, but he also pointed out just how unusual such an arrangement was in a European context.[37]

Nevertheless, persuading people that it is the grandsons of Cináed mac Ailpín who should be given the credit for the change from Pictish to Alba-based terminology is difficult, mainly because of the pre-eminent place that Cináed mac Ailpín holds in popular consciousness as a Gaelic mass-murderer of Picts, even though Cináed himself was described as king of the Picts in his obit. To this end, in 2005, Broun returned to some of the surviving sources relating to Alba, namely the longer Pictish king-list, the Irish Gaelic annals, and the *Chronicle of the Kings of Alba*.

He showed that the term 'Alba' had been known to and used by learned men in Pictland in the 860s to 870s and was later adopted as a designation for Pictland. Partly this was because the Picts regarded themselves as the people of Britain so it must have seemed appropriate to them to have called their country 'Britain', or 'Alba' in Gaelic. Therefore, the switch from Pictland to Alba did not represent something outrageously new but a continuation of an important element of Pictish identity in Gaelic, where Alba may have been a translation-loan into Gaelic of the Pictish word for their country.

However, this raises a further problem concerning how, within a few generations, Alba could be used to refer to an obviously Gaelic kingdom, the origins of which lay in the Gaelic kingdom of Dál Riata. Broun found a solution to this problem in a tenth-century text, *Míniugud Senchasa fher nAlban* (Explanation of the History of the People of Alba). This, for the first time, contained the inferred idea that the leaders of the kingdom of Alba could all claim descent from the Gaelic kingdom of Dál Riata. A further pedigree, datable to the reign of King Máel Coluim mac Donnchada (1058–1093), and appended to the manuscript that contains *Míniugud Senchasa fher nAlban* adds more detail.

This makes statements about important Albanaig kindreds that branched off the royal pedigree. It states, for example, that the genealogies of the people of Fife and the *Gabranaig* (the inhabitants of the Gowrie?) joined the royal Dál Riatan genealogy at Eochaid Buide. This led Broun to suggest that some or all of the main kingroups found in Dál Riata settled in key areas of Pictland: Cenél Comgaill (Cowal) in Strathearn; a branch of Cenél nGabráin (Kintyre) in the Gowrie, and part of Cenél nOengusa

37 Ibid., 19.

(Islay) to Angus. These settlements could have occurred as early as the seventh century. The final point made by Broun in this article was that the adoption of Alba may not have been a conscious rejection of 'Pictishness' but instead one product of a gradual change in language to that increasingly spoken by the ruling elites in Pictland/Alba, Gaelic.[38]

It is, however, during the last six or so years that huge advances have been made in defining Alba, Scotia, and the geography of pre-1100 north Britain. Broun has once again been at the forefront of these developments, but he has been aided and abetted by Dumville, Fraser, and Woolf. During this time Broun has retreated from his earlier assertion that the use of the Gaelic noun *Alba* to describe just Pictland c.900 was an outrageous change of meaning and he has instead mooted two alternative suggestions. First, noting that the noun *Britannia* occasionally appears in Welsh usage to mean just Wales, he has suggested that the Picts too might particularly have thought of themselves as 'the people of Britain', thereby answering why they also might have thought of their kingdom as 'Alba'. In this model, Alba representing Pictland was not something new but a persistence with a major part of Pictish identity, only this time in Gaelic.

His second suggestion was to further help explain the name change from Pictland to Alba. This involved the Welsh word *Prydain*, meaning Britain. Problems arise because of the existence of a second word, *Prydyn*, originally possibly a Pictish word that was used in *Y Gododdin* to refer to the Picts or Pictland. Broun has further noted that these two words were confused in texts so that *Prydain* could mean either 'Britain' or 'Pictland' and *Prydyn* could mean either 'Pictland' or 'Britain'. To cut a long story short, Broun argues that *Prydyn* was a Pictish word both for Britain and for their own country, just as *Britannia* was used to denote both 'Wales' and 'Britain'. In this model, Alba was the direct Gaelic equivalent of the Pictish word *Prydyn* and could have been a translation-loan into Gaelic of the word that the Picts used to describe their own country.[39]

And here lies the nub of the problem. If any of these theories are correct and Alba c.900 was indeed the effective equivalent of Pictland, comprising both northern and southern kingdoms of the Picts, how then did we arrive at a later situation where Alba 'proper' appears to have been defined as comprising only the lands that lay between the Forth and the Spey, with

---

38 Dauvit Broun, 'Alba: Pictish Homeland or Irish Offshoot?', in Pamela O'Neill (ed.), *Exile and Homecoming. Papers from the Fifth Australian Conference of Celtic Studies* (Sydney, 2005), 234–75.

39 Dauvit Broun, *Scottish Independence and the Idea of Britain* (King's Lynn, 2007), 79–84.

Moray a separate kingdom that had to be reconquered (if that is indeed what happened)? To lose one territory looks like carelessness on the part of the post-900 kings of Alba, but to also lose the lands of Ross, Sutherland, Caithness, and the Northern Isles is surely approaching utter negligence.

This confusing picture can be further complicated. A ninth-century entry in the *Annals of Ulster* states:

> *Amlaiph 7 Auisle do dul i Fortrenn co ngallaib Erenn 7 Alban cor innriset Cruithentuaith n-uile 7 co tucsat a ngiallo.*

> Amlaíb and Auisle went with the foreigners of Ireland and Scotland to Fortriu, plundered the entire Pictish country and took away hostages with them.[40]

The editors of this text translated 'Alban' as 'Scotland', but what does it really mean in this context? Did the author of the original entry intend 'Alba' to mean 'Britain' or one part of north Britain? If it was the latter, this surely indicates that Alba and Fortriu were different places in north Britain at a relatively early date? As if this were not confusing enough, a slightly later entry from a similar type of Gaelic source under the year-date 918 states the following:

> *As beag nach insa laithibh si ro chuirsead Foirtreannaigh agus Lochlannaig cath. As cruaidh imorro ro cuirsiot Fir Alban an cath so, úair baoí Coluim Cille ag congnamh leó, úair ra ghuidhsiod go diochra é, úair ba he a n-apstol é, agus as tríd ro ghabhsad creideamh.*

> Almost at the same time the men of Fortriu and the Norwegians fought a battle. The men of Alba fought this battle steadfastly, moreover, because Colum Cille was assisting them, for they had prayed fervently to him, since he was their apostle, and it was through him that they received faith.[41]

This latter entry appears to suggest that the terms 'Alba' and 'Fortriu' were synonymous or was the scribe just having a bad day and got his nouns mixed up? The same event also appears in the *Annals of Ulster*, but this

---

40 *Ann. Ulster*, 866.1.
41 Joan Newlon Radner, *Fragmentary Annals of Ireland* (Dublin, 1978), 168–71 [hereafter: Radner, *Fragmentary Annals*].

just refers to *Fir Alban* (the men of Alba).[42] A question that is perhaps too awful for us to contemplate is this: are we now placing too much reliance upon the annalists as accurate recorders of ethnic synonyms for the various peoples living in north Britain before *c.*1100?

But perhaps the most important theory in relation to Alba to have been advanced during the last six years is one constructed by Woolf. This is that Moray was the location of the older Pictish kingdom of Fortriu. If accepted, this fundamentally alters all of our perceptions about Pictland, Alba, and the formation of the medieval kingdom of Scotia, as Fortriu was hitherto thought to have been located south of the Mounth. This theory is discussed in the following chapter by examining the evidence relating to Moray in some detail. It seems to be crucial to our understanding of how the late-eleventh- and twelfth-century kingdom of Scotia emerged as a fully functioning and unified political unit.

Mormaer, Toísech, Cro, and Kelchyn: the structure of Albanian society

At the highest level of society in Alba we know that the royal kindred was divided into two main groupings, Clann Áeda meic Cináeda and Clann Custantín meic Cináeda, both descended from Cináed mac Ailpín. Like the Uí Neill kings in Ireland, it is probable that Clann Áeda meic Cináeda and Clann Custantín meic Cináeda each controlled different territories in Alba. While it seems likely that the core of Clann Custantín meic Cináeda lands were located south of the Mounth, it is currently impossible to tell where the Clann Áeda meic Cináeda territories were located. The sources are also quite clear that the lowest level of society in Alba was slavery. It is, however, much more difficult to uncover details concerning everyone in between these two extremes.

The impression garnered from the sources is that the rank of society immediately below the king was occupied by men known as mormaír (sing. mormaer). Perhaps surprisingly, the first references to people holding this rank occur in the Irish Gaelic Annals during the tenth century (see Table 2.1).

Writing in 1837, Skene made five key points about these men. First, that the office of mormaer was next in dignity and power to that of the king. Second, that the title was always associated with one of the great

42 *Ann. Ulster*, 918.4.

Table 2.1 **The first references to people holding the rank of mormaer occur in the Irish Gaelic Annals during the tenth century.**

918	*Raghnall dono do fuabairt iar suidhiu i llorg fer nAlban coro la ar dibh acht nad farcbath ri na mor-móer di suidibh.* (Ragnall, however, then attacked in the rear of the men of Alba and made a slaughter of them, although none of their kings or mormaír was cut off.
976	*Cellach mac Fíndgaine, Cellach mac Bairedha, Donnchadh mac Morgaínd, tri mormair Alban.* (Cellach son of Findguine, Cellach son of Bard, and Duncan son of Morgrund three mormaír in Alba).
1014	*Domhnall m. Eimhin m. Cainnigh mormhaer Marr i nAlbain.* (Domnall son of Eimen son of Cainnech mormaer of Marr in Alba).[43]

districts of Scotland. Third, that mormaír succession was hereditary in the male line. Fourth, that mormaír must also have been the leaders of great tribes. His final point was that mormaer was a Scottish Gaelic title and office.[44]

Writing almost thirty years later, Robertson concentrated more upon the office of maer, arguing that each maer was a royal official appointed to manage either Crown or fiscal lands and that the maer later became known as the thane. In this model each maer or thane was responsible both for the collection of royal dues and for the presence of the tenantry at a hosting each year. But Robertson also noted the appearance of a still greater official, the mormaer or 'Lord High Steward'. Essentially, according to Robertson, a mormaer was a maer who had been placed to manage a province or earldom rather than a thanage.[45]

Other nineteenth-century writers agreed with this assessment of the mormaer as a Crown official who acted as a steward of a province on behalf of the king, but they could not agree upon who eventually replaced the mormaer. Stuart opined that the office was replaced by the *vice-comes* (sheriff), whereas Innes saw a direct link between mormaer and *comes* (earl) as both controlled provinces.[46] This interpretation was challenged in 1932 by Watson who noted that the phonetics of the word as recorded in the

43 *Ann. Ulster*, 918.4, 1014.2; http://www.ucc.ie/celt/published/G100002/index.html Accessed 30 January 2010.
44 W. F. Skene, *The Highlanders of Scotland*, 2 vols (London, 1837), i, 79–83.
45 Robertson, *Early Kings*, i, 102–6.
46 J. Stuart (ed.), *The Book of Deer* (Edinburgh, 1869), lxxviii–lxxxi; Innes, *Scotch Legal Antiquities*, 96–97.

Book of Deer (*morair*) demonstrated that the letter 'o' was originally short so the compound must mean either 'sea-steward' or 'sea-officer', essentially *mor* followed by the compositional form of *muir* (sea). Watson did, however, also think that mormaer was the equivalent of the Latin word *comes*.[47]

This latter interpretation was comprehensively assaulted by Jackson in 1972. For him, there was no historical evidence that the 'sea-officer' ever existed; and how could such a post be later transformed into the rank of earl when some Scottish earldoms were landlocked? On the linguistic side of the argument Jackson also argued that the Pictish word for 'great' would probably have been *mōr*, with a long 'o' and, like other early Celtic languages, the Pictish word for 'official' would doubless have been *maer*. Moreover, a compound of the two would have given *morvaer* with a short 'o', exactly the form needed to explain the development of the modern Scottish Gaelic word *morair*.[48] This explanation was accepted with little fuss. Duncan, for example, wrote in 1975 that mormaer meant a 'great steward' who was effectively a territorial magnate, one of whose functions was to lead the army of that province in battle.[49]

However, during the last five years, Woolf and Fraser have both argued that Jackson was wrong and Watson's theory is to be preferred. Woolf was the first to break cover on this topic in 2007 when he suggested that the naval levy for the Gaelic kingdom of Dál Riata, organised by *prímchenéla* (chief kindreds), meant that the chiefs of the kindreds of Dál Riata may have been known as admirals. Gaelic settlers could then have brought this title eastwards as they moved into Pictland. His alternate suggestion was that mormaer could have originated either as 'great steward' or as 'sea steward' as an indigenous Pictish term.[50] While this argument is ingenious, it does explain why the title mormaer is completely unknown in all Gaelic sources until the tenth century AD when it was used to describe men from north Britain.

Some two years later, Fraser further refined Woolf's theory. He argued that one sea stewartry had retained its name in the Scottish landscape. This was Morvern, in Gaelic *A'Mhorbhairn*. In this scenario, Onuist son of Fergus, king of the Picts, took this part of Dál Riata in the 730s and then

---

47 W. J. Watson, *Bardachd Ghaidhlig: Specimens of Gaelic Poetry, 1550–1900*, 2nd edn (Stirling, 1932), 370.
48 Jackson, *Deer*, 106–8.
49 Duncan, *Kingdom*, 110–11.
50 Alex Woolf, *From Pictland to Alba, 789–1070* (Edinburgh, 2007), 342–43 [hereafter: Woolf, *Pictland to Alba*].

placed it in the hands of sea-maers with responsibilities for regional stewartries. For Fraser, this would explain how a maritime title came to be borne by Alba's great regional stewards in possession of non-maritime stewartries.[51]

However, this explanation contradicts the received etymology of Morvern, explained by Watson in 1926. According to his etymology Morvern meant 'sea gap' and the word was a compound derived from *muir* (the sea) and *bearn* (a gap).[52] This is a place-name that fits the local topography. Neither Woolf nor Fraser has explained why the received (Watson's) etymology for *A'Mhorbhairn* might be wrong and why their interpretation is preferable. Until this is explained in detail in print, it is difficult to fully accept the alternative case they make for the meaning of the word mormaer.

There is one further point to make about mormaír. Although a number of later sources directly link the two titles mormaer and Latin *comes* (earl), no text contemporary to the early twelfth century, when mormaír fade from sight in the sources and *comites* appear, ever directly equates the two titles; so it can never be assumed that one was a direct replacement for the other. In addition, unlike *comes*, there is no evidence that the office of *mormaer* was hereditary.

The title *toísech* has, if anything, generated even more historical controversy than mormaer. According to Fordun, this title was a creation of King Máel Coluim mac Cináeda (1005–1034) in the eleventh century:

> *Antiquitis vero consueverant reges suis dare militibus plus aut minus de terris suis in feodofirmam alicuius provincie porcionem vel thanagium. Nam eo tempore totum pene regnum dividebatur in thanagiis. De quibus autem cuique dedit prout placuit vel singulis annis ad firmam, ut agricolis, vel ad decem annorum seu viginti seu vite [ad] terminum cum uno saltem aut duobus heredibus, ut liberis et generosis, quibusdam itaque, sed paucis, imperpetuum, ut militibus, thanis et principibus, nec tamen adeo libere quin eorum quilibet domino regi solveret annuatim certum censum.*

From ancient times indeed kings had been in the habit of giving to their knights greater or smaller tracts from their own lands in

---

51 James E. Fraser, *From Caledonia to Pictland, Scotland to 795* (Edinburgh, 2009), 358 [hereafter: Fraser, *Caledonia to Pictland*].
52 Watson, *CPNS*, 122–23.

feu-ferme, a portion of some province or thanage. For at that time almost the whole kingdom was divided up into thanages. He apportioned these lands to each man as he thought fit either for one year at a time for ferme, as in the case of tenant farmers, or for a ferme of ten or twenty years or life with at least one or two heirs permitted, as in the case of certain freemen and gentlemen, and to some likewise (but these only a few) in perpetuity, as in the case of knights, thanes and magnates, with the restriction however that any of them should make a fixed annual payment to the lord king.[53]

As Grant remarked in 1993, despite Fordun's claim, little is actually known about the origin of thanages, even though it is thought that a thane administered a unit of land on behalf of a lordly superior, led its inhabitants in war, supervised local justice, and collected render.[54]

In fact, much of what we think we know about the *toísech* comes again from the *c.*1130 *Book of Deer*, even if that evidence is not straightforward. This is because the *Book of Deer* contains references to men described both as *toísech* and *toísech clainne* (head of a noble kindred).[55] Nineteenth-century historians were divided about such men. Some believed, for example, that the *toísech* was a tribal chief who eventually became a thane because of increasing royal authority after 1100. Broun has already discussed these fevered debates in some detail, and examined the arguments earlier commentators utilised as they attempted to reach a consensus about thanes and their responsibilities and duties.[56]

As usual, it was left to Jackson to try to sort out the mess in 1972. He achieved this by arguing that there were two kinds of *toísech* represented in the *Book of Deer* records, the royal thane and the head of a noble kindred. While the second office was known in Gaelic Ireland, Jackson found no parallel there for the royal thane and so concluded that either the former had been part of a Pictish social organisation, or the title had been borrowed from the Anglo-Saxon thane. Jackson may, however, have favoured the first explanation, since he also took the trouble to point out

53 *Chron. Fordun*, i, 186. Translation taken from: *Chron. Bower* (Watt), ii, 417.
54 A. Grant, 'Thanes and Thanages, from the Eleventh to the Fourteenth Centuries', in A. Grant and K. Stringer (eds), *Medieval Scotland* (Cambridge, 1993), pp. 39–81 [hereafter: Grant, 'Thanages']. Also see, Barrow, *Kingdom of the Scots*, 38–39.
55 Forsyth, Broun and Clancy, 'The Property Records', 137 and 141.
56 Dauvit Broun, 'The Property Records in the Book of Deer as a Source for Early Scottish Society', in Katherine Forsyth (ed.), *Studies on the Book of Deer* (Bodmin, 2008), 313–62 [hereafter: Broun, 'Records in the Book of Deer'].

that all known thanages were in the territories formerly controlled by the Picts.[57]

These arguments reached maturity in a paper presented in 2000 by Grant in which he argued that the hierarchical structure of the society of Alba, as indicated by the *Book of Deer* and interpreted by Jackson and others, only worked if it referred to a period before *c.*1130 when the property records were preserved in the *Book of Deer*.[58] According to Grant, thanages were a creation specific to Alba that could also be found in Lothian because the kings of Alba had established their overlordship there in the tenth century. Grant also saw an older parallel to thanages in English *villae regiae* (royal vills) – multiple estates whose renders belonged to the Crown – and suggested that thanages could originally have been Pictish *villae regiae* in origin.[59]

One of these issues has recently been re-examined by Broun, who concluded that the most natural reading of the *Book of Deer* property records suggested that *toísech* and *toísech clainne* were one and the same rank, namely the leader of a noble kindred who possessed a right to levy taxes and services upon finite areas of land for the king and who could also possess other lands in their own right.[60]

There is one final important point to make at this stage. In Scotland north of the Mounth every thanage seems to have been composed of an exact multiple of davochs and the most common multiple of davochs per thanage in Moray is six. This indicates that thanages, like the medieval parish, post-date the period of davoch formation in that part of north Britain, as it would have been infinitely more difficult to divide pre-existing thanages into exact multiples of davochs rather than take exact multiples of davochs and call them thanages. As with the parish, what is currently unknown is the decision process by which it was determined that certain davochs would come together to form a thanage. The evidence for those thanages found south of the Mounth has not yet been checked in the same detail but is surely worthy of further investigation.

So far this chapter has largely been discussing elites in north Britain but there is one text that provides a glimpse into the day-to-day lives of the people who would have comprised the vast majority of the population of

57 Jackson, *Deer*, 114–15.
58 Grant, 'Early Scottish State', 58.
59 Ibid., 64.
60 Broun, 'Records in the Book of Deer', 354–55.

Alba. This is the eleventh-century collection now commonly referred to as *Leges inter Brettos et Scotos* (Laws among Britons and Scots), the earliest surviving copy of which is contained in the Berne manuscript of *c.*1270.[61] Probably originally composed in Gaelic, the text only survives in French, Latin, and Scots versions and it may represent a revised version of an eleventh-century original first compiled when Scottish overlordship was completely established over Strathclyde in the 1070s. This text affords a unique opportunity to view how social status was considered in Alba because it calculates individual honour prices in cows (see Table 2.2) and therefore is exactly the same kind of evidence that is found in Irish Gaelic law texts like *Críth Gablach*.[62]

The first section of *Leges inter Brettos et Scotos* deals with *cro* (Old Gaelic: fixed compensation for death), *galnys* (Old Welsh *galanas*: either compensation for bloodfeud or to settle the feud), and *enach* (Old Gaelic: face or honour), all literally types of 'face' or 'honour prices' by which every person's standing in their community and in society at large was measured. It states that the *cro, galnys*, and *enach* of every man are alike in respect of the *enach* of their wives.[63] It is not a hierarchy of officials.

Table 2.2 **The eleventh-century collection now commonly referred to as** *Leges inter Brettos et Scotos* **(Laws among Britons and Scots) affords a unique opportunity to view how social status was considered in Alba because it calculates individual honour prices in cows.**

King of Scots	1,000 cows or	3,000 oras
A king's son or a *cunte*[64]	150 cows or	450 oras
An *cunt*'s son or thayn	100 cows	300 oras
Son of a thayn	66.66 cows	200 oras
Grandson of a thayn or an *ogthiern*	44 cows and 21.66 pence	
A rustic	16 cows	
A married woman	0.66 of the *cro* of her husband	
An unmarried woman	The same as her brother	

continues

61 http://www.stairsociety.org/Berne_MS/berne_folio61v.htm Accessed 15 July 2010.
62 Fergus Kelly, *A Guide to Early Irish Law* (Dublin, 1988), 8.
63 Ibid., 307 and 310; Dafydd Jenkins (ed.), *The Law of Hywel Dda* (Llandysul, 1986), 346.
64 The most recent editor of this text translates *cunte* as either earl or mormaer: Alice Taylor, 'Leges Scocie and the lawcodes of David I, William the Lion and Alexander II', *SHR*, 88, 2009, 207–88 [hereafter: Taylor, 'Leges Scocie'].

Table 2.2 *continued*

The following section then describes the fines for murder while in the peace of the king and of others:

Any man slain within the peace of the king	180 cows
Any man slain within the peace of the king's son or a *cunte*	90 cows
Any man slain within the peace of an *cunt*'s son or a thain	60 cows
Any man slain within the peace of a thain's son	40 cows
Any man slain within the peace of a thain's grandson	20.66 cows

This is followed by a section on *kelchyn/gelchach* (compensation for loss of status?):

Kelchyn of a king	100 cows
Kelchyn of a king's son or a *cunt*	66.66 cows
Kelchyn of an *cunt*'s son or a thayn	44 cows & 21.66 pence
Kelchyn of a thayn's son	29 cows & 11.33 pence
Kelchyn of a rustic	zero
Murder of the wife of a free man	The husband will have the kelchyn; her friends the *cro* and *galnys*
Murder of the wife of a rustic	The rustic's overlord will have the *kelchyn*; her friends the *cro* and *galnys*

The final section deals with the shedding of blood:

Blood shed from the head of an *cunte* or the king's son	9 cows
Blood shed from the head of an *cunte*'s son or a thayn	6 cows
Blood shed from the head of a thayn's son	3 cows
Blood shed from the head of a thayn's grandson	2.66 cows
Blood shed from the head of a rustic	1 cow
Blood drawn below the breath	Penalties reduced by a third
Blood drawn from an unmarried woman	Same rights as her brother
A blow that does not shed blood	10 pence[65]

The picture painted by these brief glimpses into an earlier form of law is one of a highly stratified society based around the notion of a

---

65 Lord Cooper, *Regiam Majestatem and Quoniam Attachiamenta* (Edinburgh, 1947), 276–79 [hereafter: Cooper, *Regiam Majestatem*].

kin-group in which every person's honour price was calculated according to a set number of cows. Taylor has demonstrated that this system was still used as a way of assessing society in 1221.[66] Just as the kin was responsible for the actions of its members, when a member of that kin-group was killed, wounded, or insulted, so the kin also received a payment for injury.

The Church

Writing in 2000, Barrell stated that the Scottish Church in 'the late eleventh and twelfth centuries witnessed one of those periods of spiritual revival and renewal which have characterised the Christian era'.[67] At face value there is no point in disputing this statement because it is underpinned by what later sources triumphantly tell us about the achievements of Queen Margaret and her two sons, King Alexander I and King David I, in bringing reformed monasticism to Scotia. However, it might be asked whether this perception is at all coloured by the fact that those same sources are not available for the tenth and eleventh centuries, so that we are forced to scrabble around in a dimly lit landscape looking for clues about the pre-AD 1100 Church in Alba.

This search is further hindered by a distinct lack of monumental stonework. Anyone who has visited Meigle, St Vigeans, and St Andrews (but particularly the first two) cannot help but be impressed by the sheer volume of Class II and Class III monumental stonework at these sites, all of which display prominent Christian symbolism. Yet, to all intents and purposes this sculptured stone tradition seems to have been abandoned post-AD 900 – assuming, of course, that the Class III stones actually are 'Pictish'.

By the end of the ninth century, Christianity had been present in north Britain in one form or another for around 400 years and there is little doubt that Colum Cille and his successors on Iona in combination with St Uinniau at Whithorn have grabbed the historiographic limelight to date. However, as more is discovered about the Pictish monastery at Portmahomack in Easter Ross with its evidence of vellum manufacture, so

---

66 Taylor, '*Leges Scocie*', 240–42.
67 A. D. M. Barrell, *Medieval Scotland* (Cambridge, 2000), 42 [hereafter: Barrell, *Medieval Scotland*].

new light is shed on Christianity in Pictland.[68] As yet, unfortunately, we have little idea how the Church was organised at grassroots level, although the work done on early-medieval Gaelic Ireland by Colman Etchingham may help our understanding of what was going on in Pictland and Alba.[69] What little we do know about Scotland is based upon some very brief entries in different sources.

In 848/9, for example, we hear that half of the relics of St Colum Cille were transferred from Kells in Ireland to a new church at Dunkeld, built by King Cináed mac Ailpín. There is no indication whether this was really a new church or just a new building (a slightly earlier king is also linked with founding Dunkeld), but it indicates that Cináed perhaps envisaged an important future role for Dunkeld in his Pictish kingdom. In fact, Broun has suggested that the intended relationship between Dunkeld and Clann Cinaeda meic Alpín might have been identical to that between Armagh and the Uí Néill.[70] If this suggestion is correct, it would certainly be worthwhile having a much closer look at nearby Clunie (Plate 2). This was an important fortified medieval royal estate and hunting forest with an early church and a crannog site. Given its proximity to both Dunkeld and Meigle, together with the fact that it was important enough to be mentioned along with Dunkeld in *The Chronicle of the Kings of Alba* under the year date 849, these three sites could well have been linked in a late-Pictish sacral landscape.[71]

Within sixteen years of the (re)foundation of Dunkeld, the *Annals of Ulster* list the following obit: *Conmal equonimus Tamlachta et Tuathal m. Artgusso prim-escop Fortrenn et abbas Duin Caillenn dormierunt* (Conmal, steward of Tamlacht and Tuathal son of Artgus, chief bishop of Fortriu and abbot of Dunkeld, fell asleep).[72] This is a very interesting entry because it establishes that Tuathal was bishop of an organised Church in Pictland, presumably with an established hierarchy, and a pluralist. The entry is

---

68 Carver, *Portmahomack*, Plate 7a.
69 Colmán Etchingham, *Church Organisation in Ireland AD 650 to 1000* (Kildare, 1999) [hereafter: Etchingham, *Church Organisation in Ireland*].
70 Dauvit Broun, 'Dunkeld and the Origin of Scottish Identity', in Dauvit Broun and Thomas Owen Clancy (eds), *Spes Scotorum, Hope of Scots Saint Columba, Iona and Scotland* (Edinburgh, 1999), 95–114, at 102.
71 *ES*, i, 288.
72 *Ann. Ulster*, 865.6. Etchingham suggested that the title 'prim-escop' might have been comparable to *Suí-epscop*, someone whose episcopal domains were extensive and who had been appointed to a position of particular dignity and authority [Etchingham, *Church Organisation in Ireland*, 184–85].

important for another reason: it might indicate that the abbacy of Dunkeld was not considered to have been in Fortriu in the mid-ninth century (see Chapter 3 for further discussion).

It is likely that Tuathal was not the only bishop north of the Forth–Clyde line. In 963, for example, the sources record the name of Fothud mac Brian, bishop of the islands of Alba, presumably the Western Isles.[73] But whatever the organisation of the Pictish Church, there must have been some operational problems because we are told by *The Chronicle of the Kings of Alba* that sometime between 878 and 889 King Giric mac Dúngail gave liberty to the Scottish Church, which was in servitude up to that time, after the custom and fashion of the Picts.[74] This may have amounted to nothing more than a disagreement over a form of liturgy, but this enigmatic statement was evidently important enough to the chronicler to be worthy of mention.

Alternatively, King Giric may also have been initiating a major Church reform connected with the presence of *céli Dé* (clients of God) reformers from Ireland in Pictland. In 1996, Clancy argued that a key figure responsible for the appearance of *céli Dé* communities in Pictland was Diarmait, abbot of Iona between 814 and c.831. He is known to have visited Pictland twice with relics of St Colum Cille during the reigns of two different kings in 818 and 829 and for each of these two kings the sources record either the building of a new church or the foundation of a new monastic community (Dunkeld and St Andrews).[75]

It did not take long for the *céli Dé* to gain royal favour and patronage. In 906, King Causantín mac Áeda and Bishop Cellach swore to keep the laws and disciplines of the faith and the rights of the Churches and the gospels, in the same manner as the Irish. It was probably no coincidence that Causantín retired into the *céli Dé* community at St Andrews when he relinquished his kingship in 943.[76] It also might be asked whether this latter entry and the royal patronage it describes indicates that St Andrews had by then overtaken Dunkeld in terms of ecclesiastic primacy in Alba.

During the tenth and eleventh centuries, *céli Déi* communities are either known or thought to have been operating in various sites in Alba including

73 http://www.ucc.ie/celt/published/T100005B/index.html Accessed 24 March 2010; Etchingham, *Church Organisation in Ireland*, 185.

74 *ES*, i, 365.

75 Thomas O. Clancy, 'Iona, Scotland, and the Céli Dé', in Barbara E. Crawford (ed.), *Scotland in Dark Age Britain* (St Andrews, 1996), 111–30.

76 *ES*, i, 445–47.

Brechin, Deer, Loch Leven, St Andrews, Monymusk, and Abernethy.[77] We are fortunate that some of the names of members of the Abernethy community have survived in a late-eleventh-century St Andrews' document, thereby allowing us a snapshot of the community at one point in time. This document was witnessed by (among others), '. . . Nesse and Cormac, sons of Macbeath, and Malnethe son of Beollani, priests of Abernethy, and Berbeadh, *rectoris scolarum* of Abernethy'.[78] This last office is likely the Latin equivalent of Gaelic *fer léiginn*, the head of a *scriptorium*: another man bearing the same title witnesses one of the grants in the *Book of Deer*.[79]

At both Brechin and Abernethy there are more tangible reminders of these communities in the form of the round towers that still survive to this day but which are much more commonly found in Ireland (Plate 3). It has recently been argued by Fernie that these two towers are quite late in date, *c*.1090–*c*.1130, because he saw clear signs of Anglo-Norman architectural influence (angle rolls and nook shafts around the opening on the belfry) in the stonework of the towers.[80] In contrast, Cameron has argued that their architectural history is more complicated. At Abernethy he noted different phases of building work and suggested that the earlier eleventh century might be a more appropriate date, while at Brechin he suggested that a tenth-century date was more likely.[81]

Apart from the *céli Dé* communities there are also a number of references to pre-1100 bishops in Alba, most often relating to the sees of St Andrews and Glasgow, but some of these only appear in later sources like Bower's *Scotichronicon*. This does not invalidate them as historical figures, but a degree of caution has to be employed. When figures like the named bishops of St Andrews can be independently verified by other sources, they are often given the title *ardescop Alban* (chief bishop of Alba).[82] Little is known about what this meant in practical terms, and the situation is further complicated because of the claims of primacy over the Scottish Church known to have been made by York during the eleventh century, and the parallel campaigns to raise St Andrews to metropolitan

77 Cowan and Easson, *Religious Houses*, 46–54 [hereafter: *MRHS*].
78 *ESC*, no. 14.
79 Forsyth, Broun and Clancy, 'The Property Records', 138–39.
80 Eric Fernie, 'Early Church Architecture in Scotland', *PSAS*, 116 (1986), 393–411.
81 N. Cameron, 'St Rule's Church, St Andrews, and early stone-built churches in Scotland', *PSAS*, 124, 1994, 367–78.
82 *Ann. Ulster*, 1093.2.

status.[83] There are two further problems that, if they can be solved, are key to gaining greater understanding of the eleventh-century Church in Alba. First, how was the Church structured at a local level and, second, how was provision made for ordinary people?

In an important article published in 1989, Barrow examined the structure of the medieval Church in Badenoch, Strathavon and Strathspey, looking for evidence of pre-parochial ecclesiastic activity. He argued for a direct link between earlier units of secular lordship and medieval parishes, speculating that during the process of parochial creation there was a tendency to make a parish out of every shire or thanage. However, he also noted that some parishes contained more than one thanage and there were also instances where no link between thanage and parish could be established.

For Barrow, the key to this pre-AD 1100 provision of ecclesiastic care was the davoch, and he mooted that at 'some remote period' there was an intention to provide a place of worship, baptism, and burial in many davochs and half-davochs. Then, in the period of parochial formation during the twelfth and thirteenth centuries (his words), one of these davoch or half-davoch churches was selected to become a parochial church, with the rest becoming either dependent chapels or falling out of use. Such a hypothesis, according to him, had the added benefit of explaining the large numbers of ecclesiastic-related place-names in the landscape that are far in excess of the known number of parishes.[84]

In 1992, Rogers examined the establishment of the parochial system in Perthshire and argued that almost all of the seventy-two parishes in Perthshire had been created before c.1200. Furthermore, beyond the union of parishes and the creation of a small number of new units, the parishes that had been formed by 1200 remained unchanged until the 1890–91 alterations in parochial boundaries. He also argued that the legal establishment of teind rights (a tax defined as a tenth of everything that was renewed each year) had the effect of hardening boundaries and fossilising the patterns of territorial organisation and settlement in Scotland during the twelfth century. After all, no member of society in any specific area would want to

---

83 Dauvit Broun, 'The Church of St Andrews and its Foundation Legend in the Early Twelfth Century: Recovering the Full Text of Version A of the Foundation Legend', in Simon Taylor (ed.), *Kings, Clerics and Chronicles in Scotland, 500–1297* (Bodmin, 2000), 108–14.

84 G. W. S. Barrow, 'Badenoch and Strathspey, 1130–1312: 2 The Church', *Northern Scotland*, 9, 1989, 1–16 [hereafter: Barrow, 'Badenoch and Strathspey: 2'].

be in the situation whereby they were legally forced to pay teinds to more than one parish church. Like Barrow, Rogers suggested that the newly created medieval parishes used pre-existing local churches because of an established relationship to and status within the territorial communities that became parishes.[85]

Clancy discussed both these contributions to early Church history in 1995 and argued that they made sense, particularly in light of evidence from Ireland in their law tracts about the correspondence of structures of pastoral care and the basic unit of lordship, the *túath*. In this article Clancy also paid close attention to place-names in Scotland that contained either *annaid* (AD 800–AD 1100 term for the mother church of a local community) or the rarer *domnach* (a church). He concluded that an Irish Gaelic pastoral model with the *annaid* at its hub seemed to underpin the formalisation of the medieval parochial system in Scotland.[86]

Exactly when the latter occurred is unknown, though most commentators favour King David I (1124–1153) as the instigator. During the reign of David's grandson King William I, a reference was made in a document dated 1187 x 89 to the enforcement of the payment of teinds to local churches according to King David's decision.[87] This statement appears to refer to an assize held shortly after the beginning of David I's reign in which he allocated a tenth of his income (a teind) to the Church. Accordingly, it has been argued that by legally insisting on a regularised payment of teinds, King David also effectively created the parochial system, where a parish could be defined as a geographic area in which every member of society resident paid one-tenth of their income to a local church.[88] This general line of argument has proved to be very persuasive, leading one recent author to claim that it was actually royal policy during the reign of David I to create parishes.[89]

But, if the belief that King David I created parishes is correct, it must have involved an extraordinary burst of activity throughout twelfth-century Scotland. Presumably someone would have had to decide which lands and communities were to be included within each particular parish and then

85 John M. Rogers, 'The Formation of the Parish Unit and Community in Perthshire', unpublished PhD thesis, University of Edinburgh, 1992, 72–114 [hereafter: Rogers, 'Thesis'].
86 Thomas O. Clancy, 'Annat in Scotland and the Origins of the Parish', *Innes Review*, 46, 1995, 91–115.
87 *RRS*, ii, no. 281.
88 Duncan, *Kingdom*, 298.
89 Barrell, *Medieval Scotland*, 54–55.

inform every community in the kingdom of the decision. Furthermore, everyone liable for teinds would then have to be informed of the arrangements relating to what was taxable, how, when, and by whom their taxes would be collected. If we stop for a moment and think about the sheer amount of work that the creation of a parochial system in such a fashion entailed, it is quite remarkable that absolutely no records or references to the processes of parochial creation have survived from the reign of David I onwards, particularly since there must have been many disputes relating to the arrangements put in place. Absence of information is not proof that something did not happen, but it is nevertheless quite remarkable given the amount of other material that has survived from that king's reign.

In fact, the belief that King David I created the medieval parochial system may be flawed. First, Barrow himself clearly recognised that the decision of the undated King David I assize, no records of which have survived, may have been enforceable in just one diocese (St Andrews) rather than in all dioceses across Scotland.[90] Second, while it cannot be doubted that there was an assize concerned with the payment of teinds during the reign of King David I, the wording of the 1187 x 89 document that refers back to it (specifically in the context of St Andrews diocese) implies that the assize was more concerned with enforcing a forfeiture of one cow and one sheep from each neyf to the Crown for the non-payment of teinds. If the thane, lord, or sheriff either did not enforce this decision or withheld their own teind payments, they had to pay a fine of eight cows to the Crown.

There is one further point to consider in relation to this assize. The 1187 x 89 document that refers back to the earlier assize was produced for the benefit of Richard de Lincoln, bishop of Moray (1187–1203), after there had been no bishop of Moray in office between 1184 and 1187. More importantly, between 1179 and 1186 parts of Moray (north of Inverness) and all of Ross had been under the effective control of Donald MacWilliam, claimant to the Crown via his descent from King Donnchad mac Máel Coluim, eldest son of King Máel Coluim mac Donnchada. These, combined with a vacancy in the bishopric of Caithness, had effectively left Gregory, bishop of Ross, as the chief representative of royal authority in the north. Accordingly, the 1187 x 89 document that refers back to the assize of King David I should perhaps be viewed as one means of re-establishing royal authority across much of northern Scotland in the aftermath

90 G. W. S. Barrow, *Kingship and Unity* (Edinburgh, 1981), 73 [hereafter: Barrow, *Kingship*].

of the upheavals of the 1180s. In the same vein there is no reason why the earlier assize of King David could not also have been produced to solve a similar problem, as it is likely that large parts of the country fell outwith royal control in the period c.1130–34 when both Oengus of Moray and Máel Coluim, son of King Alexander I, led armies against the king.

Looking a little further afield, current research in England would indicate that many parochial units, as they would now be recognised, had been formed both during and after the tenth century out of a now obselete and near-invisible layer of older and larger Anglo-Saxon quasi-parishes. These older quasi-parishes can be traced through payments made by 'daughter-' to 'mother'-churches.[91] In Scotland, however, there is no such written evidence, and references to the early Church are largely confined to annalistic entries and to place-names that contain Old-Gaelic words like andóit and domnach. Nevertheless, despite the spectacular absence of records for the pre-1124 Church in Scotland, it would take extraordinary pleading to suggest that until after 1124 the senior ecclesiastic officials of the Church in the kingdoms of Pictland and Alba ignored the organised system utilised to govern the Church by their closest southern neighbour, not to mention throughout Europe. In fact, it surely would have been near impossible to administer the lands belonging to the dioceses of St Andrews and Dunkeld, for example, without some type of efficient administrative system like a quasi-parish to collect taxation, run ecclesiastic estates, and administer to their constituents.

The previous chapter has clearly demonstrated that it was the Pictish davoch that underpinned the parochial system across much of medieval Scotland north of the Mounth; in other (non-Pictish) areas, differently named units of land assessment like the officiary and the arachor also seem to underpin medieval parishes. Effectively, the intimate relationship between the davoch and the parish means that in theory parishes across the Pictish part of north Britain could have been created any time between c.900 and the beginning of the twelfth century, although the period of reform that western Christendom underwent during the eleventh century might be responsible. The question that should be asked is this: how long were the kings of Pictland or Alba with their abbots and bishops likely to have taken to initiate the parochialisation of their country when they would have been well aware of the workings of the system elsewhere in Britain and Europe?

One final point to make in this section concerns Barrow's argument that each davoch or half-davoch once possessed a church. A similar claim has recently been made for the period of parish formation in Ireland where it has been suggested that when a *túath* was granted parochial status and a parish church site was identified, the remaining pre-existing ecclesiastic sites in the *túath* began to fall out of use.[92] Barrow's theory, however, was unfortunately predicated upon an extremely narrow evidence base and, outwith his area of study, no further evidence across Moray has been found to support the assertion. Much the same point can also be made about Clancy's theory in relation to the *annaid*. This remains a comparatively rare place-name that tends to appear in distinct clusters, perhaps pointing to a different (or even earlier) form of ecclesiastic organisation. Clancy's case is further hampered by incomplete listings for this place-name element, many of which seem to refer to detached portions of land that had once been granted to a mother church.

Just as Chapter 1 demonstrated that the landscape of Alba and the territories in which its kings later established overlordship were divided into distinct units of land assessment, so the society of Alba has been shown to be similarly stratified. Based upon the kindred, everyone had an honour price that, according to *Leges inter Brettos et Scotos*, could be calculated in cows for various injuries or insults. This evidence is very close to that found in the law tracts of both Gaelic Ireland and pre-conquest Wales. The Church in Alba was also a highly structured organisation even if we do not yet fully understand the inter-relationship between the bishops of Alba and the abbots that appear so frequently in the sources. A distinct lack of evidence would appear to suggest that the dearly held belief that the medieval parochial pattern in Scotland was only created post-1124 is unsound. Since davochs and other units of land assessment clearly underpin the parochial system, and since those units of land assessment are much older than the 1120s, in theory the parochial structure in north Britain could have been created any time between the formation of these units of land assessment and 1124.

---

92 Patrick Nugent, 'The Dynamics of Parish Formation in High Medieval and Late Medieval Clare', in Elizabeth FitzPatrick and Raymond Gillespie (eds), *The Parish in Medieval and Early Modern Ireland: Community, Territory and Building* (Bodmin, 2006), 186–210.

CHAPTER THREE

Ein Volk, Ein Reich, Ein Führer? North Britain, c.1000 to c.1130

For the period between *c.*1000 and *c.*1130, understanding the roles of the medieval kingdoms and/or provinces of Strathclyde/Cumbria and Moray is crucially important to assessing the gradual evolution of the kingdom of Alba. However, trying to evaluate the processes by which Alba gradually grew into the dominant kingdom in north Britain is another matter altogether, made even more problematic by the simple fact that neither Strathclyde/Cumbria nor Moray can currently be precisely defined by historical geography.

A lack of information about either fixed territorial boundaries or areas of overlordship makes it very difficult to assess both the natural and economic resources that the respective rulers or mormaír of those areas would have had at their disposal and this, in turn, blurs our current perceptions about their respective abilities to conduct warfare in and establish overlordship over other parts of north Britain. Of these two areas, it is Moray that has hitherto attracted more historical attention. Partly this is because there are many more references to Moray than Strathclyde during the eleventh and early twelfth centuries in contemporary sources, and partly because of the key roles in the history of Alba that Moray and Moravians have been traditionally assigned by chroniclers and historians. This chapter will evaluate both areas in an attempt to solve some of the mysteries and historiography is employed to better understand how various theories have arisen and evolved across time.

Defining eleventh-century Moray

In any examination of the historiography of Moray it rapidly becomes evident that the vast majority of historians have been quite content to utilise the name 'Moray' without attempting to define the exact geographic extent of this area. This problem has reached quite remarkable proportions in work published during the last two decades where at least one collection of essays has been devoted to discussing historical problems within the boundaries of the 'province' of modern-day Morayshire, which is a relatively recent geographic entity, even though the authors were aware that the lands now considered to be in Morayshire were actually only a very small part of medieval Moray.[1]

This lack of precision regarding the geography of the province of Moray is not just a modern phenomenon. At least partly, the narrower description of Moray was based upon the eighteenth-century writings of Lachlan Shaw, who defined the county of Moray as the county of Elgin and Forres.[2] This description was probably the reason why in 1988 Barrow redefined Moray as the three river-systems of Spey, Findhorn and Nairn.[3] However, evidence relating to a narrower meaning of Moray cannot be taken back any further in time than Shaw. Accordingly, it must be discarded as a meaning pertinent to Shaw's time. In fact, given the importance of Moray, it is quite staggering that no twentieth-century historian has ever seriously attempted to define the exact geography of the area.[4]

In general, most historians have been quite happy to utilise the phrase 'Moray west of the Spey' in their writings.[5] This rather nebulous definition seems to have been ultimately based on a conflation of two separate descriptions of the provinces of Alba, both of which are contained in the tract called *De Situ Albanie* (see Chapter 1).[6] The use of this tract in an attempt to describe the geography of Moray has also led to a second problem, because *De Situ Albanie* paired Moray with Ross. Accordingly, for George Buchanan, writing in the sixteenth century, the River Spey was, 'the utmost boundary of Ross-shire.'[7] During the nineteenth century, historians like Chalmers and Burton perpetuated this belief when they discussed Moray: '. . . that dubious colony in the extreme north, sometimes called Ross'.[8]

Since the sixteenth century, historical views on this pairing have not changed in any significant way. At various times during the last three

1 For example, W. D. H. Sellar (ed.), *Moray: Province and People* (Edinburgh, 1993), where the map on page vi includes Stratha'an but excludes Strathbogie and Inverness-shire.

2 Lachlan Shaw, *The History of the Province of Moray*, 3 vols (Edinburgh, 1775), i, 185.

3 G. W. S. Barrow, 'Badenoch and Strathspey, 1130–1312: 1 Secular and Political', *Northern Scotland*, 8, 1988, 1–16, at 2 and at 10, n. 8.

4 Alex Woolf, ' "The Moray Question" and the Kingship of Alba in the Tenth and Eleventh Centuries', *SHR*, 79, 2000, 145–64 [hereafter: Woolf, 'Moray Question']

5 P. Hume Brown, *History of Scotland to the Present Time*, 3 vols (Cambridge, 1911), i, 30 [hereafter: Hume Brown, *History*].

6 Broun, 'The Seven Kingdoms', 25.

7 Buchanan, *History*, i, 349.

8 J. H. Burton, *The History of Scotland*, 8 vols (Edinburgh, 1897), i, 338 [hereafter: Burton, *Scotland*].

decades, Duncan, Barrow, and MacDonald have all suggested that Ross was originally part of the greater territory of Moray,[9] probably because the first recorded appearance of an earl of Ross does not occur until 1157,[10] some 130 years after the first appearance of the designation *mormaer Moreb* (mormaer of Moray) in 1020.[11] Another possible reason for this acceptance of Moray and Ross as forming one geographic area before *c.*1157 is that at least one other medieval Scottish province was divided into two separate regions: between 1211 and 1214 Caithness was divided into two parts by King William I when all of Sutherland was granted to Hugh Freskin.[12]

However, the assumption that Ross was not a separate province before 1157 is not a safe supposition to make, for two reasons. Firstly, Bishop MacBethad of Rosemarkie and Bishop Gregory of Moray both witnessed a royal confirmation to Dunfermline Abbey during the period 1127 x 1131.[13] If it is assumed that the dioceses of Rosemarkie and Ross were identical, and that the names were often used interchangeably, this is a clear indication that Ross was recognised as at least a separate ecclesiastic province from Moray at this time.[14] Secondly, as there are no known instances of any early medieval Scottish secular province ever containing two dioceses, it would be safer to assume that Moray and Ross were also separate secular provinces by 1127 x 31.[15] How much further back in time this separation of Moray and Ross might have gone is unknown: the history of the early Church in the north of Scotland is a very obscure topic, due mainly to missing diocesan records. However, as there is no indication in any surviving primary source that either the province or diocese of Ross were new creations in the eleventh or early twelfth century, it is probably safer to presume that the two provinces could already have been distinct territorial areas for some time.

During the last 200 years, only two historians have attempted to define the boundaries of Moray: Chalmers and Rhind. The attempt made by

---

9 Duncan, *Kingdom*, 167; Barrow, *Kingship*, 51; R. Andrew McDonald, 'Treachery in the Remotest Territories of Scotland: Northern Resistance to the Canmore Dynasty, 1130–1230', *Canadian Journal of History*, 33, 1999, 161–92, at 174 [hereafter: McDonald, 'Treachery'].

10 *Chron. Holyrood*, 151.

11 *Ann. Tig.*, ii, 359.

12 Duncan, *Kingdom*, 197.

13 G. W. S. Barrow (ed.), *The Charters of David I* (Woodbridge, 1999), 71 [hereafter: Barrow, *Chrs. David I*].

14 Duncan, *Kingdom*, 267.

15 Grant, 'Ross', 103–4, has recently argued that Ross had always been a separate province and that it came under direct Crown control in the 1070s.

Chalmers was particularly noteworthy because he was the first historian to utilise the internal evidence from the charter given by King Robert I to Thomas Randolph in 1312, which (supposedly) resurrected the earldom of Moray within named marches.[16] Unfortunately, Chalmers was more concerned with using this evidence to define the boundaries of Argyll rather than Moray. In contrast, Rhind made a real attempt to ascertain the boundaries of Moray. After examining the evidence, he concluded that the province stretched from the Spey to the Beauly Firth and from Loch Lochy, through Lochaber, skirting the bases of Cairngorm and Ben Rinnes, and back to the Spey.[17] Even this definition excluded large sections of territorial units that may originally have been part of Moray.

It is also notable that, unlike some other earldoms, lordships and dioceses in Scotland, the fourteenth-century diocese and earldom of Moray were not wholly coterminous.[18] Each of them included lands that were not present in the other. The diocese, for example, included the parishes of Cromdale, Abernethy and Aberlour, the lordship of Strathavon and the deanery of Strathbogie, none of which were part of the earldom during the fourteenth century. In contrast, in 1312 the earldom included the lordship of Lochaber when it was not part of the medieval diocese.[19] A better awareness of the geographic extents of both the secular earldom and the diocese of Moray, and how they changed over time (if at all), may help historians to better understand some of the forces that helped to shape the eleventh-century kingdom of Alba. In order to do this, however, it is necessary to use fourteenth-century evidence since that is the earliest surviving material relating to the medieval geography of Moray (*Plate 4*).

The boundaries of the diocese of Moray

There are four main points of interest in the reconstruction of the boundaries of the diocese of Moray, dated to *c.*1300. The first of these occurs on the northernmost boundary of the diocese in the parish of Convinth.

16 *RRS*, v, no. 389; George Chalmers, *Caledonia: or a Historical and Topographical Account of North Britain*, 8 vols, new edn (Paisley, 1887), i, 336 (fn.) [hereafter: Chalmers, *Caledonia*].

17 William Rhind, *Sketches of the Past and Present State of Moray* (Edinburgh, 1839), 1 [hereafter: Rhind, *Sketches*].

18 Gordon Donaldson, *Scottish Church History* (Edinburgh, 1985), 21 [hereafter: Donaldson, *Church History*].

19 Peter G. B. McNeill and Hector L. MacQueen (eds), *Atlas of Scottish History to 1707* (Edinburgh, 1996), 337 [hereafter: McNeill and MacQueen, *Atlas*].

There, the medieval diocesan boundary suddenly turned northwards away from the course of the River Beauly, to include the davoch of Erchless, before returning to follow the river once again. This sudden alteration is rather unusual, since a major river feature like the Beauly would have been an obvious boundary marker. Between 1203 and 1224 a list of the eleven davochs in the parish of Convinth gave the following names: *Gulakin, Buntach, Herkele, Cumber, ConeWy, scilicet ii dauachis, Brutach, Muy, et altera Muy, Dunyn and Fothenes . . .*[20] In a slightly later document, dated 1258 and concerning a dispute between the bishop of Moray and John Bisset, lord of the Aird, it was stated: . . . *et alia dauacha in Ros que vocatur Herchelys . . .*[21] Taken together, these two documents categorically place the davoch of Herkele/Herchelys (now Erchless) in the diocese of Moray, the lordship of the Aird, and in the province of Ross. This davoch was still a part of the diocese of Moray in the early eighteenth century.

A few miles to the south-west of Erchless the medieval diocesan boundary took another noticeable deviation, this time travelling southwards away from the River Glass to exclude the davoch of Crochail (originally in the parish of Kilmorack, diocese of Ross, before 1891) from the see of Moray, before returning to the river once more.[22] Since each of these two sudden deviations in the northern diocesan boundary of Moray involved the inclusion and exclusion of one davoch, it seems logical to suggest that there must have been an excambion of land between the two dioceses of Moray and Ross. This exchange resulted in the attachment of the davoch of Erchless in Ross to Convinth parish and the detachment of the davoch of Crochail from one of the three parishes of Kiltarlity, Glen Urquhart and Glen Moriston or Convinth.

There is a further complication. In 1312, the boundary of the earldom of Moray was recorded as following the rivers Beauly and Glass in their entirety, without any deviations.[23] This means that after 1312 the davoch of

---

20 *Moray Reg.*, no. 21.
21 Ibid., no. 122.
22 H. Shennan, *Boundaries of Counties and Parishes in Scotland as settled by the Boundary Commissioners appointed under the Local Government (Scotland) Act of 1889* (Edinburgh, 1892), 150. Under this legislation, Easter-, Mid- and Wester-Crochaill were transferred from the parish of Kilmorack to the parish of Convinth and Kiltarlity. As there is very little information relating to the dabhach of Crochail in particular, and to the parish of Kilmorack in general, it has been presumed for the purposes of this investigation that the dabhach of Crochail had been part of Kilmorack parish since the high-medieval period.
23 *RRS*, v, no. 389.

Erchless was in the diocese of Moray, the lordship of the Aird, and the earldom of Ross, but was not in the earldom and regality of Moray. Presumably, at the same time the davoch of Crochail was in the diocese of Ross and the earldoms of Moray and Ross. There is little doubt that this must have been a very complicated landholding pattern to administer during the medieval period – assuming, of course, that the description of the boundary of the earldom of Moray in the charter of 1312 was actually a contemporary description.

The second point of interest in the diocesan boundary occurs in the west, where the parishes of Glenelg, Kilmonivaig and Kilmallie are outwith the boundaries of the see. The exclusion of these three parishes from the diocese *c.*1300 is worthy of note mainly because it is possible that they had earlier been part of the province of Moray. In a charter granted by King David I to the monks of Urquhart Priory between 1145 and 1153 the monks were given: *decimam cani de Ergaithel de Muref et placitorum et tocius lucri eiusdem Ergaithel* (the tenth part of the king's cáin of Argyll of Moray and of the king's pleas and revenues from that Argyll).[24] The word *Ergaithel* in this sentence is clearly derived from the Middle Gaelic place-name *Airer Gáidel*, now spelt *Earra-Ghàidheal*, and means 'coastland of the Gael'.[25] This raises the issue of locating the 'Argyll of Moray'. It is likely that during the medieval period Argyll once stretched as far north as Loch Broom: in 1256, for example, the parishes of *Nort Argail* (now Wester Ross) were subject to the diocese of Ross.[26] Similarly, the earl of Ross held lands in *Nort Argail* (North Argyll) by 1293.[27] In 1312, it was stated that the southern border of the lands of *Nort Argail* that belonged to the earl of Ross was located immediately to the north of Glenelg.[28]

Accordingly, if it is assumed that these mid-thirteenth-century and early-fourteenth-century definitions of 'north Argyll' had not changed since the mid-twelfth century, it is likely that the 'Argyll of Moray' was originally located to the south of Glen Shiel. This means that the lands of Glenelg could have been the most northerly part of the 'Argyll of Moray'. Unfortunately, it is difficult to decide from these definitions how far

---

24 Barrow, *Chrs. David I*, 144–45.
25 Watson, *CPNS*, 21.
26 Theiner, *Monumenta*, no. 182.
27 *Acts Parl. Scot.*, i, 447 [hereafter: *APS*].
28 *RRS*, v, no. 389. Since the earldom of Ross did not originally include the lands of North Argyll, this would imply that there was originally one 'Argyll', covering much of the west coast of Scotia, and that it must have pre-dated the formation of dioceses.

southwards along the west coast the 'Argyll of Moray' stretched in the period 1145 x 53, although it might be suggested that *Ergadia que pertinet ad Scociam* (Argyll of Scotia) included the lands of Knoydart, Arisaig, Moidart, Ardnamurchan, Ardgour and Morvern, down to the Mull of Kintyre.[29] If this definition is acceptable, the 'Argyll of Moray' can really only have consisted of the districts of Glenelg, Kilmonivaig and Kilmallie. Although this may seem a rather doubtful geographic description, particularly in relation to the latter two areas, they did both border the sea-loch of Loch Linnhe. If this argument is correct, like Glenelg the lands of Kilmallie and Kilmonivaig could conceivably be described as 'coast-lands of Ergaithel de Muref' in the period 1145 x 53 and it should be noted that all three were certainly part of the earldom and regality of Moray in 1312.[30]

It has been argued that in other areas of medieval Scotland the boundaries of some earldoms, lordships and dioceses were originally coterminous, in what has been labelled a 'secular diocese'.[31] This may explain why more than half the dioceses in Scotland have a secular territorial designation, in contrast to English dioceses which were generally named after the seat of the bishop's see. If the former scenario was also applicable to Moray, there is a strong possibility that the lands of Glenelg, Kilmonivaig and Kilmallie (which probably comprised the area known as 'Argyll of Moray') which seem to have been a part of the secular province since at least 1145, had also originally been a part of the diocese of Moray.

If this is the case, a reason has to be found to account for the detachment of these three parishes from the diocese of Moray before c.1300. One possible clue may lie in the creation of the diocese of Argyll, sometime between 1183 and 1193.[32] It is known that the diocese of Argyll was largely created out of the diocese of Dunkeld. But no historian has drawn attention to the fact that the diocese of Argyll also included the three parishes of Glenelg, Kilmonivaig and Kilmallie, which were certainly part of the earldom of Moray in 1312, and which had probably been part of the

29 This definition can be extrapolated from a series of fourteenth-century charters in which the lands of Morvern and Ardnamurchan, together with the lordship of Garmoran (Moidart, Arisaig, Sunart, Morar, Knoydart and Ardgour), are clearly not regarded as part of the lordship of Lochaber [cf. Jean and R. W. Munro, *Acts of the Lords of the Isles 1336–1493* (Edinburgh, 1986), 1–2, and at 10–11; *APS*, i, 372.

30 *RRS*, v, no. 389.

31 Donaldson, *Church History*, 20–21.

32 R. Andrew McDonald, *The Kingdom of the Isles* (East Linton, 1997), 211–12 [hereafter: McDonald, *Kingdom*].

province of Moray forty years earlier. If the province and diocese of Moray were originally geographically identical, it appears that with the creation of the diocese of Argyll the diocese of Moray lost the parishes of Glenelg, Kilmonivaig and Kilmallie before 1193, and that these three parishes were then attached to the new diocese of Argyll. Of course, like any secular lord, it is doubtful that any bishop would voluntarily detach a portion of his diocese, and surrender all property and rights in that portion to another bishop, without some sort of compensation.

Bearing this last point in mind, it has already been noted by other historians that the third point of interest on the boundary of the see of Moray occurs in the south-east of the diocese. This is where the diocesan boundary turns sharply north to exclude the parishes of Mortlach and Cabrach before turning south again to include the deanery and lordship of Strathbogie. Here, it seems likely that the deanery of Strathbogie was tacked on to the original diocese of Moray when Mortlach fell out of use as an episcopal centre sometime before 1140. It is tempting to suggest that this was compensation for Moray's loss of the three western parishes of Glenelg, Kilmallie and Kilmonivaig.

While this suggestion may have some merit, there is also a second option regarding the deanery of Strathbogie and the south-eastern boundary of the diocese of Moray. This is that the lands that now comprise the parishes of Mortlach and Cabrach had been deliberately detached from the early diocese or province of Moray and given to the see of Aberdeen. On a map of the diocese of Moray this suggestion certainly looks feasible: including Mortlach and Cabrach would mean that there was originally one less sudden deviation in the diocesan boundary and that they were once part of Moray.

Of course, choosing either of these two suggestions depends almost entirely upon deciding the status and allegiance of the medieval monastery that is known to have existed at Mortlach before 1131 x 32, by which time Bishop Nechtan had translated the seat of his see from there to Old Aberdeen.[33] Since much of the earliest surviving charter evidence in the Aberdeen Registrum, including those deeds that mention this monastery, have been proven to be forgeries,[34] any attempt to decide whether Mortlach belonged to Moray before the twelfth century is fraught with difficulty.

---

33 Ian B. Cowan (ed. James Kirk), *The Medieval Church in Scotland* (Edinburgh, 1995), 98–99.
34 *Abdn Reg.*, i, xii–xiii; *RRS*, i, 43.

This process is further complicated by the fact that the sources cannot even agree which king of Alba was responsible for founding the monastery in the first instance: John of Fordun claimed that the founder was King Máel Coluim mac Cináeda in 1010; the Aberdeen Registrum claimed it was King Máel Coluim mac Donnchada in 1070.[35]

Fordun's claim that King Máel Coluim mac Cináetha founded Mortlach to commemorate a victory over the Norguigensibus is not supported by the available contemporary evidence for that period, which contains no reference to such a battle, or even to King Máel Coluim mac Cináetha campaigning in Moray. But there may be an element of truth in his story, if it is speculated that it was not King Máel Coluim mac Cináetha but King Máel Coluim mac Donnchada who originally founded the see at Mortlach to commemorate a victory. While there is no record of King Máel Coluim mac Donnchada fighting Norguigensibus c.1070, he certainly did enter Moray. The Anglo-Saxon Chronicle, under the year-date 1078, recorded that in that year King Máel Coluim mac Donnchada captured the mother of Máel Snechta mac Lulaich, all his best men, and all his treasures, and his livestock.[36]

If the Norguigensibus, whom, according to Fordun, King Máel Coluim mac Donnchada defeated at Mortlach in 1070 were actually Moravians led by Máel Snechta mac Lulaich in 1078, it is possible that at that time Mortlach may indeed have been regarded as a part of the province of Moray. Even that would not explain, however, why Mortlach was taken away from Moray and chosen by King Máel Coluim mac Donnchada as the site of a new ecclesiastic establishment to commemorate his victory. The place-name Mortlach though may itself contain a clue. It is likely that this compounded word was originally Mórthulach which, in an Irish Gaelic context, is known to have indicated an inauguration mound.[37] Mortlach was perhaps, then, originally a sacral site for the mormaír of Moray and was deliberately detached from the ecclesiastical province of Moray during the late eleventh century after the Moravians had suffered a defeat at the hands of the king of Alba.

It is difficult to decide which of the two options discussed above is correct. On balance, it is perhaps less likely that the parishes of Mortlach

35 Chron. Fordun, 182–83, Abdn. Reg., i, 250–51.
36 G. N. Garmonsway (trans. and ed.), The Anglo-Saxon Chronicle (Guernsey, 1994), 213 [hereafter: Garmonsway, A-S Chronicle].
37 Dr Simon Taylor, personal communication.

and Cabrach had originally belonged to Moray. The argument for them originally being a part of Moray depends on four suppositions: that it was King Máel Coluim mac Donnchada who founded Mortlach; that he defeated the Moravians there instead of the *Norguigensibus*; that this battle took place in 1078 rather than 1070; and, finally, that Mortlach was an important Moravian sacral site.

The final point of interest in the Moravian diocesan boundary concerns the parish of Ardersier. Although this clearly belongs to Moray in geographical terms, during the medieval period it was a part of the diocese of Ross and this can be simply explained by the fact that to any traveller coming up the east coast and intending to travel to Rosemarkie, which was probably the original seat of the diocese of Ross, Ardersier was the most obvious, and shortest, crossing point by boat. Accordingly, it may be that Ardersier had belonged to Rosemarkie ever since an ecclesiastic community had been present there, and that it continued in the possession of the bishops of Ross during the high medieval period. As well as being the shortest practical way for overland travellers to reach Rosemarkie, a ferry situated here would have been a valuable economic resource for whoever controlled it. Nevertheless, such reasoning is problematic: the 1312 charter of the earldom of Moray to Thomas Randolph did not specifically exclude Ardersier. Accordingly, if the description of the bounds of Moray in this charter is both correct and contemporary, it would seem that after 1312 the parish and lands of Ardersier were in both the diocese of Ross and the earldom of Moray.[38]

The 1312 charter of the earldom of Moray

The second piece of evidence regarding the geography of Moray is contained in the grant of the earldom of Moray from King Robert I to Thomas Randolph, probably originally issued sometime between 12 April and 29 October 1312, which defined the boundaries of the earldom. This states:

> *Incipiendo videlicet ad aquam de Spee sicut cadit in mare et sicut ascendendo per eandem aquam includendo terras de Fouchabre Rothenayk' Rothays et Bocharme per suas rectas metas et diuisas cum*

38 The parish of Ardersier remained a part of the diocese of Ross until at least 1600.

suis pertinenciis et sic ascendendo per dictam aquam de Spee vsque ad marchias de Badenach' et sic includendo omnes terras de Badenach' de Kyncardyn et /de/ Glencarni cum pertinenciis per suas rectas metas et diuisas et sic sequendo marchiam de Badenach' vsque marchiam de Louchabre et sic includendo terras de Louchabre de Maymor del Lozharketh' de Glengareth' et de Glennelg' cum pertinenciis per suas rectas metas et diuisas et sic sequendo marchiam de Glenelg' vsque ad mare versus occidentem et sic per mare vsque ad marchias borialis Ergadie que est comitis de Ross' et sic per marchias illas vsque ad marchias Rossie et sic per marchias Rossie quousque perueniatur ad aquam de Forne et sic per aquam de Forne quousque perueniatur ad mare orientale.[39]

Namely, starting at the water of Spey as it falls into the sea and then rising from that water including the lands of Fochabers, Rathenach, Rothes and Boharm by their rightful boundaries and divisions with their appurtenances and then rising by the said water of Spey up to the marches of Badenoch and then including all lands of Badenoch, of Kincardine and of Glencarnie with appurtenances by their rightful boundaries and divisions and then following the marches of Badenoch up to the marches of Lochaber and then including the lands of Lochaber, of Mamore, of Locharkaig, of Glengarry and of Glenelg with appurtenances by their rightful boundaries and divisions and then following the march of Glenelg up to the sea to the west, and then by the sea up to the northern marches of the Argyll which belongs to the earl of Ross and thus by those marches up to the marches of Ross and then along the marches of Ross until they come to the water of Forne, and then along the water of Forne until it reaches the eastern sea.

There are a number of points of interest in this description that should be discussed in more detail. First, the boundaries of the earldom and diocese of Moray are only coterminous for approximately 40 per cent of the time. If the boundaries of the earldom and diocese were never identical, this is not a problem. However, in other areas of Scotland it has been argued that the boundaries of some earldoms, lordships and dioceses were identical during the medieval period, and Moray has generally been regarded as one

---

39 *RRS*, v, no. 389.

such 'provincial diocese'.[40] This perception is perhaps strengthened by the fact that some of the lands that were in the diocese, but excluded from the 1312 charter, were part of the earldom at a later date.[41] If so, it also follows that the lands that were included within the secular boundaries, but outwith the diocesan boundaries, could also have originally been a part of the diocese of Moray at an earlier date.

The second point of interest is more specific: this is the deliberate inclusion of the four lands of Fochabers, Rathenach, Rothes and Boharm. Two of these lands, Fochabers and Rathenach, were, or had been, royal thanages during the thirteenth and early fourteenth centuries.[42] This puzzle is easily solved. The River Spey ran through all four of these lands so if that river had been used as a boundary marker in the 1312 charter it would have divided the four lands in half.

It is also immediately obvious that this part of the description of the earldom of Moray in the 1312 charter excluded the fourteen medieval parishes of Botriphnie, Glass, Essie, Rhynie, Gartly, Kinnoir, Ruthven, Rothiemay, Inverkeithny, Aberchirder, Botary, Dunbennan, Drumdelgie and Keith, all of which were contained within the diocese of Moray. The reasoning behind the exclusion of these lands may be quite simple. In 1312, all but three of these fourteen parishes (Inverkeithny, Aberchirder and Keith) belonged to David de Strathbogie, earl of Atholl, who had returned to Scotland sometime before 29 October 1312 and been granted sasine of all of his lands. The return of these northern lands, together with their exclusion from the earldom of Moray, could easily have been part of the negotiations that took place when Strathbogie came back into the allegiance of King Robert I.[43]

It is more difficult to decide why the three parishes of Keith, Aberchirder and Inverkeithny were excluded. Aberchirder and Inverkeithny also included the three thanages of Aberchirder, Netherdale and Convinth. Netherdale and Convinth were certainly forfeited by Robert I, and Alexander III had previously declared Aberchirder forfeit.[44] Presumably,

40 Donaldson, *Church History*, 20–21; Barrow, *Kingship*, 67–68.

41 *Reg. Mag. Sig.*, iv, 299 [hereafter: *RMS*].

42 Grant, 'Thanages', 73.

43 Alasdair Ross, 'Men for all Seasons? The Strathbogie Earls of Atholl and the Wars of Independence, *c.*1290–*c.*1335: Part 1 Earl John and Earl David III', *Northern Scotland*, 20, 2000, 1–30, at 15.

44 *RRS*, vi, no. 94A; Aberdeen-Banff Illustrations ii, 216–17.

all three thanages were in Crown hands in 1312. In contrast, the parish of Keith was one of the mensal properties of the bishop of Moray. It can only be presumed that Keith was excluded from the earldom by agreement between Robert I and Bishop David de Moravia.

The third point of interest in the description appears between Rothes and the lordship of Badenoch. Although the lands of Badenoch, Kincardine and Glencarnie were included within the limits of the earldom, the description of the boundaries excluded six parishes (Aberlour, Inveravon, Kirkmichael, Cromdale, Abernethy and Rothiemurchus), at least one thanage (Cromdale), and two lordships (Strathavon and Abernethy), all of which were in the medieval diocese of Moray. Once again, the solution to this question of the inclusion and exclusion of some of these lands may be simple in terms of early-fourteenth-century politics.

In 1312, the lands of Glencarnie, Kincardine and Badenoch had previously belonged to families who had continued to oppose the seizure of the throne by King Robert I in 1306. If the families who had held these lands before 1312 had done so as tenants-in-chief of the Crown, this might explain why the lands were preceded by an *includendo* clause in the charter. This does not mean that these lands had never been part of the province of Moray before 1312, only that they had been granted out to various families to be held directly of the Crown before that date. With the creation or reactivation of the earldom in 1312, these newly confiscated lands were once again specifically included in the regality and earldom of Moray.

In contrast, the parishes of Inveravon and Kirkmichael (which comprised the lordship of Strathavon) and Cromdale belonged to the earls of Fife. Although Earl Duncan did not commit himself to supporting Robert I until 1315, Earl Duncan's aunt, Isabel, was a supporter of the new king and probably helped to inaugurate him in 1306.[45] As such, these three parishes may have been excluded from the earldom of Moray to avoid offending an important supporter of the Bruce kingship.

Unfortunately, it is very difficult to explain the absence of the parish of Abernethy from the 1312 perambulation. At that time, the parish was divided into three distinct areas of lordship between the bishop of Moray, the earls of Mar, and the lord of Badenoch. Accordingly, it seems impossible to reconcile the exclusion of the parish of Abernethy when approxi-

---

45 G. W. S. Barrow, *Robert Bruce and the Community of the Realm of Scotland*, 3rd edn (Edinburgh, 1988), 278 [hereafter: Barrow, *Bruce*].

mately one-third of that parish amounted to a detached portion of the lordship of Badenoch, which was included in the 1312 charter. There are perhaps two main possibilities: first, that the detached portion of the lordship of Badenoch in Abernethy had been removed from the lands of the lordship of Badenoch in 1312 and given to another, though there is no evidence of this; second, that the original perambulation of Moray might pre-date the formation of the lordship of Badenoch.

Another parish that was excluded in this section was Rothiemurchus. This parish was certainly episcopal mensal property in 1312 and it has been argued that it was originally a royal thanage.[46] Neither of these reasons would seem to justify its exclusion from the earldom of Moray. Like the parish of Keith, Rothiemurchus may have been excluded from the earldom of Moray as a result of an agreement between Robert I and Bishop David de Moravia.

The fourth, and last, point of interest in this description concerns the *includendo* clause attached to the lordship of Lochaber (Mamore, Locharkaig, Glengarry and Glenelg). These names probably refer to the parishes of Kilmallie, Kilmonivaig and Glenelg. Before 1312, Lochaber had been the property of the Comyns of Badenoch who were (presumably) disinherited by King Robert I. If the Comyns had held Lochaber as tenants-in-chief of the Crown, this may explain why there was some doubt regarding the new status of the confiscated lordship in 1312. This does not mean that Lochaber had never been part of Moray before 1312, merely that it had been separated from the province at some point before that date and granted to the Comyns to be held directly of the Crown. In fact, assuming that the identification of 'Argyll of Moray' with the parishes of Glenelg, Kilmallie and Kilmonivaig is acceptable, it is probably correct to state that some parts of Lochaber, if not the entire lordship, had been part of the province of Moray since at least the early twelfth century. After Lochaber, the description of the secular boundaries followed the diocesan boundary until it reached the River Glass.

Even if all of the above explanations are acceptable, there remain a number of potential problems with the charter of 1312. This is because there are three occasions where the description of the boundaries clearly divides a parish in half. The first occurs on the southern boundary of the earldom when the parish of Advie in Strathspey is reached. The second and third occasions occur on the northern boundary of the perambulation in the

---

46 *Moray Reg.*, no. 29; Barrow, 'Badenoch and Strathspey: 2', 8.

parishes of Convinth and Kilmorack. However, while the 1312 perambulation may divide these parishes, it does not divide any of the davochs within those parishes but follows their boundaries precisely. This might indicate that the perambulation recorded in the 1312 charter was copied from an earlier document.

Since the 1312 grant of Moray to Thomas Randolph was the first occasion on which the earldom of Moray left direct royal control since the mid-twelfth century, it may have seemed logical to Robert I to grant Moray by the same boundaries that defined the earldom when it was first taken into Crown hands.[47] If he did, the scribe who was responsible for writing the 1312 charter could easily have copied an earlier perambulation of the boundaries of Moray for insertion into the document he was preparing. This scenario would also explain why the perambulators were not named in the document of 1312. If they had been included, anyone reading the charter would have realised that the perambulation was not contemporary. Although there is no supporting evidence, the most obvious date for an earlier perambulation to have taken place was after the defeat of Oengus of Moray in 1130, after which it is likely that Moray was taken into Crown control before being regranted.

Judging by the available evidence, it appears that the ecclesiastic boundaries of Moray changed, possibly on a number of different occasions, between *c.*1000 and *c.*1350. It has been argued that the earliest material relating to the boundaries of Moray is the description of the boundary contained within the 1312 grant of the earldom of Moray to Thomas Randolph. This perambulation, while ignoring parochial boundaries, follows davoch boundaries for approximately 95 per cent of its extent (the remaining 5 per cent is unverifiable). Since it is now certain that parishes in Moray were created from multiples of davochs, it seems logical to suggest that the description of the boundaries of Moray in the 1312 charter must pre-date the formation of parochial units. As suggested above, the most likely dating for this perambulation would have been in the years immediately following the death of Oengus of Moray in 1130, after which the earldom of Moray was taken into direct Crown control before being regranted to William fitz Duncan. Accordingly, it is possible that the 1312

---

47 Of course, King Robert I may have had no choice in the matter since much of the royal Scottish archive was taken to England by King Edward I in 1296 [R. Nicholson, *Scotland, The Later Middle Ages* (Edinburgh, 1974), 51.

charter could actually record the earliest-known extent of the secular province of Moray.

If this theory is correct, it means that some of the suggestions made by Rogers in his 1992 thesis are incorrect. He argued that the legal establishment of teind rights had the effect of hardening boundaries and fossilising patterns of territorial organisation. However, since all of the early parochial and secular boundaries in Moray are clearly based upon davoch boundaries, it would seem that boundaries and many patterns of territorial organisation were already well established in Moray before the advent of the parochial system. Depending on how old the davoch was, this means that the medieval parish boundaries of Moray helped to preserve much older territorial divisions of land.

The theory that the stated boundaries of Moray in the 1312 charter are actually much older is also attractive in that it only requires two suppositions, far fewer than any other argument. It stands in marked contrast to the vast collection of suppositions that have to be made regarding the inclusion and exclusion of various lands if the perambulation was actually contemporary with the grant of the earldom of Moray in 1312. Furthermore, if this theory regarding the early dating of the perambulation of Moray is correct, it also means that the 1312 charter preserves a superb snapshot of the extent of Moray soon after the final extinction in 1130 of its native dynasty of lords. This allows us to calculate that the Moray of c.1130 would have been comprised of approximately 250 davochs.

It has been assumed throughout this section that the earldom and bishopric of Moray were originally coterminous. If they were, it is likely that the bishopric originally extended westwards to include the three parishes of Glenelg, Kilmallie and Kilmonivaig. Then, upon the creation of the diocese of Argyll, sometime between 1183 and 1193, the bishop of Moray lost these three parishes. In return for this loss, the see of Moray gained either twenty-one or twenty-two parishes south of the Spey. Although this may seem like a rather inequitable arrangement, we have no exact idea of the respective land assessments and teind values of the two areas, nor of their respective rentals. It cannot be automatically assumed that the eastern parishes would have been more valuable than the western ones.

Although this theory is conjectural, it probably best accounts for the attachment of the deanery of Strathbogie (together with other Banffshire parishes) to the see of Moray. The alternative, that a number of Banffshire parishes had been deliberately detached from the see of

Moray, depends on at least four suppositions, none of which is particularly convincing.

The final point to make about the diocese of Moray concerns the parish of Ardersier. Although this parish could have belonged to the diocese of Ross from an early date, the fact that it was included in the perambulation of Moray in the charter of 1312 suggests that this was not always the case. Accordingly, if the theory that this perambulation was completed shortly after 1130 is correct, it is possible that the parish of Ardersier was detached from Moray after that date, possibly again during the period of reorganisation that must have occurred after the creation of the diocese of Argyll.

Usurpers, rebels, and malcontents?

Prolonged conflict attracts attention and, as a result, historians through the centuries have almost without exception castigated Moravians both for their usurpation of the kingship of Alba during the eleventh century, and for their opposition to the dynasty descended from the second marriage of King Máel Coluim mac Donnchada (1058–1093) and Queen Margaret during the late eleventh and early twelfth centuries. Medieval annals and chronicles seem to be filled with records of Moravian malcontents leading revolts against the kings of Alba and Scotia over a period of almost 110 years before 1130.

But is this Moravian reputation for violence, mayhem and revolt justified? In 1975, A. A. M. Duncan shrewdly remarked that, 'The problem of Moray is different from that of other earldoms. Here we know of too many earls and pretenders, too little of their interrelationships and aims.'[48] Despite these wise words, the political relationship between Alba and Moray is still discussed with surprising frequency from a monarchocentric perspective that favours the inevitability of primogeniture. Commentators ignore, misunderstand or minimalise the importance of the *derbfine* (four-generational kin-group) in royal Gaelic society.[49] This has occasionally led to confused discussion regarding the legitimacy of challenges which individuals connected to Moray posed to successive kings of Alba.

What is perhaps even more surprising is that no historian has yet paid attention to the fact that the medieval accounts of the Moravian penchant

48 Duncan, *Kingdom*, 167.
49 Ibid., 112.

for violence and revolt were often written long after the events they described had actually taken place. Furthermore, these accounts were almost wholly written from the perspective of the winning side, the descendants of Máel Coluim mac Donnchada and Margaret. It is not inconceivable that they contain a large degree of propaganda aimed at justifying the gradual monopolisation of the kingship of Scotia during the twelfth and thirteenth centuries by this segment of the royal kindred. Accordingly, the relationship between Alba and Moray before 1130 is perhaps as much about the practical development of the cult of kingship in high-medieval Scotia as it is about 'rebellion' and 'revolt' in one area of that kingdom.

There is at least one further vital issue in the debate regarding Moray during this period: the historiographic controversy about the political status of the region, including the question of whether it was a separate and wholly independent kingdom before 1130. Historical opinions on this matter have varied wildly over the last 300 years, although recent commentators have tended to favour the theory that Moray was a separate kingdom in north Britain before the twelfth century.

What follows will endeavour to disentangle these various threads of pre-2006 historiography to decide whether the deplorable reputation gained by the Moravians between c.1000 and 1130 is warranted. The first part examines the evidence relating to the political status of Moray and attempts to decide whether the currently popular theory that Moray was an independent kingdom is justifiable. The second part will evaluate the repercussions of Woolf's paper of 2006 in which he argued that the important Pictish kingdom of Fortriu was not located in southern Scotland but north of the Mounth. This theory has crucial repercussions for the histories of both Fortriu and Moray because it literally turns our mental map of both Pictland and Alba upside-down.

Following on from this, the discussion is devoted to assessing important individuals connected to Moray, to determine whether they have been unfairly slandered by pro-King Máel Coluim mac Donnchada sources. This former kindred seems to have died out with the killing of Oengus of Moray in 1130. Indeed, prior to 1130, Moravian 'rebellion' and 'revolt' was centred on what might be considered to have been a 'native' Moravian kindred. Although the later MacWilliams, who frequently challenged for the kingship of Scotia between 1174 and 1230, are often closely linked with Moray, in fact they do not seem to have been related to the pre-1130 leading Moravian kindred, nor is there any shred of evidence to support the theory that Moravians ever backed the MacWilliams in their various efforts to seize the kingship of Scotia.[50]

The final section of this discussion will examine the absorption of the kingdom of Strathclyde by King Máel Coluim mac Donnchada. In contrast to Moray, the establishment of their overlordship across Strathclyde by the kings of Alba has passed unremarked in Scottish sources and, as such, it is problematic to assign an exact date to this process. In constrast to Moray, it is also difficult to determine the exact extent of Strathclyde/Cumbria at any one time, making any assessment of that country's resources difficult to ascertain.

Alba and Moray: two kingdoms or one?

The popular historiographic concept that Alba and Moray may have been two separate kingdoms seems to be largely based on evidence from the writings of Bede:

> [venit] Brittaniam praedicatarus uerbum Dei prouinciis septentrion-alium Pictorum, hoc est eis quae arduis atque horrentibus montium iugis ab australibus eorum sunt regionibus sequestratae.

> He [Colum Cille] came to Britain to preach the word of God to the kingdoms of the northern Picts which are separated from the southern part of their land by steep and rugged mountains.[51]

This statement regarding the kingdom of the northern Picts became accepted as a historical 'fact' during the nineteenth century,[52] particularly as it was apparently supported by an entry from the *Annals of Ulster*.[53] Accordingly, for E. William Robertson writing in 1862, the evidence that

---

50 Alasdair Ross, 'Moray, Ulster, and the MacWilliams', in Seán Duffy (ed.), *The World of the Galloglass: Kings, Warlords and Warriors in Ireland and Scotland, 1200–1600* (Bodmin, 2007), 24–44 [hereafter: Ross, 'Moray, Ulster, and the MacWilliams'].

51 Bertram Colgrave and R. A. B. Mynors (eds), *Bede's Ecclesiastical History of the English People* (Oxford, 1969), 220–23.

52 For example: Thomas Innes, *A Critical Essay on the Ancient Inhabitants of the Northern Parts of Britain, or Scotland*, 2 vols (London, 1729), i, 88–90 [hereafter: Innes, *Essay*]; Andrew Lang, *A History of Scotland*, 4 vols (Edinburgh, 1900–07), i, 28–29 [hereafter: Lang, *History*]; Hume-Brown, *History*, i, 8.

53 *Ann. Ulster*, 782.1: *Dub Tholargg rex Pictorum citra Monoth* (Dub Tholarg, king of the Picts on this side of the Mounth).

there were two kings, Domnall mac Causantín and Giric mac Dúngail, reigning together in Alba as late as 889 meant that Scotland was still divided into two separate kingdoms, Alba and Moray. For Robertson, it was not until after the death of Giric mac Dúngail that the two kingdoms became united, although 'memories of early independence continued to linger in Moray and caused upsets for a number of centuries.'[54] This was Robertson's way of rationalising Moravian 'rebellions' between *c.*1000 and 1230. However, even for many 'pro-unionist' commentators, Scottish control of Moray after the 'union' of the Picts and Scots effectively stopped at the River Spey. Beyond this geographical boundary, the kings of Alba only exercised nominal sovereignty: successive mormaír of Moray were virtually independent princes until 'later Scottish kings succeeded in breaking the power of these dangerous subjects.'[55] In effect, the River Spey was classed as a frontier line beyond which law and order did not fully operate; an area that had to be brought under royal authority and control.

This general argument rests on a number of key assumptions. First, that the Mounth referred to by Bede and the *Annals of Ulster* was the chain of hills currently known by this name, which separates Aberdeenshire from the Mearns and extends westwards into northern Perthshire. This may not be the case. In 1926, W. J. Watson noted that in the eighth century the term 'monith' could actually have referred to quite different geographical markers, like Edinburgh (*Dún Monaidh*) or St Andrews (*Cennríghmonaid*).[56] The second assumption is that Bede possessed an understanding of the geography of Pictland that was identical to modern cartographic representations of Scotland. If, however, just for the sake of argument, Bede had based his terms of geographic reference on an understanding of classical maps of northern Britain like Ptolemy's map, his northern Picts might have inhabited Galloway, north Argyll, the Hebrides or Orkney.[57] Although this last suggestion is conjectural, Bede does seem to have had a classically inspired understanding of geography. He believed, for example, that Ireland lay to the south of Britain, just off the north coast of Spain.[58]

---

54 Robertson, *Early Kings*, i, 51–52.
55 Hume Brown, *History*, 34–36.
56 Watson, *CPNS*, 394–97. Anderson [cf. *ES*, i, 575], noted this in 1922, but he acknowledged that he had received his information from Watson.
57 For Ptolemy's map, see McNeill and MacQueen, *Atlas*, 36.
58 Peter Hunter Blair, *The World of Bede* (London, 1970), 11.

A small minority of historians have disagreed with the idea that Alba and Moray were separate kingdoms. Innes, Pinkerton and Rhind, for example, all argued that Moray had been an integral part of Alba since the 'union' of the Picts and the Scots in the ninth century. Chalmers was more robust in his defence of a 'united kingdom', going so far as to call Moray a 'fictitious monarchy'.[59] For them, any mormaer of Moray who fought against a king of Alba after *c*.850 could be classed as a rebellious subject.[60] This meant that a reason had to be found to explain why there was so much conflict between the kings of Alba and the province of Moray during the eleventh, twelfth, and thirteenth centuries.

Ethnographic differences were one possible answer: Highland Celts fighting against Teutonic Lowlanders. This solution was further aided by the imposition of a perceived nineteenth-century Highland/Lowland divide on to early medieval Moray. For example, according to Charles Rampini, writing in 1897 and constructing an ethnographic knot of Gordian proportions, the Picts of Moray were really Gaels who sided with their Celtic brethren against Norman (and Flemish) incomers. After losing their lands in the Laich of Moray to these incomers, the previous inhabitants had no other choice than to live in the Highlands and harass civilised (Lowland) people, thus becoming caterans. This explanation allowed him to class the original inhabitants of Moray as: 'a warlike and impetuous race . . . who . . . were wholly responsible for spreading a fear of any Gaelic speaking people in Lowland northern Scotland'.[61]

In contrast, both David Dalrymple and Andrew Lang preferred to class twelfth- and thirteenth-century kindreds associated with Moray as proto-Jacobites. Lang, in particular, compared various leading representatives of the MacEth and MacWilliam kindreds to Prince Charles Edward Stuart (the Young Pretender) and continually referred to them as 'pretenders' who 'raised their standards' whenever they were 'out'.[62] While it is perhaps difficult to excuse Dalrymple and Lang's use of emotive Jacobite terminology, there is little doubt that Rampini's commentary was influenced by the

---

59 Chalmers, *Caledonia*, i, 336.
60 John Pinkerton, *An Enquiry into the History of Scotland*, 2 vols, new edn (Edinburgh, 1814), ii, 185 [hereafter: Pinkerton, *Enquiry*] and Rhind, *Sketches*, 7–8.
61 Charles Rampini, *History of Moray and Nairn* (Edinburgh, 1897), 5, and at 121–23 [hereafter: Rampini, *Moray*].
62 David Dalrymple, *Annals of Scotland* (Edinburgh, 1776), 43 [hereafter: Dalrymple, *Annals*]; Lang, *History*, 88–118.

ethnographic debate over the different merits of Teutonic and Celtic ancestry which took place in Scotland in the eighteenth and nineteenth centuries.[63]

Rampini's work is notable for another reason. He was the first historian to suggest that the common Cenél Loairn ancestry of the men of Moray could have influenced their relations with the Gaels living in southern Scotland, who claimed descent from Cenél nGabráin, although he did not discuss this in any detail.[64] This suggestion was based upon the genealogy *Item Ríg Alban* in the manuscript *Leabhar Glinne Dá Locha*, compiled sometime between *c.*1120 and 1130.[65]

During the last thirty years, Rampini's suggestion has been more thoroughly evaluated, particularly by B. T. Hudson. According to him, Cenél Loairn may have migrated along the Great Glen from Dál Riata to Moray some time during the later eighth century, shortly after Oengus mac Fergusa, king of Fortriu, invaded and conquered Dál Riata in 741. Thereafter, the kindred of Cenél Loairn created a new kingdom in the north until they were eventually conquered by King Máel Coluim mac Donnchada and his descendants after 1058.[66]

Hudson also admitted, however, that there was virtually no evidence to support his argument. Other than the twelfth-century Moray genealogies, written in Ireland and preserved in four manuscripts, there is no corroborating evidence for this migration, even though a stratum of what appears to be early Gaelic place-names stretches eastwards from Inverness to Banffshire[67] and a cluster of early Gaelic church *cill* place-names in Easter

---

63 Colin Kidd, 'Teutonist ethnology and Scottish nationalist inhibition, 1780–1880', *SHR*, 74, 1995, 45–68, at 45–68.

64 Rampini, *Moray*, 122. Skene [cf. Skene, *Celtic Scotland*, i, 293] commented that the invasion by Oengus prompted the remains of both Cenél Loairn and Cenél nGabráin to seek settler ~ut elsewhere, but did not elucidate any further. In his third volume [cf. Skene, *Celtic Scotland*, iii, 365] Skene noted that the old mormaers of Moray appeared in old Irish genealogies of the tribe of Lorn.

65 M. A. O'Brien (ed.), *Corpus Genealogiarum Hiberniae*, i (Dublin, 1962), 162.e. In *Leabhar na Nuachongbála* (the Book of Leinster), compiled *c.*1152, this genealogy is called *Genelach Clainde Lulaig*. For the dating of *Leabhar Glinne Dá Locha* (more commonly known as Rawl.B.502) and *Leabhar na Nuachongbhála* [cf. Padraig Ó Riain (ed.), *Corpus Genealogiarum Sanctorum Hiberniae* (Dublin, 1985), xviii–xix].

66 Benjamin T. Hudson, *Kings of Celtic Scotland* (Westport, 1994), 128–29 [hereafter: Hudson, *Kings*]. More recently, this thesis has been accepted by both McDonald [McDonald, 'Treachery', 188–89] and Grant [Grant, 'Ross', 97].

67 Watson, *CPNS*, 229.

Ross that might indicate early Gaelic settlement in these parts of Pictland.[68] For the most part, Hudson's theory depended on acceptance of the idea that the well-documented eighth-century rivalry between Cenél Loairn and Cenél nGabráin in Dál Riata continued unabated, and completely unnoticed by annalists, into the eleventh century in Moray. Interestingly, other scholars, like Barrow, accept that the mormaír of Moray were descended from Cenél Loairn, but are noticeably reluctant to call Moray a separate kingdom.[69] This uncertainty regarding the status of Moray during the eleventh century may explain why Duncan, writing in 1975, suggested that King Máel Coluim mac Cináeda (1005–1034) was an unsuccessful king who lost control of the province of Moray after c.1020.[70] Dumville has recently revived this theory and argued that Moray was a 'separate political unit' from the tenth century, although he was strangely reluctant to call it a kingdom.[71]

However, not all historians have accepted the Moray genealogy as trustworthy. Skene, for example, effectively demonstrated that it showed signs of artificial construction.[72] More recently, Broun came to the same conclusion. According to him, the genealogy is an obvious forgery concocted by someone in Gaelic Ireland, and three different genealogies were joined together in an attempt to give the ruling Gaels in Moray a pedigree descended from Loarn mac Eirc. Two of these genealogies concern Ainbchellach, who was expelled from the kingship of Dál Riata in 698,[73] and his cousin Mongán mac Domnaill.[74] Broun has demonstrated that Mongán's genealogy was stacked on top of Ainbchellach's by an unknown scribe, because it was thought that the great-great-grandfather of Mongán was the same man as the father of Ainbchellach. To complete this list, the ancestors of Máel Snechta mac Lulaich, comprising six generations, were then added to the genealogy.[75]

---

68 Taylor, 'Early Church', 93–110.
69 Barrow, *Kingship*, 25.
70 Duncan, *Kingdom*, 100.
71 David N. Dumville, *The Churches of North Britain in the First Viking-Age* (Stranraer, 1997), map opposite 1, and at 36.
72 Skene, *Celtic Scotland*, iii, 342–46.
73 *Ann. Ulster*, 698.4.
74 The genealogies of these two men were attached to *Senchus Fer nAlban* [cf. Bannerman, *Dalriada*, 66].
75 My thanks to Professor Dauvit Broun for providing me with a summary of his unpublished paper on this subject. Dumville has recently come to the same conclusion [see David N. Dumville, 'Cethri Prímchenéla Dáil Riata', *Scottish Gaelic Studies*, 20, 2000, 170–91, at 186, hereafter: Dumville, 'Cethri Prímchenéla'].

While Broun's analysis is acceptable, it does not explain why the attempt was made to link Máel Snechta to Cenél Loairn in the first instance. Recently Woolf argued that even if Máel Snechta and his predecessors thought the link between themselves and Cenél Loairn to be important, this could not be demonstrated to have been the case. He thought that, had they done so, the 'Irish antiquarian' responsible for fabricating the genealogy would hardly have needed to go to such obvious trouble to construct the link.[76] While this may be a valid point, the comment as such is perhaps typical of historical discussion concerning this pedigree in that it assumes that the genealogy was constructed on behalf of, and for, a member of the Moravian kindred.

This may not be the case. It is equally possible that the pedigree attached to the family of Máel Snechta was anti-Moravian propaganda, due to the link made between Máel Snechta and Cenél Loairn. During the late seventh and early eighth centuries, members of Cenél Loairn had briefly assumed the overkingship of Dál Riata before being ousted by members of Cenél nGabráin.[77] The *Leabhar Glinne Dá Locha*, which contains the Moravian Cenél Loairn genealogy was produced between *c.*1120 and 1130. It was during this period that King David I (1124–1153), who could claim descent from Cenél nGabráin,[78] was challenged in some way by Oengus of Moray, nephew of Máel Snechta mac Lulaich and grandson of King Lulach mac Gilla Comgáin, before Oengus was eventually killed in battle in 1130.[79]

If it is assumed that the author of the Moravian genealogy in *Leabhar Glinne Dá Locha*, or the client for whom it was made, was familiar with the history of Dál Riata, it is possible that the genealogy was deliberately constructed to provide a historical precedent for the events of 1130. It was, in effect, black propaganda. The kindred to which Oengus of Moray belonged was deliberately linked back to a Dál Riatan Cenél that had previously challenged, briefly held, and then lost forever, a kingdom to Cenél nGabráin. By being directly linked to Cenél Loairn, the Moravian kindred became two-time losers in the competition for kingship in any grand scheme of Scottish history.

Alex Woolf, writing in 2000, returned to the theory that Moray and Alba were separate kingdoms. According to him, two independent kingdoms

---

76 Woolf, 'Moray Question', 149.
77 Anderson, *Kings and Kingship*, 179–81.
78 Ibid., 256–57.
79 *Ann. Ulster*, 1130.4.

existed in northern Britain, but only for a short period during the eleventh century. Woolf envisaged a scenario where between 1034 and c.1058 there were actually two kings of Alba who were forced to split the kingdom between them.[80] This scenario is based on a number of points. Firstly, beginning with the death of Findlaech mac Ruaidri in 1020, and continuing to the death of Lulach mac Gilla Comgáin in 1058, all of the leading members of the Moray dynasty were described as *rí Alban* in their death notices, whenever they were given a royal title. Woolf also argued that this term seemed to have been reserved for the descendants of Cináed mac Ailpín in the chronicles of the time, at least until 1020.[81]

His second point was based on evidence from Gaelic Ireland where the kingship of Tara alternated between two segments, Cenél nEógain and Clann Cholmáin, each of which had discrete territorial bases. Using this example, Woolf suggested that the two royal kindreds that shared the kingship of Alba between the ninth and eleventh centuries, Clann Áeda meic Cináeda and Clann Custantín meic Cináeda, also each possessed geographically discrete territories.[82] Since the sources indicate that members of Clann Custantín meic Cináeda were constantly at odds with men in Moray, and since none of these sources indicate that Clann Áeda meic Cináeda ever faced opposition from Moray, Woolf concluded that Moray was the home territory of Clann Áeda meic Cináeda.[83]

A potential problem with this theory is that Clann Áeda meic Cináeda had become extinct in the male line in the last decade of the tenth century. Therefore, Woolf suggested that an otherwise unattested daughter of one of the Clann Áeda meic Cináeda dynasts had married into a Moravian Gaelic kindred and become either the wife or mother of Ruaidri. This, according to Woolf, would explain why a kindred based in Moray felt that it had a right to challenge Clann Custantín meic Cináeda for the kingship of Alba, and why the members of this kindred were given the epithet *rí Alban* in their death notices between 1020 and 1085.[84] In support of this theory

---

80 Woolf, 'Moray Question', 163.
81 Ibid., 151.
82 It is possible that this model of alternating kingship had been deliberately copied from Gaelic Ireland, particularly as the sister of both Custantín mac Cináeda (862–877) and Áed meic Cináeda (877–888), Máel Muire, was married to two successive Uí Néill kings. Two of her descendants also held the title *rí Érenn* [see Herbert, 'Rí Éirenn', 69–70].
83 Woolf, 'Moray Question', 152–53 and at 156.
84 Ibid., 155.

Woolf constructed a speculative account of the history of Moray during the ninth century which described the province beginning as a Pictish province, receiving a Gaelic dynasty *c.*850, and being conquered by the Norse a generation later, before being reconquered by the men of Alba in the 890s.[85] It also allowed him to conveniently explain why later people who were allegedly closely linked to Moray, the MacWilliams, often 'rebelled' against Kings William I (1165–1214) and Alexander II (1214–1249).

The third piece of evidence utilised by Woolf was the occurrence of the epithet *rí Mureb* (king of Moray) in the death notice of Máel Snechta mac Lulaich in 1085.[86] He saw the appearance of this title as evidence that Máel Snechta mac Lulaich had voluntarily relinquished his claim to the high-kingship of Alba. According to Woolf, Máel Snechta mac Lulaich had realised that neither he nor his kin-group could compete with the newly increased economic resources of the southern kingdom of Alba since it had expanded southwards, annexing Lothian and Cumbria, giving it increased economic ties to both England and Europe. Effectively, the epithet *rí Mureb* was Máel Coluim mac Donnchada's solution to the 'Moray problem': it legitimised his family's monopolisation of the high-kingship of Alba whilst allowing Máel Snechta mac Lulaich to retain a more restricted royal title; essentially, an inferior grade of kingship.[87]

The fourth, and final, piece of evidence to which Woolf drew attention was the fact that between 1130 and *c.*1214, some primary sources had a clear distinction between the men of Alba and the men of Moray.[88] This observation seems to have been based on work by Broun who noted that between 1145 and 1153 a royal charter referred to the worthy men of Moray and Scotia, and that in 1214 an anonymous source could refer to 'Scotland' as the lands north of the Forth and south of Moray.[89] This suggested to him that for much of the tenth and eleventh centuries there were in fact two Scotlands: 'lesser Scotland', the original core of the kingdom of Alba, and 'greater Scotland', where the kings of Alba hoped to rule but had only and sporadically achieved a loose overlordship. Broun was, however, careful to

---

85 Ibid., 158.
86 *Ann. Ulster*, 1085.1.
87 Woolf, 'Moray Question', 163–64.
88 Ibid., 150.
89 Dauvit Broun, 'Defining Scotland and the Scots before the Wars of Independence', in Dauvit Broun, R. J. Finlay and Michael Lynch (eds), *Image and Identity, The Making and Re-making of Scotland Through the Ages* (Edinburgh, 1998), 4–17, at 4–6.

note that this may not be the entire story, and commented that it was striking how these definitions of the two 'Scotlands' seemed to be unaffected by the successful expansion of the kingdom after the tenth century.[90]

While some of Woolf's arguments may be valid, much of the evidence he utilised can be interpreted in a different way. Firstly, of the seven members of the Moray kindred who are mentioned in the Gaelic Annals only three were ever actually given the epithet *rí Alban*.[91]

The first of these three instances (in 1020) can be immediately discounted since the phrase *rí Alban* was added by a sixteenth-century (or later) scribe as a marginal interpolation.[92] Two further instances (in 1029 and 1058) should also perhaps be treated circumspectly. This is because they appear in the *Annals of Tigernach*, which are generally agreed to reflect contemporary usage less accurately than the *Annals of Ulster*. This leaves the epithet *mormaer Murebe* for Gilla Comgán mac Máel Brigte meic Ruaidri in the *Annals of Ulster*, as the earliest unequivocal descriptor for a leading member of a kindred based in Moray. Essentially, this man was a 'great-steward' who governed the province of Moray on behalf of a king.[93]

The second general point made by Woolf, that Clann Áeda meic Cináeda and Clann Custantín meic Cináeda each held separate territories, is likely to be correct, but identifying the core territory of Clann Áeda meic Cináeda is an altogether different matter. Woolf's choice of Moray was based on circumstantial evidence. His first argument was derived from the *Chronicle of the Kings of Alba* which stated that the Clann Custantín meic Cináeda dynast King Máel Coluim mac Domnaill (*c*.943–954) led an army into Moray and killed a person called Cellach.[94] For Woolf, this implied that Moray was not King Máel Coluim's home territory. His second argu-

---

90 Ibid., 8.

91 *Ann. Ulster*, 1020.6; *Ann. Tig.*, 1029 and at 1058.

92 *Ann. Ulster*, 1020.6, note f.

93 This title was in use in an Irish Gaelic context by at least the beginning of the eleventh century and was presumably familiar to Gaelic annalists [see Jackson, *Deer*, 108–9].

94 Anderson, *Kings and Kingship*, 252: *Cum excercitu suo Maelcolam per[r]exit in Moreb et occidit Cel[l]ach*. This material is part of the Poppleton MS, probably compiled in York 1357x64, and was given the title 'Chronicle of the Kings of Alba' by Dumville [Dumville, 'Chronicle of the Kings of Alba', 73]. Since the reign-length of the last king in this list, Cinaed mac Máel Coluim (971–975), has been left blank, it is possible that this chronicle dates to these years. Dumville, however, has suggested on linguistic evidence that it could be either twelfth- or thirteenth-century in date [Ibid., 74].

ment was based upon the *Prophecy of Berchán* which claimed that King Dub mac Máel Coluim (962–966) died in the north in Fortriu.[95] Woolf then noted that the late-fourteenth-century text *Chronica Gentis Scotorum* stated that King Dub was slain by the men of Moray at Forres.[96] The final piece of evidence used by Woolf was the appearance of the name Máel Coluim mac Cuiléin as a grantor in the Gaelic notes in the *Book of Deer*.[97] He suggested that if Máel Coluim mac Cuiléin was the son of the Clann Áeda meic Cináeda dynast Cuilén mac Indulf (966–971), then Máel Coluim mac Cuiléin may have been the head of Clann Áeda meic Cináeda at the time this grant was made to Deer Abbey. According to Woolf, the presence of this name in a grant to Deer was also evidence of the presence of Clann Áeda meic Cináeda north of the Mounth.[98]

A number of objections can be raised against all of this evidence. Firstly, it is not known who Cellach was, from which direction he invaded Moray, what he was doing in Moray, or whether he was even a member of Clann Áeda meic Cináeda or any other royal kindred in the first instance. It is not even known whether this person originated from Ireland or Alba. Secondly, while Máel Coluim mac Cuiléin could indeed have been the son of King Cuilén, the presence of this name in the *Book of Deer* can hardly be considered as strong evidence that the territory of Clann Áeda meic Cináeda was located in Moray. On this evidence, perhaps the province of Buchan, where Deer is located, would have been a more logical choice.

The final piece of Woolf's evidence that remains to be examined is the appearance of the epithet *rí Mureb* in 1085. While his argument concerning this epithet is persuasive in places, it is difficult to accept that Máel Snechta mac Lulaich *voluntarily* relinquished his, and his kindred's, claim to the high-kingship of Alba because of increasing economic and social marginal- isation. Admittedly, broadly similar examples to this did occur in Gaelic Ireland, where ousted members of royal dynasties claimed a part in the inauguration process, but these all seem to date to the sixteenth century or later.[99] Furthermore, one only has to look at the repeated challenges that members of the MacWilliam kindred made during the twelfth and

95 B. T. Hudson, *Prophecy of Berchán* (Westport, 1996), 88 [hereafter: Hudson, *Berchán*].
96 *Chron. Fordun*, 168.
97 Jackson, *Deer*, 31.
98 Woolf, 'Moray Question', 157–58.
99 Francis J. Byrne, *Irish Kings and High-Kings*, 2nd edn (Dublin, 2001), 21 [hereafter: Byrne, *Irish Kings*].

thirteenth centuries in Scotia, before the deliberate and complete extinction
of their family in 1230 by King Alexander II (1214–1249), to realise that such
claims to kingship in medieval Scotia were never voluntarily abandoned.

Even if this argument were to be accepted, however, it still cannot
account for the unique epithet *rí Mureb*. It is difficult to decide precisely
what the Gaelic annalist in Ireland meant by the title, or whether this
phrase should be translated literally to mean 'king of a kingdom'. In
medieval Ireland the word *rí* had a number of different meanings including
'head of a kindred', 'chief of a district', and 'head of a monastery'.[100] Since we
know nothing about this scribe, his ethnicity, and his world-view, we
should be extremely cautious about straightforwardly accepting his use of
this title to mean that Máel Snechta mac Lulaich was an inaugurated king
of Moray. For example, was the scribe an 'Irish' Gael who tried to convert
the title of mormaer into something that his main audience would readily
understand: *rí Mureb*, chief of the district of Moray? Alternatively, perhaps
a close analogy can be found in the epithets given to various members of
the leading Gaelic kindreds in western Scotland during the early fourteenth century. Here, for example, the lords of Argyll and Garmoran are
called *ri Oirir Gaedeal* (king of Argyll) and *ri Innsi Gall* (king of the islands
of the strangers) in their respective epitaphs in the Annals of Connacht.[101]
In these two examples it is clear that these particular men were never kings
of independent countries.

Though the argument regarding the definition of the phrase *rí Mureb* is
a matter of choice, historians need not translate it literally in the modern
sense of the word. Apart from the unique occurrence of the phrase *rí
Mureb* in 1085, and perhaps an entry under the year-date 1130 when a
similar title may have been implied,[102] there is no indication in any
medieval primary source that Moray was ever a separate kingdom.
Although it is dangerous to argue from negative evidence, the silence is
deafening and, had Moray been an independent kingdom, even for a short
time during the late eleventh and early twelfth centuries, some sort of
reference to this might have been expected to survive in at least one
medieval source in western Christendom.

Putting these considerations to one side for the moment, there is one
other fundamental problem with Woolf's theory. It ignored a major piece of

100 RIA, *DIL*, R.52.49.
101 A. Martin Freeman (ed.), *Annála Connacht* (Dublin, 1983), 1318.8.
102 *Ann. Ulster*, 1130.4.

evidence concerning Gruoch, daughter of Boite mac Cináeda, and wife of the mormaer of Moray, Gilla Comgáin mac Máel Brigte.[103] Opinions vary as to whether Boite was a son of King Cináed mac Máel Coluim (971–995) or King Cináed mac Duib (Kenneth III, *c.*997–1005). These options would make Boite either a cousin or brother of Máel Coluim mac Cináeda.[104] In one sense, and at least as far as this argument is concerned, it does not really matter from which of these two kings Boite was descended. All three men, together with King Máel Coluim mac Cináeda, belonged to the same branch of the royal dynasty, Clann Custantín meic Cináeda.

King Máel Coluim mac Cináeda's only surviving child appears to have been Bethóc, who was married to Crínán, abbot of Dunkeld. By the late 1020s, then, the evidence indicates that the royal succession in Alba would have been limited to sons of either Gruoch or Bethóc, or to any sons of Boite, all of whom would have been a part of the kindred of Clann Custantín meic Cináeda. In 1027, the *Annals of Ulster* record that Dunkeld was completely burned.[105] We are not told why, or by whom. It is perhaps unlikely that the attack was at the behest of King Máel Coluim mac Cináeda, since his son-in-law was abbot of Dunkeld. Therefore, it is possible that this may have been an attack on the family of Bethóc, and by inference King Máel Coluim mac Cináeda, by someone representing a rival claim to the kingship of Alba. According to the available evidence, and since Clann Áeda meic Cináeda was extinct by this time, the most obvious suspects would be the only other known members of Clann Custantín meic Cináeda: the immediate kindred of Boite mac Cináeda.

It is likely that the attack on Dunkeld had drastic repercussions. Within six years, two mormaír of Moray and an individual only referred to as 'M. mac Boite mac Cináeda' were all dead. While the *Annals of Ulster* state that M. mac Boite mac Cináeda was killed by King Máel Coluim mac Cináeda,[106]

---

103 *ESC,* 5–6.

104 Both Skene [Skene, *Celtic Scotland,* i, 399] and Duncan [Duncan, *Kingdom,* 113] prefer the option that Boite was a brother of Máel Coluim mac Cináeda.

105 *Ann. Ulster,* 1027.7.

106 Ibid., 1033.7. A number of commentators, including the editors of the *Annals of Ulster*, argue that the capital 'M.' is not a personal name but an indication that the entry relates to a grandson (*mac meic*) of Boite. However, if this was the case, then both he, his father, and Boite would have had to be dead before 1034. This is not impossible, just improbable, given that Gruoch, his aunt, survived for a number of years and that King Lulach is described as *nepos filii Boide* in 1058. Accordingly, it is possible to speculate that 'M' may have been meant to represent Máel Coluim.

it is always assumed by historians that it was MacBethad mac Findláich who killed the mormaer Máel Coluim mac Máel Brigte in 1029 and who burned Gilla Comgáin mac Máel Brigte to death in 1032.[107] This is because Gilla Comgáin mac Máel Brigte was named as one of the brothers who had killed MacBethad's father, Findlaech mac Ruaidri.[108] Although this theory has proved popular, an entirely different scenario can be constructed.

If Gruoch was married to Gilla Comgáin mac Máel Brigte before 1020, one of the two known segments of the leading Moravian Gaelic kindred was now closely associated with the royal segment of Clann Custantín meic Cináeda descended from Boite mac Cináeda. Moreover, this segment of Clann Custantín meic Cináeda might be expected to supply the next king of Alba, since King Máel Coluim mac Cináeda is not known to have fathered any sons. Accordingly, the murder of Findlaech mac Ruaidri in 1020 perhaps represented an attack on the senior segment of the native Moravian Gaelic kindred by the junior branch, represented by Gilla Comgáin mac Máel Brigte and Máel Coluim mac Máel Brigte, acting in concert with members of Clann Custantín meic Cináeda. This might have had the effect of providing a new and large power base for one branch of Clann Custantín meic Cináeda in the north, so that they might more successfully prosecute their claim to supply the next high-king of Alba. If this were the case, responsibility for the deaths of Máel Coluim mac Máel Brigte and Gilla Comgáin mac Máel Brigte might not lie with MacBethad mac Findláich but with King Máel Coluim mac Cináeda if the latter was determined that his own grandson would eventually succeed him in the kingship.

Even if this was not the case, the marriage between Gruoch and Gilla Comgáin mac Máel Brigte is a much more obvious and logical explanation for the rise to prominence of a Moravian Gaelic kindred than the theory advanced by Woolf: namely, that there was a hypothetical marriage between a member of the Moravian kindred and a hypothetical daughter of a Clann Áeda meic Cináeda dynast.

In addition, what is invariably glossed over by historians is the fact that all the known segments of the royal Scottish kindred – with the obvious exception of Boite mac Cináeda's line – seem to fail in the male line during the early eleventh century. Therefore, King Máel Coluim mac Cináeda may have murdered the son of Boite to ensure that one of his own

---

107 Ibid., 1032.2; *Ann. Tig.*, ii, 369.
108 *Ann. Tig*, ii, 359.

grandchildren acquired at least a chance of succeeding him in the kingship. The deliberate murder of this man would have had the added attraction of keeping overall power in Alba within King Máel Coluim's segment of Clann Custantín meic Cináeda. This interpretation may be crucial because it is generally recognised, at least as far as the evidence from early medieval Gaelic Ireland is concerned, that the right to compete for kingship could not be passed through the female line.[109]

The murder of the son of Boite by Máel Coluim mac Cináeda thus assumes an added significance, particularly if Máel Coluim knew in 1033 that he himself was unlikely to produce an heir. Consequently, it seems doubtful whether the fighting between the descendants of Gruoch and the descendants of Bethóc would have occurred at all if the son of Boite had not been murdered. Similarly perhaps, it seems unlikely that MacBethad and his kindred would ever have become involved in fighting for the kingship of Alba if Gruoch had not married into their kindred and produced a son, Lulach mac Gilla Comgáin.

In this scenario, there is no solid proof that Moray was an independent kingdom between the death of King Lulach mac Gilla Comgáin in 1058 and the death of Oengus in 1130. Instead, the earliest reliable description of a member of the leading Moravian Gaelic kindred was as a mormaer: someone who probably governed a region for the high-king of Alba. It has also been demonstrated that the theory regarding the presence of Clann Áeda meic Cináeda in the north is equally unreliable, and that the leading Moravian Gaelic kindred most probably rose in status because of a marriage into the kindred of Gruoch who belonged to Clann Custantín meic Cináeda.

However, all of this applies to a relatively small segment of time between the 1020s and 1130. The status of Moray before the 1020s was until recently at best unclear. In late 2006, Woolf returned to 'The Moray Question' once again and, in a quite stunning paper, literally turned the geography of both Pictland and Alba upside-down by arguing that the important Pictish kingdom of Fortriu was located in northern Scotland. The implications of this for both Alba and Moray are discussed in the following section.

109 T. Charles-Edwards, *Early Irish and Welsh Kingship* (Oxford, 1993), 89–110.

Moray, Fortriu, and Alba: two kingdoms or three?

Since the nineteenth century, most historians of Scotland have believed
that the important Pictish kingdom of Fortriu was based south of the
Mounth, perhaps comprising west Fife, Clackmannanshire, Strathearn,
and Menteith. Key to this process were the maps and writings of E. W.
Robertson and W. F. Skene, who both identified Fortriu with western
Perthshire and Strathearn and as the first province described in *De Situ
Albanie* (DSb):[110]

> *Quelibet igitur istarum partium regio tunc uocabatur et erat quia*
> *unaqueque earum subregionem in se habebat. Inde est ut hii septem*
> *fratres predicti p<ro> septem regibus habebantur septem regulos sub se*
> *habentes. Iste septem fratres regnum Albanie in septem regna*
> *diuiserunt et unusquisque in tempore suo in suo regno regnauit.*
> *Primum regnum fuit sicut mihi uerus relator retulit Andreas uidelicet*
> *et uir uenerabilis Katanensis episcopus natione Scottus et Dunfermelis*
> *monachus ab illa aqua optima que Scottice uocata est Froch Britannice*
> *Werid Romane uero Scottewatre id est aqua Scottorum q[uia] regna*
> *Scottorum et Anglorum diuidit et currit iuxta oppidum de Striuelin*
> *usque ad flumen aliud nobile quod uocatum est Tae. S[e]c[un]d[u]m*
> *reg[nu]m ad Hilef sicut mare circuit usque ad montem aquilonali plaga*
> *de Striuelin qui uocatur Athran. Tertium regnum ab Hilef usque ad De.*
> *Quartum regnum ex De usque ad magnum et mirabile flumen quod*
> *uocatur Spe maiorem et meliorem totius Scotie. Quintum regnum de*
> *Spe usque ad montem Bru[m]alban. Sextum regnum fuit Mure<f> et*
> *Ros. Septimum regnum erat A[r]rega[i]thel.*[111]

Each of these parts, therefore, was called a region, and that was
because each one of them had within itself a sub-region. Thence it is
that these seven foresaid brothers were held to be seven kings, having
under themselves seven sub-kings. These seven brothers divided the
realm of Albany into seven realms, and each one reigned in his own
time in his own realm. The first realm was, just as a true relator

---

110 Robertson, *Early Kings*, i, title page map, and at 33; W. F. Skene, *Celtic Scotland*, i, 207, 340.
111 Anderson, *Kings and Kingship*, 242–43. Translation taken from: David Howlett, 'The
     Structure of iDe Situ Albanie', in Simon Taylor (ed.), *Kings, Clerics and Chronicles in Scotland
     500–1297* (Bodmin, 2000), 124–45, at 138–39.

related to me, Andrew, that is, and a venerable man, bishop of Caithness, a Scot by nation and a monk of Dunfermline, from that excellent water which is called in Scottish Froch, in British the Werid, in Romance, in truth, Scot Water, that is Water of the Scots, because it divides the realms of the Scots and the English, and it runs alongside the town of Stirling as far as that other noble river that is called Tay. The second realm is to the River Isla, just as the sea goes about as far as the mountain in the northern territory of Stirling which is called Athran. The third realm from Isla as far as the Dee. The fourth realm from the Dee as far as the great and wonderful river which is called the Spey, the greatest and best of the whole of Scotland. The fifth realm from the Spey as far as the mountain Druimm nAlban. The sixth realm was Moray and Ross. The seventh realm was Argyll.

Despite obvious difficulties with both texts of *De Situ Albanie*, this geographic identification withstood the test of time unquestioned until 2006, when Alex Woolf noticed that Skene's only evidence for locating Fortriu in Strathearn and Menteith consisted of two pieces of information from separate texts. The first was a battle noted in the *Chronicle of the Kings of Alba* during the reign of Custantín mac Áeda (900–943):

Constantinus filius Edij tenuit regnum .xl. annos cuius tercio anno Normanni predauerunt Duncaldem omnemque Albaniam. In sequenti utique anno occisi sunt in Sraith Herenn Normanni.[112]

Custantin mac Aeda held the kingdom forty years. In his third year the northmen plundered Dunkeld and all Alba. The very next year [904] the Northmen were slain in Sraith Herenn.

The second piece of information came from an entry in the *Annals of Ulster* for AD 904:

Imhar ua hImhair do marbad la firu Fortrenn, 7 ár már n-imbi.

Imar grandson of Imar was killed by the men of Fortriu, and there was great slaughter around him.[113]

---

112 Anderson, *Kings and Kingship*, 251.
113 *Ann. Ulster*, 904.4.

Taken together, these two pieces of evidence led Skene to assume that Strathearn was in Fortriu because that was where the men of Fortriu had killed Imar and, since he knew that Strathearn was located in southern Scotland, then that was where Fortriu must also have been located.[114] However, as Woolf pointed out, there are two Strathearn place-names in Scotland, north and south of the Mounth, and this made Skene's location of *Straith Herenn* to the south of the Mounth far from certain. The northerly example corresponds to the valley of the River Findhorn, Strath Éireann, south of Inverness.[115]

Woolf then examined two different accounts of the death of King Dubh mac Máel Coluim. The first of these, the *Prophecy of Berchan*, states that King Dubh was killed in Fortriu. The second, from the X-group of king lists, states that Dubh was slain at Forres in Moray. This was further evidence to suggest that Fortriu could once have been located north of the Mounth.[116]

However, the most important evidence to support Woolf's theory is found in two English sources. The first of these is that part of *Historia Regum Anglorum* which describes Æthelstan's expedition into Scotland in 934:

> *Diende hostes subegit, Scotiam usque Dunfoeder et Wertermorum terrestri exercitu uastauit, nauali uero usque Catanes depopulatus est.*

> After this he subdued his enemies and wasted Scotland as far as Dunottar and Wertermor, and with his navy depopulated as far as Caithness.

Woolf showed that *Werter*, the first element of *Wertermorum*, had been previously recognised as deriving from *Uerturiones* and that the second element, OE -*mor*, could mean either moor, waste, damp land or, high waste ground, a mountain. Therefore, since Fortriu seems to be descended from *Verturiones*,[117] *Wertermorum* must have meant either the 'moor/swamp of Fortriu' or 'mountain of Fortriu'. He then suggested that

---

114 Alex Woolf, 'Dún Nechtain, Fortriu and the Geography of the Picts', *SHR*, 85, 2006, 182–201, at 192 [hereafter: Woolf, 'Dún Nechtain'].

115 Watson, *CPNS*, 230.

116 Woolf, 'Dún Nechtain', 196.

117 Watson, *CPNS*, 68.

the first definition could easily refer to the pre-improvement Laich of Moray around Loch Spynie.[118]

The second English source that Woolf utilised was an entry in the 'Northern recension' of the *Anglo-Saxon Chronicle*, a hypothetical text reconstructed from common features of the D, E, and F Anglo-Saxon Chronicle manuscripts. The important passage in question consists of a translation from Bede's *Historia Ecclesiastica*:

> *An.dlxv. her feng Æðelbriht to Cantwara rice 7 heold .liii. wintra. On his dagum sende Gregorius \us/ fulluht, 7 Columba messapreost com to Pyhtum 7 hi gecyrde to Cristes geleafan – þet sind þone wærteres be norðum morum . . .*

> Here Æðelberht obtained the sovereignty of the Cantwara and held it fifty-three winters. In his days Gregory sent us baptism and Columba, a mass-priest, came to the Picts and they chose to believe in Christ – that is then, *wærteres* benorth the 'moors' – . . .[119]

According to Woolf the key word in this passage was *wærteres* which was used as the translation of the Latin phrase *prouinciis septentrionalium Pictorum*:

> *[venit] Brittaniam praedicatarus uerbum Dei prouinciis septentrion-alium Pictorum, hoc est eis quae arduis atque horrentibus montium iugis ab australibus eorum sunt regionibus sequestratae.*

> He [Colum Cille] came to Britain to preach the word of God to the kingdoms of the northern Picts which are separated from the southern part of their land by steep and rugged mountains.[120]

All of which meant that *wærteres* in English stood for *prouinciis septentri-onalium Pictorum* and that *morum* must have stood for Latin *montium*. As far as Woolf was concerned, this was an explicit statement that in tenth-century Northumbria Fortriu was understood to have been the lands of the

---

118 Woolf, 'Dún Nechtain', 197.
119 Ibid., 198.
120 Bertram Colgrave and R. A. B. Mynors (eds), *Bede's Ecclesiastical History of the English People* (Oxford, 1969), 220–23.

northern Picts, north of the Mounth. This fundamentally alters historical perceptions concerning the pre-900 kingdom of the Picts because the kings of Fortriu that are mentioned in the Irish annals seem to have been pre-eminent amongst their peers who were kings of other Pictish provinces.

Perhaps the most (in)famous king of the Picts was Onuist son of Wrguist, possibly a native of the Mearns, who rose to pre-eminence by either killing or defeating his rivals to the high-kingship of the Picts and who established his overlordship across Fortriu, reigning between 728 and 761. As James Fraser has recently shown, he was the first Pictish king known to have invaded Northumbria, the first Pictish king known to have invaded Strathclyde, and he may even have invaded Ireland during his 33-year career.[121] In English records he was regarded as a 'despotic butcher', which tells us a great deal about his perceived effectiveness as king of the Picts.[122] For Fraser, Onuist was also the king who laid the foundations for the eventual annexation of both Lothian and Strathclyde by the kings of Alba in the tenth and eleventh centuries.

All of which leaves one fundamental problem: it now seems impossible to determine the historical extent of Fortriu. Fraser has argued that it could have included Atholl (*Áth Fochla* – north pass or way), but we currently have no idea how far east and north it extended into Aberdeenshire, Banffshire, Ross, Sutherland, and Caithness. Equally, although we know that Brude mac Bili, king of Fortriu, 'destroyed' the Orkneys in 682, there is not enough evidence to say whether later kings of Fortriu hung on to this prize in the longer term.[123]

Perhaps an even greater problem associated with all of the above is that any attempt to uncover the process by which Fortriu disintegrated into a number of disparate territories in northern Scotland without leaving any distinct traces in the onomastic record also currently seems impossible. It has been opined that Moray could originally have been qualified as *Muréb Fortrenn* and Ross as *Ros Fortrenn* yet this suggestion must remain speculative because there are no attested records of such place-names.[124] But all is not quite lost: while the primary source material relating to Moray has been searched in some detail, the same cannot be said of the whole of Ross and it may be that a sustained search of that material

---

121 Fraser, *Caledonia to Pictland*, 287.
122 *SAEC*, 57.
123 *Ann. Ulster*, 682.4.
124 Woolf, 'Dún Nechtain', 193.

may turn up a preserved reference to a place-name containing the Fortriu element.

What is clear is that the last dated reference to Fortriu in any of the Irish Annals appears in the year 918: *As beag nach isna laithibh si ro chuirsead Foirtreannaigh et Lochlannaig cath* (Almost at the same time the men of Fortriu and the Norwegians fought a battle).[125] The first recorded instance of the place-name Moray in those same sources does not occur until 1020 in the *Annals of Tigernach* when the death of Findlaech mac Ruaidri (father of King Macbethad mac Findlaích), was recorded: *Fíndlaech mac Ruaidhrí mormaer Moreb a filiis fratris suí Mael Brighdi occisus est* (Findlaech son of Ruaidri, mormaer of Moray, was killed by the sons of his brother Mael Brigte).[126] The name Moray next appears in the *Annals of Ulster* in 1032: *Gilla Comgan m. Mael Brighde, mormaer Murebe, do loscadh co coecait do dainibh ime* (Gilla Comgán son of Mael Brigte, mormaer of Moray, was burned together with fifty people).[127] This means that during this 102–114-year period the kingdom of Fortriu, either in physical terms or as an accepted concept of regal overlordship in what had been northern Pictland, was dismantled and replaced either by the term 'Moray' or by references to its constituent parts, like Caithness, Ross, and Moray, as the regnal and political focus of the kingdom of Alba increasingly shifted southwards. Unfortunately, historical research is not yet at a stage where it can be decided whether 'Moray' was an old name for a constituent part of Fortriu or whether it was a new name given to a large part of Fortriu when the latter, once the territory of the northern Picts, ceased to exist as a regal and territorial reality.

Pannonians, pirates, and Pictish wives: the medieval origin legend of the people of Moray

To add further spice to this conundrum, the people of Moray once occupied a unique position in the literature of medieval Scotland because they possessed their own origin legend, separate from those of the Picts and Scots. The text *Chronica Gentis Scotorum*, which is thought to have been

---

125 Radner, *Fragmentary Annals*, 169.
126 http://www.ucc.ie/celt/published/G100002/index.html T1020.8.
127 *Ann. Ulster*, 1032.2. The editors of this text translated the word 'mormaer' as 'earl'. I have chosen to retain the original word as it is not certain that the two terms are interchangeable.

completed sometime between 1371 and 1385 by John of Fordun, describes
when, and why, the Moravians first settled in Britain:

*Imperatoris illius nequissimi Neronis vecordia segnicieque non incog-
nitis, spes pristine libertatis recuperande nonnullis est exorta gentibus.
Innumera mala Romani suis diebus perpessi sunt. Nam, legionibus
orientis Parthi jugo subducis, Armeniam ab eis receptam servire coge-
bant. Brittania quidem a circumsitis est diminuta peneque vastata
populis. Germanos insuper et Pannonios novo motu rebellare volentes,
Romani domabant exercitus. Itaque Moravia Pannonie regio quedem
juxta Danubii flumen, ut sepe solebat, per sedicionem excitata, Roderico
duce rebellans, totam ipsius patrie tutricem legionem, dolo circum-
ventam, occidit. Hos quippe Moravios ante privignus Augusti Cesaris
Tiberius, nondum imperator cede cruenta ferme delevit. Quamobrem
propinque provinciarum legiones, sceleris huiusmodi faccione percepta,
discernunt quod vel eorum majores, videlicet Moraviorum, punirent
gladio, sive perpetuo deinceps dampnatos exilio relegarent. Rodericus
igitur adveniencium impetus legionum, pavore territus, ferre non susti-
nens, cum suis exul, classe referta victualibus, per Danubii flumen mare
peciit, ac arte piratica sinus varios borealis Occeani predando circum-
iens, ad mare Belgicum se transtulit. Igitur dum ibidem per tempus
aliquod adversando Romanis mare transcurreret, ac multis infesta-
cionibus Gallie portus et Britannie suasque naves afficeret, Pictis
demum, inter quos antea sepius moram fecerat, quiescere volens,
perpetuo federe manus dabat. Quorum ilico multitudine numerosiores
Picti multoque forciores effecti, contra Britones ad bella procedere
continuo Scotos hortantur. Quod et factum est. Nam sua componentes in
unum agmina, nullius adversarii timentes impetum, Britanniam
advolant, et post multos hominum hinc inde discursus gravesque provinciarum vastaciones ad propria redire contendunt. Quibus interea cum
predis pluribus et spoliis margine regnorum revertentibus, Romane
gentis legionum dux Marius Britonumque patricius occurrens, eos,
utrimque sevissima cede commissa, fugere compulit, perempto prius in
acie Moraviorum principe Roderico. Hos enim Moravios Gaufridus
fuisse Pictos de Scithia scriptis imposuit, et bene. Nam omnes a mari
Baltico regiones usque Danubium olim inferior Scithia dicebatur. Ex
quarum una venientes se Pictis perpetuo conjunxerunt. Reversus
vero domi Pictorum populus post fugam confuse penitus, necnon et
acephale genti Moravie, cuius princeps in bello cecidit, filias in uxores et*

amplam dedit patriam excolendam, cui pristine regiones Moravie secundum Galfridum Katanie tradentes nomine, cum Pictis insuper commanserunt.

Since the madness and inactivity of that most wicked emperor Nero did not go unnoticed, hope arose in several nations of recovering their ancient liberty. The Romans suffered innumerable disasters in his days. For the Parthians sent the legions of the east under the yoke, recovered Armenia, and subjected it to servitude. The Roman province of Britain was reduced in size and almost devastated by the surrounding peoples. Moreover, the Germans and Pannonians were planning fresh revolt, but were subdued by the Roman armies. So Moravia, a region of Pannonia near the River Danube, as often before, was roused to revolt, and rebelled under the leadership of Roderick. They stealthily surrounded and killed the whole of the legion that protected their country. Earlier these Moravians had been almost destroyed in savage slaughter by Tiberius the stepson of Caesar Augustus, before he became emperor. So when the legions of the neighbouring provinces heard about the perpetration of this kind of crime, they decided that they should either punish the Moravian leaders with the sword, or condemn them immediately to exile and banish them. So Roderick took fright, and without waiting to endure the attacks of the advancing legions, went into exile with his followers, after fitting out a fleet of ships with provisions, and sailing along the River Danube to the sea. He turned pirate, and after sailing round the various bays of the northern ocean, plundering as he went, he crossed over to the Belgic Sea. So while he was traversing the sea there over a period of time in opposition to the Romans, he made many attacks on the ports of Gaul and Britain and on their ships. He finally joined forces in a perpetual treaty with the Picts, with whom he had often stayed when he wished to have breathing space. So the Picts increased in numbers and in strength with the addition of these people. Immediately they urged the Scots to proceed to war against the Britons, and this was done. For with combined forces and fearing the attack of no adversary, they hurried to Britain, and after many raids in all directions by their men and severe devastation of the Roman provinces, they were anxious to return to their own homes. Meanwhile, as they were returning laden with much spoil and booty, on the border of their kingdoms they were intercepted by Marius the commander of the Roman legions and patrician of the Britons, and forced to flee, after savage slaughter had been inflicted on both sides, and after the death in battle of the Moravian prince Roderick. Now Geoffrey asserted in his history that these Moravians were Picts from Scythia, and quite rightly too. For all regions from the Baltic Sea right to the Danube were once upon a time called Lower Scythia, from one of which regions they came and joined forces with the Picts forever. The people of the Picts returned home after the rout in utter confusion, and gave their daughters as wives to the leaderless people of Moravia, whose prince had fallen in battle, and a large extent of land for them to cultivate. To this land they gave the name of their old region of Moravia, ie Catania, according to Geoffrey, and they lived side by side with the Picts thereafter.[128]

Not all later Scottish historians either knew of or chose to repeat this origin legend. For example, while Walter Bower (1385–1449) chose to repeat it, neither Andrew Wyntoun (1350–1423) nor John Mair (1467–1550) included it in their respective works. In fact, the Moravian origin legend next appeared in Boece's Chronicles of Scotland, though Boece (1465–1536) characteristically changed the story in a number of ways. According to him, the Murrays were a Germanic people with strong bodies and plenty of courage. They, together with their leader Roderick, landed in Lothian where the Picts warmly welcomed them.[129] Boece then followed Fordun and described how many Murrays fell in battle against the Romans. After the battle, those Murrays who escaped from the field of slaughter were given lands by King Corbred: namely, all the lands lying between the River Spey and Inverness. These lands were renamed 'Murraye Land' and the Murrays were then given Scottish virgins to marry so that the two races might come closer together.[130]

While this is essentially the same story that was related by Fordun, Boece must have been uncomfortable with some of the pseudo-historical anti-Moravian material in *Chronica Gentis Scotorum*. Accordingly, in Boece's work there is no sign of the Moravians rebelling against Rome, nor is there any indication that they were ever pirates. In addition, they were given a different landing place in Scotland and it is just possible that Boece altered

---

128 *Chron. Fordun*, 57–58. Translation taken from *Chron. Bower* (Watt), i, 236–39.
129 *Chron. Boece*, 144.
130 Ibid., 148.

the storyline at this point to help explain why members of the Murray (originally, de Moravia) family held lands in southern Scotland during his lifetime. However, Boece still had to explain how the Murrays could settle in Moray, given that it was already populated. He solved this problem by making all the previous pseudo-historical inhabitants of Moravia into rebels who had been expelled.[131] This was clearly based upon an exceedingly enigmatic entry in the *Chronicle of Holyrood* which states: *Et rex Malcolmus Mureviensis transtulit* (And King Malcolm transported/ translated the men of Moray).[132] After this alleged ethnic cleansing, the way was clear for loyal Murrays to settle in the north.

John Leslie (1527–1596) essentially followed the Moravian story as related by Boece. The Moravians were thrown out of Germany and came to live in Albion. Shortly after arriving they fought a battle in alliance with the Picts and Scots under the command of King Corbred. Because they were so manly upon the field of battle, Corbred granted the Moravians all the lands upon the River Spey as a reward for their services. The Moravians then expelled the previous inhabitants of these lands, the rebellious Vararis, settled their new lands (which they called Moray), and grew into one nation with the Scots.[133] Although George Buchanan (1506–1582) evidently chose not to include the Moravian origin legend in his work, it did appear in other general historical writings. In 1639, for example, it was used and adapted by Robert Gordon (1580–1656) to help explain the arrival of the Gordons in northern Scotland.[134]

Lachlan Shaw (1686–1777), writing in 1775, appears to have been the first author to dispute the historicity of this legend. It is clear from his work that Shaw regarded the Moravian origin tale as a complete falsehood, and he disparaged Boece's version of events by claiming that the European land of Pannonia (Moravia) was in fact called *Marcomania*, the inhabitants *Marcomani*, by classical authors. According to Shaw, this was ample proof that the Moravians could not have originated in Pannonia.[135] In fact, Shaw much preferred the theory that the inhabitants of Moray were descended

---

131 Ibid., 148.
132 *Chron. Holyrood*, 142.
133 Dalrymple, *Annals*, 157–59.
134 Robert Gordon, *A Genealogical History of the Earldom of Sutherland, from its Origin to the Year 1630; Written by Sir Robert Gordon of Gordonstoun, Baronet. With a Continuation to the Year 1651* (Edinburgh, 1813), 13–15.
135 Shaw, *Moray*, i, 41.

from Picts who had travelled from the shores of the mouth of the Baltic Sea (Scythia) to settle in Scotland.[136] Despite this rebuttal, however, the Moravian origin legend survived in one form or another until the end of the nineteenth century. The last occasion upon which it was given a public airing seems to have been in the work of James Suter, published in 1887.[137]

The origin legend from *Chronica Gentis Scotorum* aims to make three key points about the Moravians. First, it was usual for Moravians to rebel against authority. Second, the Moravians were pirates who plundered the seas around Britain. Finally, the Moravians came to live in north Britain and were closely linked to the Picts and Scots. This is obviously an attempt to relate an origin legend for a section of the population of Scotland other than the Picts and Scots. It is clearly trying to demonstrate that the Moravians were originally a separate race of people, who only later became associated with the other races in north Britain. In one sense it does not really matter that there may be no kernel of historical truth in this story, which has clearly borrowed some of its elements from earlier Gaelic and Pictish origin legends.[138] What does matter is that someone wanted people to believe that the Moravians had been savage fighters and rebellious pirates virtually since recorded history began. This makes it unlikely that this was an origin legend created by Moravians themselves, though it is impossible at this stage to reject the notion that it might be an adapted later version of an original Moravian origin legend.

Obviously, these points raise the question of whether it was Fordun who created the Moravian origin legend, or whether he copied it from an earlier source. The text of *Chronica Gentis Scotorum* has recently been re-evaluated by Broun. According to his initial findings, Fordun may have written only the actual *Chronica* section (the first five and a half books) of *Chronica Gentis Scotorum*. It is within these five and a half books that the Moravian origin legend first appears. However, Broun also noted that some of *Chronica Gentis Scotorum* was a rewrite of the early part of *Gesta Annalia I* and that it also incorporated information from at least one other text.[139] Accordingly, it is possible that Fordun had copied the Moravian

136 Ibid., iii, 26–27.

137 James Suter, *Memorabilia of Inverness* (Inverness, 1887), 2.

138 *Chron. Bower* (Watt), i, 373.

139 Dauvit Broun, 'A New Look at *Gesta Annalia* Attributed to John of Fordun', in Barbara E. Crawford (ed.), *Church, Chronicle and Learning in Medieval and Early Renaissance Scotland* (Edinburgh, 1999), pp. 9–30, at 20 [hereafter: Broun, 'Gesta Annalia'].

origin legend from an earlier Scottish historical work. It is now known that this earlier work was written by Richard Vairement (Veremundus), a European, a member of the *céli Dé* of St Andrews, and chancellor of Queen Marie de Coucy, wife of King Alexander II.[140]

Indeed, Broun has recently labelled Vairement as the 'Scottish Monmouth' and textual analysis demonstrates that Vairement's history was largely based upon Geoffrey of Monmouth's *Historia Regum Britanniae* and a small collection of texts that included a legendary account of the journeys of Gaedel, Scota and Éber from Egypt and Greece to Ireland, a legend of the stone of Scone, and a king-list that began with King Cináed mac Alpín. In Broun's estimation, Vairement wrote in the 1260s.[141] Indeed, two references to Geoffrey are included within the text of the Moravian origin legend. This provides a point of comparison, even though the only origin legend about peoples living in north Britain in *Historia Regum Britanniae* relates to the Picts:[142]

> Marius, the son of Arvirargus, succeeded him in the kingship. He was a man of great prudence and wisdom. A little later on in his reign a certain King of the Picts called Sodric came from Scythia with a large fleet and landed in the northern part of Britain which is called Albany. He began to ravage Marius' lands. Marius thereupon collected his men together and marched to meet Sodric. He fought a number of battles against him and finally killed him and won a great victory. In token of his triumph Marius set up a stone in the district, which was afterwards called Westmorland after him. The inscription carved on it records his memory down to this very day. Once Sodric was killed and the people who had come with him were beaten, Marius gave them the part of Albany called Caithness to live in. The land had been desert and untilled for many a long day, for noone lived there. Since they had no wives, the Picts asked the Britons for their daughters and kinswomen; but the Britons refused to marry off their womenfolk to such manner of men. Having suffered this rebuff, the Picts crossed over to Ireland and married women from that country. Children were born to these women and in this way the Picts increased their numbers.[142]

140 Dauvit Broun, *Scottish Independence and the Idea of Britain* (King's Lynn, 2007), 257.
141 Ibid., 258–60.
142 Lewis Thorpe (ed. and trans.), *The History of the Kings of Britain* (Middlesex, 1966), 123.

Clearly, there are strong similarities between the Pictish origin legend in *Historia Regum Britanniae* and the Moravian origin legend in *Chronica Gentis Scotorum*, even though they each describe a different body of people. For example, both tales name King Marius of Britain, both describe a battle in which King Sodric/Prince Roderick were killed, both mention Caithness, and both mention the fact that the Picts/Moravians acquired their wives from another race of people. This would suggest that the Pictish origin legend in *Historia Regum Britanniae* was the exemplar for the Moravian origin legend. If so, it means that the Moravian origin legend was created sometime between c.1136, when *Historia Regum Britanniae* was completed, and the 1260s. All of which indicates that the Moravian origin legend was created with the specific intention of being hostile to Moravians and there are two precedents for such a scenario.

Broun has examined two Scottish king-lists that were produced sometime between 1198 and December 1214. The first of these, known as the *Verse Chronicle*, lists the kings of Pictland, Alba and Scotia from Cináed mac Alpín to William I in Latin elegiac couplets. This king-list displays a remarkable antipathy towards the Moravians as it categorically, but untruthfully, states that two kings of Alba met their deaths in Moray: Dubh mac Máel Coluim ('death at the hands of the men of Moray') and Máel Coluim mac Domnaill ('he fell by the deceit and guile of an apostate people').

According to Broun, the basis for this denigrating commentary on Moray and Moravians is revealed in the treatment of King Donnchad mac Máel Coluim by the *Verse Chronicle*. King Donnchad is the only king of Scotia whom the author of the *Verse Chronicle* deliberately discredited. Broun argued that the reasoning behind this treatment could be found in the activities of Donnchad's descendants, the MacWilliams, who had launched a number of challenges against the descendants of King Máel Coluim mac Donnchada (Malcolm III) since the mid-twelfth century. Because many of the MacWilliam kindred landed in Moray and Ross before launching their attacks on the kings of Scotia, the inhabitants of those areas also became closely associated with rebellion against the Crown.

The second king-list that Broun examined is found in the *Chronicle of Melrose*. The first part of this king-list begins with the succession of King Máel Coluim mac Donnchada and finishes with the birth of Prince Alexander in 1198. This part can therefore be dated to 1198 x 1214. A continuation in a different hand then carries the list on to the birth of Alexander

III on 21 January 1264. According to Broun, the first part of this king-list was written with the senior male line of the royal family very much in mind. It is the only extant Scottish king-list which deliberately begins with King Máel Coluim mac Donnchada, and which follows the reigns of the king's descendants from his second marriage to Queen Margaret. There is a heavy emphasis on hereditary rights to kingship and on primogeniture. For example, we are told that King Máel Coluim mac Donnchada's brother, King Donald bán mac Donnchada, usurped the kingship and sent the legitimate heirs, the sons of Queen Margaret, into exile. Furthermore, the king-list also describes King Donnchad mac Máel Coluim as illegitimate, thus damning his progeny and their offspring. Thus, both of these king-lists are heavily committed to King Alexander II's right to rule in Scotia, to the extent that previous legitimate kings are categorised as either usurpers or illegitimate. As with the *Verse Chronicle*, Broun argues that the king-list in the *Chronicle of Melrose* was inspired by the repeated MacWilliam challenges faced by King Alexander II.[143]

Given the production of at least two pieces of anti-MacWilliam propaganda during the reign of King Alexander II, it is possible that the Moravian origin legend was also produced to denigrate them. It is extremely negative about all the Moravian people, and thus by inference about the members of the MacWilliam kindred who were closely associated with the province of Moray because their progenitor, William fitz Duncan, had been earl of that province. Propaganda of this nature may also help to explain why Geoffrey of Monmouth's Pictish King Sodric is downgraded in status to a Prince Roderick in the Moravian origin legend.

Also important is that the name of the prince in the Moravian origin tale is Roderick. It is surely no coincidence that one of the leaders of the last MacWilliam rising in 1228, against King Alexander II, was also called Roderick.[144] If the name of the Moravian prince in the origin legend was based on contemporary thirteenth-century events, this would provide a date of *c*.1214 x 1230 for the original narrative used by Vairement, whose text was copied at a later date by John of Fordun. The activities of the MacWilliams may also account for the reason why the Pannonians were turned into pirates in the origin legend. The sources are quite clear that

---

143 Dauvit Broun, 'Contemporary Perspectives on Alexander II's Succession: The Evidence of King-lists', in R. D. Oram (ed.), *The Reign of Alexander II, 1214–49* (Leiden, 2005), 79–98 [hereafter: Broun, 'Contemporary Perspectives'].

144 *Chron. Bower* (Watt), v, 117.

most of the members of the MacWilliam kindred who invaded Scotia did so from the sea.

Of course, formulating this Moravian origin legend also meant that the received pseudo-history of Scotland was radically altered. From this point onwards the Scots were descended from three, not two, separate races. It is just possible that this deliberate alteration in the pseudo-history of the Scots indicates how far Crown propagandists supporting the descendants of Queen Margaret were willing to go in order to denigrate and marginalise one segment of the royal kindred. It is also perhaps a measure of how serious a threat was posed by the MacWilliams to kings of Scotia.

In fact, it is likely that the person, or persons, responsible for creating the Moravian origin legend realised that he or they were radically rewriting Scottish history, and that this is why the legend contains the long and curious argument that Pannonia was really part of Lower Scythia. During the medieval period people believed that the Picts originated in Scythia. Therefore, perhaps the author of the origin tale was attempting to prove that the Moravians were also really just Picts, but from a slightly different region of continental Europe. However, it must have been felt that this argument was weak and this may be why the message is reinforced by the revelation that the Moravians were very rapidly absorbed into the native Pictish population in north Britain, following which they all lived happily ever after. It is unfortunate that no source has recorded what the Moravians themselves thought about this rewriting of their history, particularly as one of the most successful eleventh-century kings of Alba happened to be a native Moravian.

There is one further possibility to consider. Until a modern edition of *Chronica Gentis Scotorum* is completed, it will be difficult to prove any direct link between the Moravian origin legend in that text and any borrowing of the same story from Vairement's earlier history. This means that we currently cannot completely discount the possibility that the Moravian origin legend is a genuine product of the fourteenth century.

It has already been suggested by Boardman that Fordun had assembled and expanded *Chronica Gentis Scotorum* for the third son of King Edward III of England, John of Gaunt. To this can be added the facts that King David II (1329–1371) had attempted to make John of Gaunt his heir and had granted the earldom of Moray to Gaunt's father-in-law, Henry of Lancaster, in 1359. Within these contexts, it is impossible to dismiss the notion that the Moravian origin legend was a piece of fourteenth-century propaganda, designed to lessen the impact of the loss of a Scottish earldom to an English

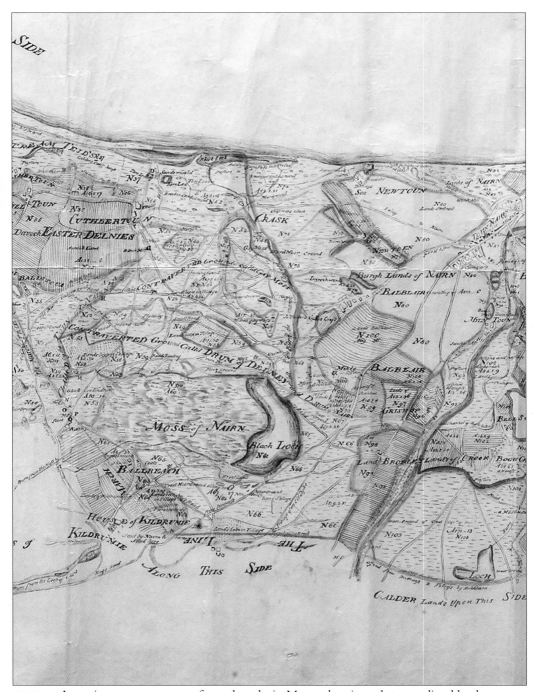

PLATE 1. A pre-improvement map of two davochs in Moray, showing what a medieval landscape might have looked like (Reproduced by permission of Highland Council Archives, Inverness: HCA/D88)

PLATE 2. The remains of the stepped–mound fortifications at Clunie

PLATE 3. The round tower at Abernethy

PLATE 4. The seat of the diocese of Moray, Elgin Cathedral

PLATE 5. The remains of the Priory on St Serf's Island, Loch Leven

PLATE 6. Kelso Abbey. The monks of Selkirk moved to their new site at Kelso *c.*1127

PLATE 7. Inchcolm Abbey

prince. By making Moravians inveterate troublemakers since the Roman period, relating their numerous historic misdeeds might have been designed to underplay the impact of King David II's plans for northern Scotland and the succession.

King MacBethad mac Findláich: the view from Scotia

The period of Moravian history between the 1020s and 1130, spanning approximately 110 years and ending with the death of Oengus of Moray, is dominated by one man, King MacBethad mac Findláich (1040–1057). To a large extent the notoriety that has been attached to this king's name is the product of a Shakespearean play, although the majority of medieval and early-modern Scottish chroniclers and historians have also had a large part to play in this process. In fact, this concentration on MacBethad has been detrimental to the study of the other Moravian dynasts who appear in the historical record between *c.*1020 and 1130.

There is no evidence to prove that after the death of Gilla Comgáin mac Máel Brigte, mormaer of Moray in 1032 he was succeeded by MacBethad mac Findláich.[145] The only possible clue about MacBethad's status after that event is that he was referred to as *duce* in the Latin chronicle of Marianus Scottus.[146] The noun *dux* can mean 'earl', 'leader', 'commander' or 'duke',[147] and was probably used by the chronicler to indicate that MacBethad was a person of high status in Alba. The argument that MacBethad was mormaer of Moray by 1040 is probably more secure because he successfully challenged and killed King Donnchad mac Crínáin on 14 August 1040 at *Bothngouane*,[148] possibly Pitgaveny near Elgin.

Medieval Scottish chroniclers did not hesitate to voice their opinion of this murder. John of Fordun was clearly not impressed by the deed. Just before MacBethad's appearance in the chronicle, Fordun stated that the

---

145 The entry for 1027 in the *Anglo-Saxon Chronicle* which contains a reference to a King Mælbeth [cf. Garmonsway, *A-S Chronicle*, 159], cannot refer to MacBethad, even if an emendation of four years is allowed, because he clearly was not mormaer of Moray at this time. Unless, of course, MacBethad was mormaer of another province of Alba by this date.

146 Georg Heinrich Pertz (ed.), *Monumenta Germaniae Historica, Scriptores* (1884), v, 557 [hereafter: Pertz, *Monumenta*].

147 R. E. Latham and D. R. Howlett, *Dictionary of Medieval Latin from British Sources* (London, 1975), iii, 740.

148 *Chron. Melrose*, 22.

royal dynasty had already experienced trouble with an ancient family of conspirators who had murdered both the great-grandfather and grandfather of King Donnchad mac Crínáin. This set the scene very nicely, establishing MacBethad as the leading representative of a troublesome family of traitors. To the reader of Fordun, having had MacBethad closely associated with a tradition of murderous treachery, it comes as no surprise when he eventually murders King Donnchad. As far as Fordun was concerned, this act was unforgivable. The new king of Alba was a murderous usurper.[149] But, according to Fordun, King MacBethad was not just a usurper, he was also a tyrant. Every one of his actions was controlled by a lust for power. Because King MacBethad was not wanted by the people of Alba, he could only hold on to power through military strength and by establishing a reign of utter terror. Any threat to his kingship resulted in banishment, executions, imprisonment and confiscation of property.[150] Such a viewpoint is not surprising given that one of Fordun's chief concerns was the royal Scottish succession and the right to kingship.

In the *Chronica*, Fordun clearly distinguished primogeniture from an older form of Scottish kingship. He explained the older form of kingship:

Hoc autem illis ideo fiebat diebus, quoniam et eis et Pictis plerisque regnorum regibus, etiam et imperii quibusdam principibus, eadem succedendi lex erat, ut regis cujusque decedentis frater aut filius fratris, si filio regis aetate fuerat ac habilitate regendi potior, quamvis gradu remotior, ipsum praecederet ad regendum. Non enim sanguinis proximitas, sed perfectae pubertatis habilitas hunc vel illum regni throno sustulit ad regnandum. Hujusmodi vero regnationis constitutio prius invaluit, quia primitivae gentis exigua paucitas, cum esset numero brevi, certam in acquirendo sibi sive servando cum libertate sedem, undique belli exposita, non solum sui regni, sed etiam corporum abhorrens regimen tradi juvenibus, hanc legem statuit praetaxatam.[151]

Now this was the practice in those days, since both Scots and the Picts and also the majority of kings of kingdoms and certain rulers of the empire had the same law of succession, namely that if the brother of

149 *Chron. Fordun*, 187–88.
150 Ibid., 188–89.
151 Ibid., 144.

each deceased king or the son of his brother was superior to the king's son in years and ability to rule, he took precedence over the king's son to the throne, although he was more distant in degree. For it was not proximity of blood but the ability that comes with maturity that raised one or the other to the reign on the throne of the kingdom. It was the tiny size of the population in early times, few in number as they were, that caused the custom of this kind of succeeding to the throne to prevail. It was in trying to acquire or preserve for themselves a settled abode in freedom that they established this aforementioned law. For since they were exposed to wars on all sides, they shrank from handing over to youths control not just over their kingdom but even over their lives.

This is a reasonably accurate description of the royal *derbfine* (true kin, literally the male descendants of the same great-grandfather) in Gaelic Ireland,[152] which enabled the most able adult male of a particular generation from among the *rígdamnai* (king-material) to assume the kingship.[153] Fordun obviously thought that the same conditions had once applied to Scotland. But Fordun also claimed that the rules of succession changed during the reign of King Cináed mac Máel Coluim. Basically, the king of Alba had received information that the law of succession of emperors had been changed on the Continent. Each potential candidate had to be elected by seven electors before he could begin his personal rule:

Hiis de mutatione successionum rumoribus auditis, rex Kenethus priscorum regni sui regum, hactenus intricate regnantium, successionis ritum aboleri voluit, et sobolem propriae generationis, post quemlibet regem, prae ceteris diademate decorari. Habebat autem ipse filium illustrem, Malcolmum nomine, cui regnum ascribi proposuit toto nisu. Statuit igitur omni consensu principum, paucis primitivae successionis fautoribus exceptis, ut regi cuique decedenti de cetero filius aut filia, nepos et neptis, seu liniae collateralis frater aut soror, aut saltem quisquis alius, regi decedenti superstes sanguine proximus, succedere debeat, unius diei licet aetatis infans, cum dicatur, 'Aetas regis in fide subditorum consistit', nulla lege deinceps in hujus contrarium praevalente.

---

152 Fergus Kelly, *A Guide to Early Irish Law* (Dublin, 1988), 12–14.
153 Byrne, *Irish Kings*, 35, and at 122–23.

Hearing these rumours about a change in the law of succession, King Kenneth wished to abolish the custom of succession observed by the ancient kings in his kingdom, who up to this time had reigned in complicated succession, and he wished that after any king his offspring of legitimate birth should be adorned with the diadem of kingdom in preference to all others. He himself had a distinguished son Malcolm, to whom he was absolutely determined that the kingdom should be assigned. Therefore he decreed with the consent of all the nobles apart from a few supporters of the ancient custom of succession that every king on his death should in future be succeeded by his son or daughter, his grandson or granddaughter, or his brother or sister in the collateral line or, failing these, any other survivor of the late king who was nearest to him in blood, even if he was an infant one day old, since it is said: 'The age of the king rests with the loyalty of his subjects.' And henceforth no law to the opposite effect was to prevail.[154]

Apart from Fordun, writing in the late fourteenth century, there is no other evidence that the rules of succession were altered during the reign of King Cináed mac Máel Coluim (971–995). Nevertheless, the idea that seven electors apparently elected a king was widely believed. Examples include the seven earls of Scotland, and the seven electors of Germany with their 'ancient right' to elect a king of the Romans.[155] Fordun perhaps invented this passage, using these examples to inform his argument, inserting the information where he thought a change in the rules of succession should have taken place. Consequently, beginning with the reign of King Máel Coluim mac Cináeda (1005–1034), Fordun was able to label each successive king as either 'lawful' or 'unlawful', depending on whether they had succeeded according to the new rule which governed kingship. Fordun seems to have regarded the introduction of primogeniture as almost a cultural advance that brought Scotland into line with the more developed European kingdoms, thereby setting the scene for the eventual dynastic triumph of that branch of the royal dynasty descended from Queen Margaret and King Máel Coluim mac Donnchada.

It is perhaps ironic, leaving the theme of primogeniture to one side for the moment, that Fordun's view of King MacBethad stands in complete contrast to the Gaelic view of the man:

154 *Chron. Fordun*, 172.
155 Barrow, *Bruce*, 44–45.

Íarsin nos géabha in rí dercc,
ríghe Alban ard dreach-leircc
íar n-ár Gaoidheal íar n-ár Gall
nos géabha fíalrí Fortrenn.

In rúadh fionn-bhuidhe foda
bidh aoibhinn dhamhsa occu
bidh lomlán Alba thíar thoir
fri ríghe an deircc dhásachtaigh.

Fiche blíadhan is deich mblíadhna
for Albain ardrí ríaghla
for lár Scoine sceithfidh fuil
fescur aidhche íar n-amárgain.

After that the red king will take sovereignty,
the kingship of noble Alba of hilly aspect;
after slaughter of Gaels, after slaughter of strangers
the generous king of Fortriu will take sovereignty.

The red, tall, golden-haired one
he will be pleasant to me among them,
Alba will be brimful west and east
during the reign of the furious red one.

Thirty years over Alba
a high-king ruling,
in the middle of Scone he will spew blood
on the evening of a night after a duel.[156]

This favourable assessment of King MacBethad's kingship indicates that his reign was successful though perhaps not too much should be read into the fact that this source also refers to MacBethad as 'king of Fortriu' as it is a

156 Hudson, *Berchán*, 54. With amended translation by A. Ross. The thirty-year reign-length assigned to MacBethad is problematic since he is known to have ruled for only seventeen years. Hudson suggested that the figure of thirty years was reasonably accurate if it was reckoned from the date that Máel Coluim mac Máel Brigte died in 1029, upon which MacBethad assumed the kingship of Cenél Loairn. Since the link between MacBethad, his Moravian kindred, and Cenél Loairn has been shown to be false [cf. Dumville, 'Cethri Prímchenéla', 186], this theory can now be discounted. Perhaps the most reasonable explanation for this mistake is that the manuscripts containing the Scottish section of the prophecy are known to have been copied and emended over a period of *c.*700 years.

problematic text. The same kind of personal assessment is reiterated in a piece of prose about MacBethad that was inserted into the main text of the Melrose Chronicle:

> *In cui[us] regno f[er]tile te[m]p[us] erat hunc tamen i[n] Lufnaut t[run]cauit morte c[ru]dele Duncani nat[us] no[m]i[n]e malcolom[us].*

And in his reign there were productive seasons but Duncan's son, named Malcolm, cut him off by a cruel death in Lumphanan.[157]

On balance, it is more likely that these last two pieces of evidence are the more accurate evaluations of MacBethad's reign. Marianus Scottus, for example, stated that in 1050 King MacBethad was in Rome where he scattered money like seed to the poor.[158] Regardless of whether this profligacy actually occurred, the very fact that MacBethad was able to leave Alba for an extended period of time, travel to Rome, and still have a kingdom to come back to, would tend to make a mockery of Fordun's comments about the king's supposed evil tyranny. Nevertheless, Fordun's opinion of MacBethad was followed by Bower. He labelled MacBethad's reign a 'corrupt period'.[159]

Scottish historical perceptions of King MacBethad changed dramatically in Andrew Wyntoun's chronicle in the fifteenth century. Although Wyntoun still cast MacBethad's murder of Donnchad as treason, he gave a much more balanced view of the new king. Wyntoun noted that MacBethad's reign was bountiful (on both land and sea), that the king was an excellent upholder of justice, that he did a great deal of good for the Church, and that MacBethad went on pilgrimage to Rome where he distributed silver.[160] While two of these assertions are already familiar, Wyntoun was the first chronicler to state that MacBethad was considered to be a good justiciar and that he had also worked profitably with the Church. Assuming that Wyntoun did not invent this information himself, it seems likely that he had access to a separate account of King MacBethad's reign.

What form this source might have taken, or where it was kept, is unknown. There are, however, two factors that should be taken into

---

157   *Chron. Melrose*, 22.
158   Pertz, *Monumenta*, v, 558.
159   *Chron. Bower* (Watt), ii, 398–99.
160   *Chron. Wyntoun*, iv, 277.

account. Firstly, it is known that Wyntoun was elected to the priory of St Serf's on Loch Leven *c.*1393.[161] Secondly, one of only two surviving records of charters granted by King MacBethad concerns a grant of lands to the *céli Dé* community of Loch Leven (Plate 5).[162] This may be nothing more than coincidence, but it may be that the later ecclesiastic community on St Serf's isle, consisting of Augustinian canons dependent upon St Andrews,[163] remembered MacBethad as a generous patron of the earlier ecclesiastic community on the island.

This perception is perhaps strengthened by the fact that Wyntoun's chronicle is the only surviving medieval Scottish account that contains anti-Canmore material. Wyntoun stated that King Máel Coluim mac Donnchada (1058–1093) was a bastard, born of the miller's daughter of Forteviot.[164] It is possible, given the similarities between the two tales, that this story could have been based on an early-twelfth-century tradition concerning the parentage of William the Conqueror, since both of these men ruled at the same time and both men usurped a throne. William's mother, Herleva, was alleged to be the daughter of Fulbert, a *pollincter* (tanner) from Falaise.[165] More puzzling is why Wyntoun inserted this information about King Máel Coluim mac Donnchada in the first instance.

A possible clue may lie in a charter dated to 1150 x 53, in which King David I granted the island of Loch Leven to St Andrews Cathedral priory. This stated that if the members of the *céli Dé* community already on the island were willing to adopt the order of canons regular, they could remain on the island in peace. If not, they were to be ejected.[166] Perhaps this charter caused enough resentment among the *céli Dé* of St Serf's Island to result in the deliberate creation of a tradition that cast aspersions upon the parentage of King David I, namely, King Máel Coluim mac Donnchada. If so, it is possible that Wyntoun did not invent the story concerning the parentage of King Máel Coluim mac Donnchada himself, but was instead drawing on an older tradition from the Loch Leven community.

---

161 Ibid., i, xxvii.
162 *ESC*, 5–6.
163 Barrow, *Chrs. David I*, 154–55.
164 *Chron. Wyntoun*, iv, 256–57.
165 Elisabeth M. C. Van Houts, 'The Origins of Herleva, Mother of William the Conqueror', *EHR*, 101, 1986, 399–404.
166 Barrow, *Chrs. David I*, 154–55.

The perception that the Loch Leven community possessed its own traditions, whether oral or written, concerning King MacBethad appears to be supported by the other pieces of information that Wyntoun provided. It is clear that MacBethad was considered to have been of supernatural birth after a meeting between his mother and a fair stranger in a wood. The man is once referred to as 'ferly wise'. This phrase may be derived from the Old Norse word *ferligr* (monstrous, dreadful).[167] This is also the first time that the three 'werd sisteris', who became famous in the much later play by Shakespeare, appear in MacBethad-related literature. It is at this point in Wyntoun's chronicle that we are informed of the threefold path that MacBethad will follow to the kingship. Firstly, he will be thane of Crwmbathy (Cromarty). Secondly, that he will become thane of Moray. Finally, that he will become king of Alba. MacBethad is the only king of Alba to be credited with supernatural aspects in historical accounts.

Wyntoun was also the first Scottish chronicler to indicate that MacBethad was related to King Donnchad mac Crínáin (Duncan I, 1034–1040). Wyntoun described the death of King Donnchad mac Crínáin in terms of MacBethad killing his 'eme' (uncle): 'He murtherist his eme in Elgyne, And usurpit his kinrik syne.'[168] It is quite clear that Wyntoun was describing the relationship between King Donnchad and MacBethad at this point because he also gave a description of MacBethad killing Gilla Comgáin mac Máel Brigte at a later point in the chronicle. In relating this second murder, Wyntoun described Gilla Comgáin mac Máel Brigte as MacBethad's 'eme', before relating how MacBethad took his uncle's widow to wife: 'The fantasy thus of his dreyme, Mowit hym mast to sla his eme, As he did al furthe in deide, As before yhe herde me rede, And Dame Grewok, his emys wiff, Tuk, and lede with hir his lif.'[169]

Unfortunately, Wyntoun never provided any further clues towards the relationship between King Donnchad and MacBethad other than stating that MacBethad had been fostered by King Donnchad and that he was the king's 'syster son'.[170] At an earlier point in the chronicle, when he was discussing the reign of King Máel Coluim mac Cináeda, Wyntoun did state that King Máel Coluim had left no son, only a daughter (Bethóc). However, Wyntoun did

167 M. Robinson, *Scots Dictionary* (Edinburgh, 1999), 193.
168 *Chron. Wyntoun*, iv, 258.
169 Ibid., 275.
170 Ibid., 259.

not claim that Bethóc was King Máel Coluim's only daughter, just that she was his lawful heir.[171] In the fifteenth-century context of Wyntoun's chronicle, this might just mean that Bethóc was King Máel Coluim mac Cináeda's eldest daughter. It is tempting to suggest that Wyntoun invented the relationship between King Donnchad and MacBethad, mainly because no earlier Scottish source provides supporting evidence. But Wyntoun clearly had access to a source about MacBethad that was not used by either Fordun or Bower. Therefore, the evidence of a family relationship could have been derived from that source.

It is possible that Wyntoun's information regarding the relationship between the family of King Donnchad and MacBethad was originally derived from an English source. At the outset of the Great Cause in 1290, King Edward I of England asked many English ecclesiastic houses to search their records for proof of English royal superiority over Scotland. One of the many monastic houses that sent extracts from their records to the king of England during 1291 was Huntingdon. Its extract began with a king-list that ran from King Alpín (840s) to King Donnchad mac Crínáin. This was then followed by an extract about the reign of King MacBethad which included the following information:

Comes Northumbrie Sywardus Scociam ingressus, Maket Rege[m] nepote[m] d[i]c[t]i Malc[olmi]. cu[m] .xv. a[n]n[is] reg[na]ret; a reg[no] fugav[it]. Et Malcol[mo] fil[io] Du[n]cani regn[um] suu[m] restituit.

Having invaded Scotland, Siward, earl of Northumbria, chased out of that kingdom King MacBethad, nephew of the said Malcolm, after he had reigned for fifteen years; And Malcolm son of Duncan recovered his kingdom.[172]

There would appear to be no reason why the information about MacBethad's relationship to King Máel Coluim mac Cináeda should have been a late-thirteenth-century addition by the canons of Huntingdon. It is unlikely that King Edward I's political cause in 1291 would have benefited from the insertion of such information, whether true or false. Therefore,

171 Ibid., 201.
172 W. F. Skene (ed.), *Chronicles of the Picts, Chronicles of the Scots and Other Memorials of Scottish History* (Edinburgh, 1867), 210.

assuming that the Huntingdon canons had not confused the relationship between King Máel Coluim mac Cináeda and MacBethad with the known relationship between King Máel Coluim mac Cináeda and King Donnchad mac Crínáin, it is likely that the canons of Huntingdon had copied the information about the family relationship between King Máel Coluim mac Cináeda and King MacBethad from an earlier manuscript. Indeed, recent work by Broun has shown that the immediate ancestor of the Huntingdon king-list, which preceded the section on MacBethad, was an earlier text datable to between 1165 and 1214.[173] What we cannot know is whether the information about MacBethad was also a part of this earlier manuscript.

In other respects, the Huntingdon entry is reasonably accurate, and this may add some validity to its claim that MacBethad was related to King Máel Coluim mac Cináeda. A number of sources state that Earl Siward did invade Alba in 1054, although this would have been the fourteenth year of MacBethad's reign, not the fifteenth.[174] Also, the long connection during the twelfth century between the earldom of Huntingdon and the kings of Scotia, when successive kings of Scots held this title and lands in the earldom and honour of Huntingdon, raises the possibility that all of the information in this extract could be correct.[175]

The really interesting question in all of this, however, is whether all the information collected by King Edward I during the Great Cause, and particularly the contribution from Huntingdon, was shown to the *probi homines* of Scotland. If it was, this may be the ultimate source of Wyntoun's information about the family relationship between King Donnchad mac Crínáin and King MacBethad, although this theory would require Wyntoun to have altered the relationship by making MacBethad a nephew of King Donnchad mac Crínáin rather than of King Máel Coluim mac Cináeda. If the Huntingdon chronicle was not the source of Wyntoun's statement, there are now two independent sources that claim some sort of close kindred affinity between King MacBethad and Clann Custantín meic Cináeda.

The alternative scenario is that MacBethad was indeed a usurper. In a comprehensive analysis of royal kindreds in Ireland, Ó Corráin has

---

173 Dauvit Broun, *The Irish Identity of the Kingdom of the Scots* (Woodbridge, 1999), 144 [hereafter: Broun, *Irish Identity*].
174 For example, *Ann. Ulster*, 1054.6.
175 Duncan, *Kingdom*, 134–35.

demonstrated that 27 per cent of kings fell outwith the royal *derbfine*, and of this last figure 8.5 per cent were completely outside any royal *derbfine*.[176] While no such analysis has been undertaken for early medieval Scotland – and there are dangers in applying solutions from Gaelic Ireland to problems in Gaelic Scotland – it is just possible that MacBethad mac Findláich may not have had a recognised claim to the kingship of Alba. This theory, though, is only tenable if two good and possibly independent sources, Wyntoun and the Huntingdon material, are ignored.

In contrast to Wyntoun's chronicle, John Mair was either not familiar with material related to MacBethad or chose not to use it. He had very little to say about King MacBethad other than commenting that he was a usurper. Mair also followed Fordun and Bower by insisting that King Máel Coluim mac Cináeda only had one daughter, Bethóc.[177] Hector Boece both followed and elaborated on Wyntoun's chronicle. Boece was the first historian to provide a name for King MacBethad's mother and he stated categorically that she was a daughter of King Donnchad mac Crínáin.[178] Boece was also the first chronicler to provide a motive that explained MacBethad's murder of King Donnchad. He stated that King Donnchad made his eldest son, Máel Coluim, prince of Cumbria. This grant made MacBethad jealous because he now thought that he would never be king. It was at this point in Boece's narrative that MacBethad realised that if King Donnchad were slain, he would be next in line for the kingship. Boece gives two reasons for this. Firstly, with the exception of Donnchad's children, MacBethad was nearest in blood to the king. Secondly, that Donnchad's children were too young to reign.[179] In effect, Boece was reporting the old method of succession, which had been used in Scotland before the advent of primogeniture, to provide some sort of legitimacy for MacBethad usurping the throne.

This curious tension in Boece's treatment of MacBethad is mirrored in other ways. For example, Boece was the first historian to attempt to find a reason why a tyrannical King MacBethad was not deposed by his subjects. In contrast to Fordun, who thought that the length of MacBethad's reign was due to the spiritual illness and lethargy of a people deprived of their

---

176 Donnchadh Ó Corráin, 'Irish Regnal Succession, a Reappraisal', *Studia Hibernica*, 11, 1971, 7–39, at 28.

177 Archibald Constable (ed. and trans.), *A History of Greater Britain as well England as Scotland* (Edinburgh, 1892), 118–21 [hereafter: Constable, *History*].

178 *Chron. Boece*, ii, 143.

179 Ibid., 150–51.

true king,[180] Boece argued that MacBethad was an evil king who pretended to be an excellent king. In short, MacBethad fooled his subjects into thinking that he was not a tyrant.[181]

However, this could not last. After ten years, according to Boece, King MacBethad's true nature reasserted itself. The reader was provided with two reasons for this sudden change. Firstly, MacBethad imagined that he had the complete support of his subjects because of his ten-year-long period of good rule. Secondly, MacBethad began to lose his sanity and imagined that others might want to get rid of him, just as he had got rid of King Donnchad.[182] In consequence, MacBethad became what Boece imagined a tyrant should be. He became totally ruthless, slaying, for example, the whole of MacDuff's family, and also placed spies in all the houses of all the nobility.[183]

Even though John Leslie's history was partly based on the work of Boece, he treated King MacBethad in a completely different manner. Leslie did not provide his readers with background material about MacBethad. Instead, he first appeared during the reign of King Donnchad when the king delegated a number of administrative duties to him. Because MacBethad performed these tasks well, King Donnchad, by inference, was an excellent and prudent ruler. MacBethad owed his position of power to the king.[184] It is possible that Leslie chose this scenario to make King Donnchad's murder seem like even more of a crime. It was not until MacBethad became king that Leslie mentioned that he was a grandson of King Máel Coluim mac Cináeda. Thereafter, Leslie generally followed the story as related by Boece, with one important difference: Leslie was unwilling to credit MacBethad with any redeeming qualities and refused to admit that King MacBethad had ten good years before he returned to his tyrannical ways. Leslie even credited one of King MacBethad's successors, King Máel Coluim mac Donnchada, with the pilgrimage to Rome, rather than MacBethad himself.[185]

On the whole, George Buchanan followed Boece's perceptions regarding King MacBethad. However, Buchanan's observations tend to be more

---

180 *Chron. Fordun*, 205.
181 *Chron. Boece*, ii, 151–53.
182 Ibid., 154.
183 Ibid., 155–56.
184 Dalrymple, *Annals*, 304–05.
185 Ibid., 308.

succinct and in consequence, MacBethad was portrayed as a man of extremes. At first, Buchanan described MacBethad as a man of penetrating genius, high spirit and unbounded ambition. But the king later underwent a severe degeneration into wanton cruelty, during which he killed a number of important nobles.[186] In common with Boece, Buchanan divided MacBethad's reign into two periods. The second of these periods, according to Buchanan, equalled the cruelty of the most barbarous tyrants.[187] Given the reputation that King MacBethad gained in the writings of six fifteenth- and sixteenth-century historians, it comes as something of a surprise that his name did not appear in the writings of that great historian of Moray, Lachlan Shaw.

In contrast to the earlier writers, most of the eighteenth- and nineteenth-century historians were agreed that Donnchad was a usurper and that MacBethad should have been the rightful king.[188] The main reason given for this was that there was an alternate system of succession operating between two segments of the royal kindreds in Alba. Therefore, Donnchad should not have succeeded his grandfather, King Máel Coluim mac Cináeda: MacBethad, either as a relation of Máel Coluim mac Cináeda, or as guardian and representative of his stepson, Lulach mac Gilla Comgáin, had a better right under law.[189] It was also frequently noted by these historians that earlier Scottish chroniclers, beginning with Fordun in the late fourteenth century, manipulated the royal succession in their works to produce an unbroken line of Scottish kings stretching back into prehistory. In earlier works of this type, and as an interloper in the line of succession, MacBethad became a monster whose character was transformed into a diabolic personality.[190]

In more recent times, both Duncan and Barrow have accepted that the accession of Donnchad mac Crínáin to the high-kingship of Alba was contrary to the normal practices of Scottish kingship of that period: King Máel Coluim mac Cináeda had manipulated the rules of succession to

---

186 J. Aikman (trans.), *The History of Scotland*, 6 vols (Glasgow and Edinburgh, 1827–29), i, 328–32 [hereafter: Aikman, *Scotland*].

187 Ibid., 336.

188 Burton, *Scotland*, i, 345; Pinkerton, *Enquiry*, 196. The exceptions were Dalrymple, Hume-Brown and Chalmers, who described MacBethad's killing of King Donnchad mac Crínáin as 'the odious crime' [see Dalrymple, *Annals*, 2; Hume Brown, *History*, 43 and Chalmers, *Caledonia*, i, 408].

189 Lang, *History*, 53.

190 Hume Brown, *History*, 43.

ensure that his grandson by his daughter Bethóc followed him in the kingship. Both reject the relatively late evidence from the thirteenth-century Chronicle of Huntingdon that MacBethad mac Findláich was related to Máel Coluim mac Cináeda, and both are even more careful to avoid stating who should have succeeded Máel Coluim.[191]

These arguments do not help to explain the right by which MacBethad mac Findláich was able to claim the high-kingship of Alba if he was not related to King Máel Coluim mac Cináeda in the first instance. In fact, the last historian to develop an elegant solution to this problem was W. F. Skene. According to him, it was Earl Thorfinn of Caithness and Orkney who was the real aggressor, concealing his identity – as a grandson of Máel Coluim mac Cináeda – by using the alias Karli Hundason. The killing of Donnchad was the joint work of Thorfinn and MacBethad and they proceeded to divide the kingdom of Alba between them.[192] This suggestion did not gain widespread popularity among historians, although it was adapted by later novelists.[193]

There is one further important point to make at this juncture: since Macbethad was the first attested Moravian to become king of Alba, could he also have been the king who successfully oversaw the amalgamation of Alba and Moray?

MacBethad – the view from the north

The identity of Karli Hundason has exercised the minds of many generations of historians. He only appears in one source concerned with the history of northern Scotland during the eleventh century, the *Orkneyinga Saga*, probably written in Iceland between 1192 and 1200.[194] The *Orkneyinga Saga* is a complicated source for a historian. The author relied on both poetry and oral tradition for information, and the picture is further complicated by the fact that the original *Orkneyinga Saga* was used as a source for a work called *Heimskringla*, compiled c.1230. When the *Orkneyinga Saga* was then revised at a later date, *Heimskringla* was used as a source for that revision.[195]

---

191 For example, Duncan, *Kingdom*, 112–13.
192 Skene, *Celtic Scotland*, i, 404–5.
193 For example, Dorothy Dunnett, *King Hereafter* (London, 1982).
194 Hermann Pálsson and Paul Edwards (trans.), *Orkneyinga Saga*, 9–10.
195 Ibid., 11.

The *Orkneyinga Saga* mentions many important figures in northern Scotland by name: Earl MacBethad,[196] Earl Mael-Brigte,[197] Earl Finnleik,[198] and Earl Máel Coluim of Moray.[199] Other crucial pieces of information are also found. For example, the reader is informed that Earl Sigurd *digri* (the stout) married a daughter of King Máel Coluim of Scotland.[200] One of their sons, Earl Thorfinn, is one of the greatest heroes in the saga. King Máel Coluim mac Donnchada (Malcolm III) is also named as the second husband of Ingibjorg of Orkney.[201] Of the five kings of Alba between 1005 and 1094, three were not directly named as kings (of Scotland) in the saga: Donnchad mac Crínáin, MacBethad mac Findláich and Lulach mac Gilla Comgáin.

References to conflict in northern Scotland appear in a second source, *Njal's Saga*, written *c.*1280.[202] In this text, one chapter describes a battle in northern Scotland at Duncansby Head between Earl Sigurd *digri* and two Scottish earls, Hundi and Melsnati, which must have taken place before Earl Sigurd's death at Clontarf in Ireland in 1014.[203]

The first point to note is that these two texts give the names of important men, often connected to Caithness, Moray and Ross, in the late tenth and early eleventh centuries. Some of these names are already familiar. Earl Mael-Brigte (or rather his tooth) is identified as the killer of Earl Sigurd *hinn riki* (the mighty) who died *c.*892. Earl Melsnati (pre-1014) is probably the Norse equivalent of the Gaelic name Máel Snechta. Earl Finnleik, again pre-1014, is probably MacBethad's father Findlaech mac Ruaidri. In contrast, the identities of Earl MacBethad and Earl Máel Coluim of Moray are more problematic. Earl MacBethad, for example, appears in the saga within a chronology that suggests he lived during the latter half of the tenth century. In contrast, the chronology for Earl Máel Coluim of Moray suggests a date during the twelfth century.

At least some of these names may be genuine: Mael-Brigte, MacBethad and Melsnati all appear again as personal names among the leading Moray

196 Ibid., 35.
197 Ibid., 27–28.
198 Ibid., 36.
199 Ibid., 218.
200 Ibid., 38.
201 Ibid., 76.
202 Magnus Magnusson and Hermann Pálsson, *Njal's Saga* (London, 1987), 9 [hereafter: Magnusson and Pálsson, *Njal's Saga*].
203 Ibid., 182–83.

kindred during the eleventh century. This might suggest that these three men also belonged to the same Moravian kindred. However, as far as Earl Máel Coluim of Moray is concerned, no source provides information about the identity of the leading member of the Moravian kindred between the death of Máel Snechta mac Lulaich in 1085 and the death of Oengus in 1130. If, however, Oengus did not immediately replace Máel Snechta in 1085, then it is possible that an Earl Máel Coluim could have been the next mormaer of the province.[204]

This leaves Karli Hundason, king of Alba, as the only unidentified northerner in the *Orkneyinga Saga*. In an important article published in 1993, Cowan argued that Karli could be equated with King MacBethad mac Findláich. This theory was based on a number of points. Firstly, since King Donnchad mac Crínáin was considered to be an obscure king by both English and Gaelic annalists, it would not be surprising if he was similarly treated in the *Orkneyinga Saga*, particularly as he seems to have mostly operated in a southern orbit. Secondly, both the *Orkneyinga Saga* and *Njal's Saga* describe a battle in northern Scotland between native earls and the Orkneymen, won by Earl Sigurd *digri*. In the first description, the *Orkneyinga Saga*, his opponent at Skitten was Earl Finnleik. On the second, in *Njal's Saga*, his opponents at Duncansby Head were Earl Hundi and Earl Melsnati. If both these accounts described the same battle, Cowan argued that Earl Finnleik and Earl Hundi were the same person. Accordingly, the son of Earl Hundi/Earl Finnleik must have been Karli Hundason, MacBethad mac Findláich.[205] This identification has been accepted by other historians.[206]

Cowan admitted that this theory depended on accepting that the author of *Njal's Saga* had shifted the site of the battle from Skitten to Duncansby Head (a distance of 10 miles), which would, he thought, have been a more familiar site to that particular author.[207] There may, however, be a greater problem with his theory: there are other references to a person called Hundi in the *Orkneyinga Saga*, and it is clear that this Hundi was Scandinavian.

---

204 This Earl Malcolm can probably be identified with Máel Coluim MacEth. See Chapter 4 for further discussion of this.
205 Edward J. Cowan, 'The Historical Macbeth', in W. D. H. Sellar (ed.), *Moray: Province and People* (Edinburgh, 1993), 117–42, at 125–26 [hereafter: Cowan, 'Historical Macbeth'].
206 Barbara Crawford, *Scandinavian Scotland* (Exeter, 1987), 72 [hereafter: Crawford, *Scandinavian Scotland*].
207 Cowan, 'Historical Macbeth', 126.

The *Orkneyinga Saga* is quite clear that Hvelp, or Hundi, was a son of Earl Sigurd *digri*, who died in 1014.[208] Accordingly, Hundi must have been a grandson of King Máel Coluim mac Cináeda (Malcolm II, 1005–1034), since Earl Sigurd was married to a daughter of King Máel Coluim, unless Sigurd had another wife, all record of whom has been lost. This identification is problematic for two reasons. Firstly, if the story in *Njal's Saga* is correct, and unless there were two important men called Hundi alive at the same time, it means that Earl Hundi must have fought against his father, Earl Sigurd *digri*, at the Battle of Duncansby Head. However, such a scenario is not impossible.

Secondly, and perhaps more importantly, if Karli Hundason was a son of this Earl Hundi, the *Orkneyinga Saga* is quite clear that Karli was a king of Alba. In another passage King Karli was described as fighting Earl Thorfinn, who was a grandson of King Máel Coluim mac Cináeda, on at least two occasions. After the second battle between these two men, the saga claims that Earl Thorfinn conquered Sutherland and Ross and chased his opponent as far south as Fife.[209]

This leaves two options. The first is that there were, in fact, two important men called Hundi in northern Scotland during the first part of the eleventh century. One was the son of Earl Sigurd *digri*, the other was either Donnchad mac Crínáin or MacBethad mac Findláich. Deciding which of the latter two was known as Hundi depends on both shifting the site of a battle, and accepting that the saga writers ignored King Donnchad mac Crínáin. The second option is that the texts of both *Njal's Saga* and the *Orkneyinga Saga* have either become corrupted during transmission, or that the authors invented particular aspects of their stories, including some fictitious characters.[210] This second option is perhaps the more likely.

King Lulach mac Gilla Comgáin and his kin

King MacBethad was succeeded as *ardrí Alban* by his stepson, Lulach mac Gilla Comgáin and it is unlikely that King Lulach would have been described as *ardrí* had he not been inaugurated at Scone. This would suggest that although Máel Coluim mac Donnchada had slain King

---

208 Pálsson and Edwards, *Orkneyinga Saga*, 37.
209 Ibid., 50–56.
210 The author of Njal's Saga certainly invented minor characters and was not overly concerned with historical accuracy [cf. Magnusson and Pálsson, *Njal's Saga*, 24].

MacBethad, he may have lost the battle at Lumphanan in August 1057. According to Marianus Scottus, King Lulach reigned from 8 September 1057 to 17 March 1058 when he was killed at Essie in Strathbogie.[211] If so, and since MacBethad died on 15 August, Lulach was perhaps not inaugurated at Scone until after MacBethad had been buried. A number of surviving king-lists add the information that King Lulach *fatuus* (stupid) was killed at Essie in Strathbogie and subsequently buried on Iona.[212] We also know that King Lulach was married and had at least two children, even if we do not know the name of his wife. One of these children was Máel Snechta mac Lulaich, the other an unnamed daughter whose son Oengus was killed at Stracathro in 1130.

In contrast to King MacBethad, King Lulach mac Gilla Comgáin is only discussed very briefly in Scottish historical works. This is probably due to his very short reign and the paucity of information. In *Chronica Gentis Scotorum*, for example, we are told that Lulach *fatuus* was inaugurated at Scone immediately after the death of King MacBethad by people who supported 'this kind of crime'.[213] Clearly, Fordun regarded the inauguration as an unlawful act even though Máel Coluim mac Donnchada was not yet king of Alba. On the whole, Bower's description of these events tended to follow Fordun although he did add information not found in *Chronica Gentis Scotorum*. In fact, this new information, gleaned from the Melrose Chronicle, was quite sympathetic towards King Lulach and it introduced a direct contradiction, *infelix* (unlucky) as opposed to *fatuus* (stupid), into Scottish historical perceptions of King Lulach:

> *Mensibus infelix Lulach tribus extiterat rex,*
> *armis eiusdem Malcolmi cecidit.*
> *Fata viri fuerunt in Strathbolgin apud Esseg,*
> *quo sic incaute rex miser occubuit.*

The unlucky Lulach was king for three months,
He was slain by the sword of the same Malcolm.

---

211 Pertz, *Monumenta*, v, 558.
212 For example, Anderson, *Kings and Kingship*, 268. Scottish sources cannot agree on the reign-length of Lulach. Most give him either four or four and a half months, although the figure varies between one month and four years [cf. *ES*, i, 603]. Only the text known as the *Duan Albanach* gives a figure (7 months) close to Marianus Scottus [see K. H. Jackson, 'The Duan Albanach', *SHR*, 36, 1957, 125–37].
213 *Chron. Fordun*, 205.

The man met his fate in Essie in Strathbogie,
where the unhappy king was thus rashly slain.[214]

This same tension, which was again left unresolved, also appeared in Wyntoun's chronicle.[215] John Mair, on the other hand, merely contented himself with commenting that Lulach was dead before King Máel Coluim mac Donnchada was inaugurated.[216] Scottish historical perceptions about King Lulach changed once again in the writings of Boece, where the taking of the throne by King Lulach was relegated to a rebellion that occurred after King Máel Coluim mac Donnchada began his reign as king of Alba.

Leslie took this re-interpretation one step further:

> In king Malcolme, his tyme, ane was, his name Luthlat, surnamed the fool, his father machabie, as in the maist ancient Histories, and of maist Antiquitie, is maid mentioune; This man, I say, throuch ambitioune, makes to invade the Realme, quhen Malcolme war slayne, to sit in the Kingis sait. Bot his gret audacitie and fuilhardines, With all his partaikeris cost him his lyfe: quha althoch was nocht reknet in the number of the kingis, was nochttheles decoiret with the kingis sepulchre in Iona.[217]

In effect, Leslie moved Lulach's 'invasion' to the end of the reign of King Máel Coluim mac Donnchada and attempted to deny King Lulach any official royal status. It is perhaps unlikely, however, that this was deliberate. Leslie could well have confused the reign of Lulach with the short reign of King Domnall bán mac Donnchada (1093–1097).

Buchanan shifted Lulach's 'rebellion' back into the correct chronology. He placed the events after the death of King MacBethad but only after King Máel Coluim mac Donnchada had been inaugurated at Scone. This had the effect of making Lulach a traitor to his sovereign. As if this were not enough, Buchanan emphasised King Lulach's nickname: *Lulach fatuus*, given to him on account of his stupidity.[218] This seems to emphasise

---

214 *Chron. Melrose*, 24. This perception of Lulach is perhaps mirrored in the *Annals of Tigernach* which state that he was slain *per dolum* (through treachery) [cf. *Ann. Tig.*, ii, 290).

215 *Chron. Wyntoun*, iv, 305.

216 Constable, *History*, 123.

217 Dalrymple, *Historie*, 317.

218 Aikman, *Scotland*, i, 337–38.

Buchanan's opinion about the utter futility of rebellion against the lawful monarch. The influence of these opinions of Boece, Leslie and Buchanan can still be found in modern historical accounts of Lulach. This may explain why Duncan, for example, commented that Lulach was only recognised as king 'by some people',[219] even though Lulach was a member of the royal *derbfine* and belonged to Clann Custantín meic Cináeda. In fact, no historian seems prepared to admit that Máel Coluim mac Donnchada had to kill two high-kings of Alba in order to secure his own reign as *ardrí Alban*. This is probably testament to the enduring nature of the pro-primogeniture, and pro-Máel Coluim mac Donnchada/Margaret, propaganda circulating in medieval chronicles.

One final point remains to be explored in connection to the deaths of both King Macbethad and King Lulach. This is the assumption that Máel Coluim mac Donnchada invaded Alba from the south in both 1057 and 1058, based largely on evidence that he had been appointed king of Strathclyde in 1054 by Earl Siward. Since it is now known that the new king of Strathclyde in 1054 was a member of that kingdom's ruling dynasty and not Máel Coluim mac Donnchada, it is possible to speculate that the latter may have invaded Alba from an entirely different direction. This theory depends on one crucial point: this is that Ingibjorg, the wife of Máel Coluim mac Donnchada, was the daughter of Earl Thorfinn *hinn riki* rather than his wife.[220]

In 1058 the *Annals of Tigernach* record a massive invasion of Britain:

Longes la mac ríg Lochland, co nGallaib Índsi Orcc [ocus] Indsi Gall [ocus] Atha cliath, do gabail rigi Saxan, acht nocor' deonaig Dia sin.

A fleet led by the son of the king of Norway, with the foreigners of the Orkneys and the Hebrides and Dublin, to seize the kingdom of England; but to this God consented not.[221]

---

219 Duncan, *Kingdom*, 100.
220 Crawford, *Scandinavian Scotland*, 77, argues that Ingebjorg was Earl Thorfinn's wife. This is based on evidence from the Orkneyinga Saga that is not wholly reliable. Also, it is stated that Thorfinn was 75 years old upon his death in 1065. If Ingebjorg was his widow and still capable of bearing children to Máel Coluim mac Donnchada after 1065, she must have been very much younger than Thorfinn. It is perhaps doubtful that an earl of Orkney would have waited 40–50 years before marrying.
221 *Ann. Tig.*, ii, 399.

If Ingibjorg was the daughter of Earl Thorfinn, and if it is further assumed that her marriage to Máel Coluim mac Donnchada was either agreed upon or fact, it is surely possible that Máel Coluim took advantage of this dynastic link, and of the disruption caused by this massive invasion, to invade Alba from the north and kill Kings Macbethad and Lulach. With the benefit of hindsight we can now see that these two killings and the establishment of Máel Coluim mac Donnchada's progeny in the kingdom of Alba proved to be decisive in the long-term future of this northern kingdom, but it was not a quick or easy process.

Máel Snechta mac Lulaich

After the killing of King Lulach mac Gilla Comgáin, the primary sources are quiet about Moray for twenty years until 1078. Under that year-date, the *Anglo-Saxon Chronicle* records that King Máel Coluim mac Donnchada, 'captured the mother of Máel Snechta, all his best men, and all his treasures, and his livestock, and he himself escaped with difficulty'.[222] This entry refers to Máel Snechta mac Lulaich, as far as we know the only son of King Lulach mac Gilla Comgáin.

Clearly this must have been a major expedition which we assume took place in Moray, and which involved the capture of the dowager queen of Alba. As if this were not bad enough, it is likely that depriving Máel Snechta of all his treasures and his livestock would have effectively bankrupted him, leaving him unable to dispense patronage in an age when wealth was frequently measured in cattle. Yet the *Anglo-Saxon Chronicle* is the only surviving near-contemporary source to describe these events and historians are left to speculate why King Máel Coluim mac Donnchada felt it necessary to undertake these measures. One possible answer may be found in a later source, *Chronica Gentis Scotorum*, which relates a story about a plot to kill King Máel Coluim.[223]

Evidently, Fordun copied this tale from an earlier manuscript written by Turgot, bishop of St Andrews.[224] We are never told exactly when the plot occurred, or the identity of the 'knight' who was intending to assassinate the king. The assassin is merely described as, 'a chief noble'. In any event, Fordun related that King Máel Coluim was told of the plot but insisted on

222 Garmonsway, *A-S Chronicle*, 213.
223 *Chron. Fordun*, 206–7.
224 *Chron. Bower* (Watt), iii, 193.

going hunting with the traitor anyway. When they were in the woods, King Máel Coluim made a long speech to the traitor, who then saw the error of his ways and realised that he had been a madman to think about killing the king. The knight repented, King Máel Coluim forgave him (not forgetting to take hostages), and the knight then became a loyal subject.[225] If there is any truth in this tale, it may be based on the events of 1078 as related by the *Anglo-Saxon Chronicle*.

Walter Bower, Andrew Wyntoun and John Mair also related the basic details of this story as found in *Chronica Gentis Scotorum*.[226] Hector Boece, on the other hand, added more detail to the tale. According to him, the Moravians, the men of Ross, the men of Caithness, and the men of the Isles slew all the king's servants and ministers of justice in the north. With the assistance of a person that Boece referred to as 'MacDuncane', the rebels thrived on theft and slaughter. To put down the insurrection, King Máel Coluim and MacDuff advanced to the Spey where they routed the malcontents.[227] It is tempting to suggest that Boece used the name 'MacDuncane' because he was familiar with the twelfth- and thirteenth-century activities of the MacWilliam kindred descended from William fitz Duncan.

John Leslie added much more detail to this story. He placed the sequence of events between the years 1072 and 1079 and, like Boece, began the story with a rebellion in Caithness and Ross. King Máel Coluim, together with MacDuff, travelled north and confronted his enemies across the River Spey. However, through the intercession of some bishops, the enemy returned to the king's peace and he won a bloodless victory. The next day, before going hunting, King Máel Coluim discovered that some of his nobility had wanted to kill him. He chose as his hunting companion a 'certan noble of ane illustre stock' who the king was certain was organising the plot. King Máel Coluim challenged the man to single combat, but, before they could come to blows, the noble's conscience got the better of him and he humbled himself before the king. He was pardoned.[228]

It is difficult to know what to make of Leslie's version of this event. Although he had clearly read Boece, Leslie placed the event in a chronological sequence during which, according to the *Anglo-Saxon Chronicle*, there

---

225 *Chron. Fordun*, 206–7.
226 *Chron. Bower* (Watt), iii, 31–35; *Chron. Wyntoun*, iv, 327–33. The editors of *Scotichronicon* suggest that the story may relate to Máel Snechta mac Lulaich.
227 *Chron. Boece*, ii, 282–83.
228 Dalrymple, *Historie*, 313–14.

was some sort of conflict between Máel Snechta and King Máel Coluim. The detail about the intercession of some bishops to settle the conflict is also a new detail and it is possible that Leslie added this information himself. Leslie was bishop of Ross after 1565 and may have had access to older historiographical material that has since been lost along with the muniments of that see. Consequently, it is impossible to reject his sequence of events entirely, and the story first related in *Chronica Gentis Scotorum* may well be an attempt to describe the conflict between Máel Snechta and King Máel Coluim. George Buchanan also knew this story, although he limited the rebellion to Moray, Ross and Caithness, and did not include the section describing the hunt during which King Máel Coluim identified the traitor.[229] After Buchanan, Máel Snechta does not figure prominently, if at all, in Scottish historiography.

If 1078 was the point in time when King Máel Coluim and his dynasty took full control of Moray, it is a shame that the surviving sources do not tell us this; but whatever happened it is clear that Máel Snechta mac Lulaich survived to live another seven years when, according to the *Annals of Ulster*, he 'ended his life happily'.[230] According to normal usage this would indicate that Máel Snechta mac Lulaich had become a monk before he died in 1085, which is entirely believable given the events of 1078. However, that same obit also refers to Máel Snechta mac Lulaich as, '*rí Mureb*' (king of Moray) though this need not be an unsurmountable problem if one of the alternate meanings of the word '*rí*' is accepted.

The only other piece of evidence relating to Máel Snechta is found in the Gaelic *notitiae* in the *Book of Deer*. This recorded that Máel Snechta mac Lulaich gave *Pett Malduib* to Drostán.[231] If we are correct in assuming that this portion of land lay relatively close to Deer in Buchan, it is difficult to explain by what right Máel Snechta possessed these lands unless, of course, what we are seeing here is a shadowy glimpse of lands that had once been considered to have been in Fortriu.

Oengus mac ingine Lulaich

As far as the sources are concerned, Máel Snechta mac Lulaich was either childless or none of his progeny survived to adulthood. This is because the

229 Aikman, *Scotland*, i, 332.
230 *Ann. Ulster*, 1085.1.
231 Forsyth, Broun and Clancy, 'The Property Records', 138–39.

final member of the Moray kindred to appear in primary Gaelic sources is
Aengus mac ingine Lulaich, who died at the Battle of Stracathro in 1130.
Virtually nothing is known about this man, other than his mother was the
unnamed daughter of King Lulach mac Gilla Comgáin. This lack of knowledge about Oengus is compounded by the fact that he never appears in any
of the surviving charters from the reign of King David I (1124–1153). As a
consequence, it is not known what title Oengus possessed, what his long-
term political aims were, and whether he bore any deep-seated long-term
grudges against the people descended from King Máel Coluim mac
Donnchada and Queen Margaret. The only contemporary information
comes from his obit:

> *Bellum itir fhiru Alban [ocus] feru Moreb i torcradar .iiii. mile
> d'fheraibh Moréb im a righ .i. Oenghus m. ingine Luluigh; . . .*

> A battle between the men of Alba and the men of Moray in which
> four thousand of the men of Moray fell with their king .i. Aengus son
> of the daughter of Lulach; . . .[232]

As with Máel Snechta, it is difficult to determine exactly what the annalist
meant by the use of the word *rí* on this occasion. Once again it could just
be a matter of perspective. While Oengus may well have seemed like a king
to the annalist, and to the men under his command, as far as King David I
was concerned Oengus may just have been one of his magnates. In this
respect, it is noticeable that the text of *Gesta Annalia I*, completed sometime before April 1285 but probably based on an earlier text written by
Vairement, referred to Oengus as *comes* (earl).[233] Since this earlier text may
have been compiled at Dunfermline c.1250,[234] it is doubtful whether *comes*
was a contemporary title for Oengus. If this was the key moment when
Moray was finally fully absorbed into the kingdom of Scotia, it had been a
long and bloody path lasting some seventy-two years after the death of
King Lulach mac Gilla Comgáin.

---

232 *Ann. Ulster*, 1130.4. The editors of the 1983 edition of the *Annals of Ulster* translated the word
     Alba as Scotland. I have preferred to give this as Alba.
233 *Chron. Fordun*, 256.
234 *Chron. Bower* (Watt), iii, xvii–xviii.

Strathclyde/Cumbria

In contrast to Moray, very little is known about the second kingdom that came to be incorporated into Alba during the eleventh and early twelfth centuries. It is common knowledge that before 870 *Ail Cluaithe* (the Rock of the Clyde) was probably the most important stronghold of a *gentes* ruled by the kings of Dumbarton Rock. This is the only pre-900 kingdom in north Britain for which no contemporary name has survived and this is surprising since the ruling kindred of Dumbarton occasionally played leading roles in the politics of north Britain before AD 900. The people of the Rock were north Britains and spoke a P-Celtic or Brittonic language, usually referred to as Cumbric. Apart from occasional references to their activities in various annals, they have left us only one composition, the stanza called the 'Strathclyde interpolation', in *Y Gododdin*:

> I saw an array that came from Kintyre,
> who brought themselves as a sacrifice to a holocaust.
> I saw a second [array] who had come down from their settlement,
> who had been roused by the grandson of Neithon.
> I saw mighty men who came with the dawn.
> And it was Donald Brecc's head that the ravens gnawed.[235]

Thanks to other sources, this stanza has been identified as describing a conflict in December 642 in Strathcarron (south of Stirling) between Eugein son of Beli, king of the Rock of the Clyde, and Domnall Brecc, king of Dál Riata, where the latter was killed.[236] The historical boundaries of the kingdom based upon Dumbarton Rock and how they may have fluctuated over time are currently unknown, and it can only be vaguely seen as a negative imprint from what we know about the other (sometimes equally vague) boundaries of other contemporary kingdoms in north Britain.

It is generally agreed that the kingdom centred upon the Rock of the Clyde came to an end in 870 when Dumbarton Rock was besieged for four months and taken by Vikings. The evidence for this comes from the Gaelic annals and this information is also reflected in the archaeological record.[237] Within two years of this siege a seemingly new name for a kingdom in the Glasgow area appears in the sources:

235 John T. Koch, *The Gododdin of Aneirin* (Cardiff, 1997), 27.
236 Bannerman, *Dalriada*, 102–3.
237 *Ann. Ulster*, 870.6.

Artghal, rex Britanorum Sratha Cluade, consilio Custantini filii Cinaedho occisus est.

Artgal, king of the Britons of Strathclyde, was killed at the instigation of Constantine son of Cinaed.[238]

Unfortunately, we cannot tell from the historical sources alone exactly how Strathclyde related to the earlier kingdom based upon Dumbarton Rock and whether the former was just a continuation of an earlier kingdom under a different name or something new. While the ruling kindred of Strathclyde certainly claimed continuity of authority from the earlier kings of Dumbarton Rock, other crucial aspects were thought to have changed. For example, it was argued that post-870 a new sacral and judicial focus appeared in Strathclyde at Govan with its ecclesiastic site dedicated to St Constantine, the Govan sarcophagus, and the fantastic collection of hogback monuments and recumbent slabs. Close by is an archaeological feature called 'Doomster Hill' that has been positively identified as a stepped *ting*-mound upon which judicial assemblies would have been held.

This perception has changed in recent years. Archaeology has now demonstrated that some of the early-Christian Govan burials span the fifth and sixth centuries AD and that the *vallum* had been built by the eighth century, making Govan an important site long before the ninth-century destruction of the fortress upon Dumbarton Rock.[239] It has been suggested that this may have been in part due to Govan's proximity to the Brittonic royal estate at Partick on the opposite bank of the River Clyde and this proposal also seems to imply some kind of physical landed continuity between the kings of Dumbarton Rock pre-870 and the post-870 kingdom of Strathclyde.[240] This kingdom may have engaged in widespread maritime activity since two large islands lying at the south-eastern tip of Bute at the mouth of the Firth of Clyde were once known to Norsemen as *Kumreyjar* (the Cumbric islands).[241]

While there may have been some territorial continuity between the kingdom of Dumbarton Rock and Strathclyde pre- and post-870, the

---

238 Ibid., 872.5.
239 Stephen T. Driscoll, *Govan from Cradle to Grave* (Glasgow, 2004), 8.
240 Ibid., 20–22.
241 P. A. Wilson, 'On the use of the terms 'Strathclyde' and 'Cumbria', *Transactions of the Cumberland and Westmorland Antiquarian and Archaeological Society*, 66, 1966, 57–92, at 68 [hereafter: Wilson, 'Strathclyde and Cumbria'].

ethnicity of the kings of Strathclyde post-870 has caused something of a long-running historical spat. In 1962, Kirby, using evidence from Fordun's *Chronica Gentis Scotorum*, argued that Strathclyde/Cumbria were separate kingdoms by the tenth century and that post-*c.*915 the king of the Cumbrians was always the designated successor (tanist) to the kingship of Alba.[242] In this scenario the kings of Strathclyde post-870 were Gaels. Writing four years later, P. A. Wilson made an exhaustive evaluation of the terms 'Strathclyde' and 'Cumbria' and, while he cautiously accepted that Strathclyde/Cumbria may indeed have become a Scottish appanage in the tenth century, he also persuasively demonstrated that these two terms in fact referred to the same kingdom, one which would have stretched far to the south of the Solway Firth.[243]

A. P. Smyth, writing in 1984, chose to follow both of the arguments presented by Kirby and Wilson. Smyth accepted that Strathclyde/Cumbria were one kingdom but argued that Strathclyde passed into Scottish Gaelic hands sometime between 870 and 916 as the two kingdoms of Strathclyde and Alba gradually merged, and that from the latter date Strathclyde was the 'dower kingdom for the tanist to the Scottish throne'.[244]

Writing in 1993, Macquarrie treated Smyth's interpretation with some caution. Quite rightly, Macquarrie was suspicious of the fact that no source earlier than Fordun referred to the Alba-Strathclyde tanist 'arrangement'. In fact, he argued that because older native Welsh names reappeared in written sources whenever annalists and other writers were recording information relating to the ruling kindred of that kingdom, the native Dumbarton Rock/Strathclyde ruling kindred had undergone a cultural resurgence after the tenth century until their eventual demise in 1018.[245]

In the most recent article on this topic, Dauvit Broun wholly rejected the notion that Gaels had any political dominance over tenth-century Strathclyde, with the exception of a form of occasional overlordship. According to Broun, during this period the 'on-going' kingdom of Strathclyde remained demonstrably Brythonic with its own dynasty of native kings, none of whom had

---

242 D. P. Kirby, 'Strathclyde and Cumbria: a survey of historical development to 1092', *Transactions of the Cumberland and Westmorland Antiquarian and Archaeological Society*, 62, 1962, 77–94, at 86–87.

243 Wilson, 'Strathclyde and Cumbria', 57–92.

244 A. P. Smyth, *Warlords and Holy Men* (Edinburgh, 1984), 218–22.

245 Alan Macquarrie, 'The Kings of Strathclyde, *c.*400–1018', in Alexander Grant and Keith J. Stringer (eds), *Medieval Scotland: Crown, Lordship and Community* (Edinburgh, 1993), 1–19.

Gaelic fathers. He also pointed out that during the late ninth century, the kings of Picts/Alba were themselves involved in a struggle for political survival and it was thus unlikely that they would have been attempting to expand their domain by conquering Strathclyde. For Broun, the idea that Strathclyde was born out of a Gaelic-Norse carve-up of the area after the destruction of Dumbarton Rock was untenable because it rested on just three pieces of evidence: the destruction of the fortification upon Dumbarton Rock; the killing of King Arthgal of Dumbarton in 872, and the identity of the St Constantine commemorated at Govan.[246]

A. A. M. Duncan, writing in 2002, unravelled yet another important strand of Strathclyde's history. He demonstrated that an important (undated) piece of Strathclyde-related evidence found in the writings of William of Malmesbury had been misinterpreted:

> *Siwardum Northimbrensium, qui iussu eius cum Scottorum rege Macbetha congressus uita regnoque spoliauit, ibidemque Malcolmum filium regis Cumbrorum regem instituit.*

> Siward, earl of Northumbria, on his [Edward's] instructions attacked Macbeth, king of the Scots, deprived him of his life and throne, and installed Malcolm, son of the king of the Cumbrians, in his place.[247]

Quite rightly, Duncan firstly pointed out MacBethad mac Findláich cannot have been deprived of his life and the kingship of Alba at this time since Siward died in 1055 and MacBethad was not killed until 1057. Duncan then demonstrated that Malmesbury's writings were based upon a collection of material, now lost, including a lost version of the *Anglo-Saxon Chronicle*, which was best represented in the chronicle written by John of Worcester sometime between 1124 and 1140.[248] In this more accurate version of events, Siward invaded Alba, fought with MacBethad, and killed many Scots. Thereafter, Earl Siward elevated Máel Coluim, son of the king of the Cumbrians, to kingship in Cumbria. In this latter version of events Máel

---

246 Dauvit Broun, 'The Welsh Identity of the Kingdom of Strathclyde *c.*900–*c.*1200', *The Innes Review*, 55, no. 2, 2004, 111–80, at 126–27 [hereafter: Broun, 'Welsh Identity'].

247 R. A. B. Mynors and Rodney M. Thomson (eds), *Gesta Regum Anglorum*, 2 vols (Oxford, 1998 and 1999), i, 348–49 [hereafter: Mynors and Thomson, *Gesta Regum Anglorum*].

248 Antonia Gransden, *Historical Writing in England, c.550–c.1307*, 2 vols (London, 1974), i, 144.

Coluim was not made king in MacBethad's place and MacBethad did not lose his life.[249]

Surely, as Duncan has argued, if this Máel Coluim had been the same person as the future King Máel Coluim mac Donnchada in these sources he would have been referred to as 'son of Donnchadh' or as 'son of the king of Alba'. This then led Duncan to identify Máel Coluim, son of the king of the Cumbrians, as someone who could either have been a son of Owen the Bald, king of Strathclyde in 1018, or the son of Owen's unrecorded successor in the kingship of Strathclyde.[250] If this scenario is correct, it leaves one outstanding question: if Earl Siward did in fact restore the Cumbrian Máel Coluim to kingship in 1054, how had he (or his father) lost it in the first instance?

Broun found a solution to this problem. He envisaged a three-way struggle for dominance in the south-west between the *Gall-Gaídil*, the rulers of Northumbria, and the Scots, in which the creation of the kingdom of Galloway by 1034 crippled Strathclyde by depriving it of its western maritime territories. Furthermore, Broun drew attention to an entry in the *Annals of Tigernach* in 1030 that noted 'a ravaging of Britons by the Northumbrians and the Foreigners of Dublin' and argued that this entry referred to the Strathclyde Britons rather than to Welshmen.[251] It is easy to envisage a mortally wounded kingdom being torn apart by ruthless competitors under such pressure and, since Earl Siward had the heir of Strathclyde in his possession before raising him to kingship in 1054, it seems likely that the Northumbrians had absorbed the greater part of Strathclyde by the middle of the eleventh century.

Broun made two further important observations. The first of these was that Máel Coluim's Cumbrian kingship may not have survived for long after the death of Earl Siward in 1055. However, there is no way of telling how accurate this observation is, and the picture is further complicated by the fact that between the 1050s and the c.1070s Strathclyde probably remained under northern English domination. The evidence for this is supplied by an early-twelfth-century source from York, claiming that two bishops of Glasgow were consecrated by Cynesige, archbishop of York, most likely after he received his pallium in 1055.[252] Second, the kingdom of

---

249 Duncan, *Kingship*, 38.
250 Ibid., 41.
251 Broun, 'Welsh Identity', 136–38.
252 Norman Shead, 'The Origins of the Medieval Diocese of Glasgow', *Scottish Historical Review*, 48, 1969, 220–24 [hereafter Shead, 'Origins of Glasgow'].

Strathclyde cannot have survived beyond the 1070s, by which time King Máel Coluim mac Donnchada was clearly in control of part of that kingdom. That at least was the opinion of an early-twelfth-century northern English chronicler who, in describing a raid upon northern England by King Máel Coluim mac Donnchada in 1070, commented that he already possessed *Cumberland* which he did not possess by right but had subdued by force.[253]

All of this means that a large part of the kingdom of Strathclyde must have permanently fallen under the overlordship of the Scots sometime between the last attested appearance of Máel Coluim, son of the king of the Cumbrians, in 1054 and the 1070s. The establishment of this overlordship was clearly a success since David mac Máel Coluim, youngest son of King Máel Coluim mac Donnchada and Queen Margaret, was designated *princeps* (ruler) of the Cumbrians before he became king of Scotia in 1124.[254] It is, however, a great shame that any account describing how Scottish overlordship was established over Strathclyde does not seem to have survived in the chronicle record.

One possibility might be the events of 1061 when King Máel Coluim mac Donnchada is recorded as having devastated Northumberland and 'violated Lindesfarne'. It is not difficult to envisage a scenario whereby that part of the old kingdom of Strathclyde which was under Northumbrian control was taken by the Scots at the same time.[255] Perhaps an equally likely candidate might be the years 1066–67. The death of King Harald and the establishment of William I as king of England surely would have been an ideal opportunity for a belligerent neighbouring king to predate upon the dislocation and disturbances caused by the Norman invasion of England.

Amidst all of these territorial upheavals it is even more unfortunate that no native Strathclyde record has survived to tell us what they thought about the various calamaties that befell their kingdom during the eleventh century. A related and equally interesting conundrum is the question of when, and under what circumstances, the inhabitants of Strathclyde stopped speaking the P-Celtic Cumbric language akin to modern Welsh. This process now seems as mysterious to us as the disappearance of Pictish.

Broun has investigated this question by looking at the appearance of Cumbric personal names in the documentary records, but he argued

---

253 *SAEC*, 92.
254 Barrow, *Chrs. David I*, 60–61.
255 *SAEC*, 86.

cogently that such evidence is not conclusive. Next looking for 'peoples addresses' in royal charters, he only found one undisputed example of the term 'Welsh' in a charter of King Máel Coluim IV (1153–1165). According to Broun, this was very fragile evidence upon which to base a claim that the Welsh were still a recognisable ethnic group in twelfth-century Scotland.[256]

Broun then drew attention to the legal text now know as *Leges inter Brettos et Scotos* (laws among Britons and Scots).[257] Duncan, writing about this text in 1975, suggested that it could be eleventh-century in date, and perhaps formulated during the establishment of Scottish overlordship in Strathclyde.[258] As we have already seen, this text contains a set of honour prices that were paid in cows, the fine depending upon the rank of the victim, and contains both Gaelic and Brittonic legal terms.[259] Two such are the Gaelic (*cró*) and Welsh (*galanas*) terms for compensation for homicide, and the text appears to have been compiled in an attempt to harmonise two different law codes through equivalency. *Leges inter Brettos et Scotos* may also have been a text known to King Edward I of England since the 'customs of the Scots and Brets' was forbidden in the legal section of *Ordinacio facta per dominum regem super stabilitate terre Scocie* (An ordinance made by the king for the good order of the land of Scotland) of 1305.[260] Broun, however, was undecided whether *Leges inter Brettos et Scotos* represented evidence for the continuing vitality of the Cumbric culture and language.[261]

Nevertheless, the very fact that this text exists perhaps gives an idea of how Scottish overlordship in Strathclyde was established by King Máel Coluim mac Donnchada. Though an English source claimed this overlordship had been achieved by force, *Leges inter Brettos et Scotos* would indicate that King Máel Coluim mac Donnchada was not intent upon complete conquest and the imposition of a foreign law code upon the inhabitants of Strathclyde, but was instead content to work with and around the existing legal framework of that country.

But perhaps Broun's most important argument for continued cultural vitality in Strathclyde/Cumbria was that the boundaries of the kingdom

---

256 Broun, 'Welsh Identity', 124.
257 http://www.stairsociety.org/Berne_MS/berne_folio61v.htm Accessed 15 July 2010.
258 Duncan, *Kingdom*, 107.
259 Cooper, *Regiam Majestatem*, 276–79.
260 E. L. G. Stones (ed.), *Anglo-Scottish Relations, 1174–1328* (Oxford, 1965), 251.
261 Broun, 'Welsh Identity', 125.

were preserved as the boundaries of the medieval diocese of Glasgow.[262] If true, this would show the extent of the foreign territory annexed by King Máel Coluim mac Donnchada and his successors as they established their permanent overlordship over Strathclyde/Cumbria during the latter half of the eleventh century. However, such an interpretation is problematic for one simple reason.

This is the appearance of a named unit of land assessment, the arachor, in the primary documentation relating to the northern part of the diocese of Glasgow, the Lennox. Writing in 1973, Barrow directly equated this unit of land assessment both to the ploughgate and specifically to arable land, using much the same argument that he had used to evaluate the Pictish davoch.[263] Writing more recently, Neville followed Barrow's lead and also equated the arachor with arable, going so far as to argue that it described a bounded area of arable land. In addition, Neville argued that the Lennox arachor was the equivalent of a 'Scottish carucate' (Scottish ploughgate) of 104 acres.[264] To be fair to Neville, this is what the sources seem to be recording: . . . *tres quartarias carucate terre de Auchincloich inferiori, que Scotice vocatur arachor . . .*[265]

However, the same sources directly contradict this equation, since some of them provide perambulations of arachors that run from the mountain tops down to the side of Loch Lomond. Clearly, the typical arachor did not just contain arable but was identical in content to many other European units of land assessment. Namely, each arachor contained all of the resources required by communities to survive from year to year: arable, meadows, fishing, access to woodland and peat, grazing and shielings. Again, like other European units of land assessment, the people who inhabited arachors were required to render various services to a superior lord, including armed service. But perhaps the clearest indication of the nature of the land in the Lennox and how it was managed comes from the charter record, where it was stipulated that the inhabitants of arachors should provide food service for the common army of the king in the form of a set number of cheeses.[266] This surely indicates

---

262 Ibid., 113–14

263 Barrow, *Kingdom of the Scots*, 246–47.

264 Cynthia J. Neville, *Native Lordship in Anglo-Norman Scotland: The Earldoms of Strathearn and Lennox, 1170–1350* (Dublin, 2005), 99–100.

265 Maitland Club, *Cartularium Comitatus de Levenax ab initio seculi decimi tertii usque ad annum M.CCC.XCVIII* (Edinburgh, 1833), 38.

266 Ibid., 19, 23.

that pastoralism rather than arable formed the mainstay of the economy of the Lennox.

With regard to the geographic spread of arachors, it is crucial to realise that they are confined to the Lennox, never appearing south of the River Clyde. This would imply that, at least in terms of secular tax assessment, the Lennox was once separate from the other secular lands that comprised the post-1100 bishopric of Glasgow. In turn, this would imply that the history of the kingdom of Strathclyde must be more nuanced than has been recently argued, even though much of this history is now lost to us. Unfortunately, it is now very difficult (if not impossible) to decide whether the areas that comprise the Lennox and the remainder of the kingdom of Strathclyde were still separate territories or already conjoined when they became subject to Scottish overlordship under King Máel Coluim mac Donnchada in the 1070s.

If the definition of Alba *c.*1000 as the lands that lay between the River Forth and the River Spey is accepted, it is quite remarkable that this small territory relatively quickly came to dominate adjacent territories like Moray and Strathclyde, territories that together probably contained greater resources than those found in Alba itself. As far as Moray is concerned this process seems fairly straightforward and we know that it involved the killing of two inaugurated kings of Alba, MacBethad mac Findláich and Lulach mac Gilla Comgáin, by Máel Coluim mac Donnchada, and the eventual extinction of the leading Moravian kindred in 1130 by those loyal to King David I. What cannot be satisfactorily decided is whether these killings of a political elite formed part of a long-term plan to fully integrate Moray into Alba, or whether that process had already been largely accomplished during the reign of King MacBethad mac Findláich and what followed afterwards merely amounted to lingering resentment on the part of Moravians against the royal kindred represented by King Máel Coluim mac Donnchada because he had killed two Moravian kings of Alba.

It is fortunate that the resources gained by the kings of Alba by establishing their overlordship across Moray can now be tentatively estimated. If Moray before 1130 was comparable in size to the earldom later given to Thomas Randolph by King Robert I in 1312, it is likely that the kings of Alba added the natural and human resources of about 250 davochs to their patrimony, these davochs stretching from the estuary of the River Spey across to the western sea lochs of Lochaber and Glenelg. This would probably have amounted to an extra 1,000 fighting men if secular fighting service was asked for and infinitely more if full Scottish service was demanded from each davoch in Moray. Perhaps even more importantly, the absorption of Moray would have given the kings of Alba access to the western seaboard of north Britain and the trade routes between Ireland and Scandinavia.

If Moray and its inhabitants resented being absorbed by Alba and were more than willing to show their discontent, by contrast Strathclyde and its population appear to have quietly accepted their eventual fate with next to no comment. It may be that the seeming unremarkability of the disappearance of Strathclyde as a separate kingdom just reflects the sudden totality of the takeover by King Máel Coluim mac Donnchada in combination with acceptance of his overlordship by the chief kindreds of Strathclyde. Or had King MacBethad mac Findláich already prepared the ground for a take over by subsequent kings of Alba? The fact that Earl Siward had to attack MacBethad in order to establish Máel Coluim, son of the king of the Cumbrians, in Strathclyde/Cumbria would imply that the independence of that kingdom had already been severely compromised by Alba before Máel Coluim mac Donnchada was inaugurated. Since neither of MacBethad's immediate predecessors was ever linked to the overlordship of Strathclyde, he would seem to be the most likely candidate for expanding the royal overlordship of Alba southwards and the final absorption of Strathclyde into Alba can be approximately pinned down to the 1070s.

It is easy to see why absorption of Strathclyde might also have seemed like an attractive long-term proposition to kings of Alba. It would have opened access into the Firth of Clyde and the wider western seaboard as well as adding large mainland territories south of the Clyde estuary to Alba. However, unlike Moray, it is difficult to even estimate what the final absorption of Strathclyde into Alba would have meant to King Máel Coluim mac Donnchada in practical terms. As already indicated, there is no standard unit of land assessment across the territories that are thought to have once been within the bounds of eleventh-century Strathclyde and so no evaluation of the tax gains to Alba in both manpower and rents in kind can currently be calculated until much more research in this field is undertaken both north and south of the River Clyde.

CHAPTER FOUR

King Máel Coluim Mac Donnchada

Enemies, domestic and foreign

There is plenty of evidence that the royal kindreds of Alba regularly engaged in murder to remove their dynastic rivals, but, as far as we know, no previous claimant to the kingship of Alba had ever killed two lawfully inaugurated kings to advance his own claims. It can only be assumed that Máel Coluim mac Donnchada had got fed up waiting, had weighed the risks involved, and calculated that the chances of swift vengeance from the kindred of both MacBethad and Lulach were low. It is also interesting to note that Bower's description of the inauguration of Máel Coluim mac Donnchada is quickly followed by a note that states: 'At that time there was famine and plague in the whole earth.'[1] While Bower does not precisely date the first appearance of these twin horsemen of the apocalypse, their well-attested presence in Britain in 1058 might suggest that Máel Coluim mac Donnchada had utilised this opportunity to attack southwards into Scotia from the Northern Isles while people in Scotia were severely debilitated by a pandemic.

We know that King Lulach was killed on 17 March 1058 at Essie, yet Bower dates Máel Coluim's inauguration to 25 April, around five weeks after the death of the previous king. This period contrasts strongly with the almost indecent haste in which many later twelfth- and thirteenth-century kings of Scotia were inaugurated, though King William I was more relaxed because two weeks passed between the death of his brother and his own inauguration.[2] In this context five weeks seems a very long time to wait for inauguration and so it might be questioned whether the death of King Lulach ended all opposition to Máel Coluim mac Donnchada.

It is perhaps a measure of Máel Coluim's effectiveness once inaugurated as king that there only seems to have been one domestic plot against him during the course of his thirty-five-year reign, assuming that the events associated with Máel Snechta mac Lulaich and the plot against the

---

1 *Chron. Bower* (Watt), iii, 23.
2 Broun, 'Contemporary Perspectives', 79–81.

king described in *Chronica Gentis Scotorum* were one and the same (see Chapter 3). This apparent lack of domestic rivalry may help explain why King Máel Coluim was able to focus his attentions elsewhere: he was either directly involved in or supported five major invasions of north England during his reign, together with a number of other lesser raids. Almost all of our detailed information about these invasions and raids comes from English sources.

Within a year of his inauguration, King Máel Coluim is on record as having visited King Edward the Confessor in England in the company of the archbishop of York, the bishop of Durham, and Earl Tostig of Northumberland.[3] No source explains the purpose of this visit, though it has been suggested that it might have been undertaken to recover English estates in Northampton which had either traditionally belonged to the kings of Alba or which had been granted to Máel Coluim during his earlier exile in England.[4] It could also have been connected to the restoration of Máel Coluim, son of the king of the Cumbrians by Earl Siward in 1054, if that territory had previously been subject to the overlordship of King MacBethad (see Chapter 3).

Two years later in 1061, while Earl Tostig was accompanying the new archbishop of York to Rome so that the latter might receive his pallium, King Máel Coluim ravaged Northumberland and it has been suggested that this raid, which went unpunished by King Edward, was a response to an unrequited betrothal. Duncan, basing his argument on information later supplied by Orderic Vitalis, has suggested that King Máel Coluim had been bethrothed to Princess Margaret on his earlier visit to England in 1059, but that subsequent English failure to keep their side of the bargain had forced Máel Coluim into taking military action to force the issue.[5] While possible, this solution is speculative because no source provides information about the destiny of Queen Ingibjorg, whether she died or was repudiated for Princess Margaret. Whether this absence of information indicates complete disinterest in or embarrassment about her fate is unknown.

3 *SAEC*, 86.

4 Duncan, *Kingdom*, 117; E. W. M. Balfour-Melville, 'A Northamptonshire Estate of Malcolm Canmore', *SHR*, 27, 1948, 101–2.

5 M. Chibnall (ed.), *The Ecclesiastical History of Orderic Vitalis*, 6 vols (Oxford, 1968–80), iv, 270–71 [hereafter: Chibnall, *Orderic Vitalis*]; Duncan, *Kingship*, 43.

But what is really mysterious about King Máel Coluim's actions at this time is this: if he was seriously exploring the possibility of expanding his overlordship further south into Northumberland, then the events of 1066 surely would have provided cover for such an allegedly opportunistic king to try and capitalise on widespread unrest. Yet, although King Máel Coluim gave shelter to Earl Tostig when the latter was expelled from England in 1065, and so may have known about Tostig and King Harald's plans to invade England, the king of Scotia remained aloof from the aftermaths of the battles of both Stamford Bridge and Hastings. There is a strong sense that he was carefully waiting to see what transpired. In late 1066, there may have been a great deal of uncertainty about the future of England and an ambitious king of Scotia might normally have been expected to exploit the situation.

To a great extent King Máel Coluim's hand was forced in 1068 when the leading Northumbrians, Edgar Ætheling, and princesses Margaret and Christina, arrived in Scotia, assuming that he had not invited them in the first instance. From this point Scotia was a refuge for the heirs to King Edward the Confessor and these events must have forced a reassessment in both Scottish and Norman foreign policies. There was more unrest in northern England in 1069 when the new French earl was murdered, and it seems that many of the Anglo-Saxon refugees in Scotia returned south in an attempt to force regime change. This, however, was balked in the autumn of 1069 when Danish support was withdrawn. English sources indicate that Ætheling and his sisters returned north the following year to seek refuge again in Scotia.

That year (1070) King Máel Coluim invaded southwards in what English sources describe as a devastating raid in what seems to have been a deliberate attempt to subdue Northumberland. He and his forces moved east from Cumberland across Teesdale and Cleveland before proceeding north to Durham. Symeon of Durham described King Máel Coluim savagely overrunning the lands of St Cuthbert, burning churches and their congregations, robbing, and murdering. According to the same source, a retaliatory raid by Earl Gospatrick of Northumberland upon Cumberland, then under King Máel Coluim's overlordship, resulted in Máel Coluim losing his temper:

Qua licentia accepta, miseria etiam erat videre quae in Anglos faciebant: sense et vetulae alii gladiis obtruncantur, alii ut porci ad esum destinati lanceis confodiuntur. Rapti ab uberibus matrum parvuli in altum

*aera projiciuntur, unde recidentes lancearum acuminibus excipiuntur
hastilibus confertim solo infixis; hac crudelitate pro ludorum spectaculo
delectabantur bestiis crudeliores Scotti . . . Juventes vero et juvenculae
et quicumque operibus ac laboribus idonei videbantur, ante faciem
hostium vincti compelluntur, ut perpetuo exilio in servos at ancillas
redigantur . . . Repleta est ergo Scotia servis et ancillis Anglici generis, ita
ut etiam usque hodie nulla non dicto villula, sed nec domuncula sine his
valeat inveniri.*

When they had received this permission, it was pitiable even to see
what they did against the English: old men and women were some
beheaded by swords, others struck with spears like pigs destined for
food. Torn from their mother's breasts babes were tossed high in the
air, and caught on the spikes of spears fixed close together on the
ground: the Scots, crueller than beasts, delighted in this cruelty as in
the sight of games . . . But the youths and girls, and all who seemed fit
for work and toil, were bound and driven in front of the enemy, to be
made slaves and handmaids in perpetual exile . . . Therefore Scotland
was filled with slaves and handmaids of English race, so that even this
day cannot be found, I say not a hamlet, but even a hut without them.[6]

It must have been shortly after his return to Scotia that King Máel Coluim
and Princess Margaret married and it is likely that this, in combination
with the earlier raid upon Northumberland, galvanised King William I of
England into action. King Máel Coluim now was not just harbouring
exiles, but any children of this new marriage would possess strong claims
to both Alba and England. From this point in time Scotia would have
figured prominently in the foreign policy decisions of the new Norman
kings of England and it is a shame that there is no record of what the
mormaír and other Scots of lesser status thought about Máel Coluim's decision to marry Margaret. Given her status, everyone must have known that
there could be long-term consequences arising from this match, and the
names that King Máel Coluim and Queen Margaret gave to their first four
sons would have removed any lingering doubts about this: Edward, Edgar,
Edmund, and Æthelred. These were the names given to the son (King
Edward, 899–924), grandson (King Edmund, 939–946), great-grandson

6 Thomas Arnold (ed.), *Symeonis Monachi Opera et Collectanea* (Edinburgh, 1868), 88.
Translation taken from: *SEAC*, 92–93.

(King Edgar, 957–975), and great-great-grandson (King Æthelred II, 978–1016) of King Ælfred the Great of Wessex.

It is also this marriage that makes King William I's decision to invade Scotia in 1072 seem unavoidable. According to the *Anglo-Saxon Chronicle*, this was a two-pronged attack by sea and land, and the English advanced as far northwards as Abernethy where the two kings met and reached an agreement. At least this is how Scottish sources present the solution even though it was the Scots who seem to have made the only concessions. Máel Coluim's eldest son by Queen Ingibjorg, Donnchad mac Máel Coluim, was taken hostage, Edward Ætheling left for exile in Europe, and King Máel Coluim performed homage to King William for the lands that he held in England. If King William made any concessions, they are nowhere recorded.[7]

There is one further point to make about this meeting. If it is considered unlikely that the two kings would have arranged to meet in a rural back-water somewhere in Scotia, the fact that Abernethy was the chosen meeting-place would indicate that it was already a place of great significance at that time, despite what some architectural historians might argue about the date of the round tower. Abernethy is also within easy riding or a half-day march of Scone and the eleventh-century sacral centre of Scotia. Accordingly, it might be questioned whether it was the seizure (either actual or imminent) of this royal landscape by King William that brought King Máel Coluim to the negotiating table.

The fact that his eldest son was a hostage in England does not seem to have unduly troubled King Máel Coluim when he invaded England again between 15 August and 8 September 1079, reaching the River Tyne. The *Anglo-Saxon Chronicle* recorded that the Scots slew 'hundreds', stole much treasure, and took slaves.[8] No source states the reason for this expedition, though its timing might suggest that harvest crops had been targeted Whatever the case, Máel Coluim's raid brought a military response in 1080. A Norman force under William I's son Robert invaded Scotia to Falkirk, but Robert does not seem to have wrung any significant new concessions from King Máel Coluim. On his way back south he built a new fortification on the Tyne at Newcastle.[9]

7 *Ann. Ulster*, 1072.8; SAEC, 95; ES, ii, 35–36; Garmonsway, *A-S Chronicle*, 208.
8 Garmonsway, *A-S Chronicle*, 213–14.
9 *SAEC*, 103–4.

Thereafter peace seems to have broken out between the two countries until 1091, when King Máel Coluim once again invaded Northumberland in what seems to have been part of growing friction between himself and King William II Rufus. Part of the reasoning for this raid may simply have been that Máel Coluim's brother-in-law, Edward Ætheling, had been deprived of his lands in Normandy, and he subsequently returned to exile (and protection) in Scotia.[10] The *Chronicle of Melrose* provides another rationale. According to this text, King Máel Coluim had been unjustly deprived of some lands in England.[11] On top of this, King Máel Coluim must also have been worried by growing Norman control of north England, underpinned by the creation of new lordships and the construction of more castles, including one at Carlisle.[12]

The two kings tried to reach a *rapprochement* towards the end of August 1093 when King Máel Coluim travelled south to Gloucester, safe in the knowledge that King William Rufus had provided hostages for Máel Coluim's wellbeing. The sources seem to indicate that this visit concerned previous agreements between the two, but William refused to meet with Máel Coluim unless the latter first submitted to the judgement of Anglo-Norman barons. King Máel Coluim's response was that the problem should be sorted at a meeting between the two kings on the border between the two realms, but this was rejected and the sources agree that the two kings parted in enmity. Máel Coluim travelled north to collect his army before returning south to raid in Northumberland and it was on this journey that he was ambushed and killed on 13 November. Prince Edward, his eldest son by Queen Margaret, was impaled by a lance and died two days later on 15 November.[13]

Durham, St Cuthbert, and the Church

For a man who had raided, pillaged, murdered, and enslaved his way across Northumberland on a number of occasions during his personal reign, sometimes allegedly reducing Northumbrians to cannibalism, King Máel Coluim's decision to actively lend patronage to the cult of St Cuthbert at Durham might not at first have seemed like a welcome development to many Northumbrians.

---

10 Ibid., 104–5.
11 *ES*, ii, 48.
12 *SAEC*, 108.
13 *ES*, ii, 52–53.

In recent years much ink has been spilt on the topic of St Cuthbert and his cult, and this historical activity is a reflection of just how important this cross-border saint was to people living in north Britain from the seventh century onwards. The cult of Cuthbert originated at Lindisfarne and after the saint died in AD 687 he quickly became *der Reichsheilige* (the patron saint) of Northumbria in imitation of the cult of St Martin in Gaul.[14] In the first half of the ninth century the cult of Cuthbert, accompanied by the physical remains of the saint, assumed a peripatetic existence; moving from Lindisfarne to Norham, from where the cult moved to Chester-le-Street, again for a short time to Ripon, before it eventually settled down at Durham in 998. In 1083, Bishop William de St Calais replaced the Durham secular canons with Benedictine monks and refounded the community of St Cuthbert.[15]

Because St Cuthbert had become patron saint of the kingdom of Northumbria, his cult became a major landowner through donations and, by the late eleventh century, the community was an economic force in its own right in north Britain. Details of this wealth are listed in a medieval text written by the community of St Cuthbert, *Historia De Sancto Cuthberto*. The most recent editor of this text has argued that it was written to record and legitimise the property claims made by the Cuthbertine community that had originated at Lindisfarne. The dating of this text depends on whether some eleventh-century charters within it are interpolations. If they are, the text is tenth-century in date. However, the editor on the whole favoured the idea that they were not later textual additions, which would date *Historia De Sancto Cuthberto* to the period between 1031 and 1050.[16]

Whatever the date, the list of territories claimed by the Cuthbertine community states:

---

14 Alan Thacker, 'Lindisfarne and the Origins of the Cult of St Cuthbert', in Gerald Bonner, David Rollason and Clare Stancliff (eds), *St Cuthbert, His Cult and His Community to AD 1200* (Woodbridge, 1989), 103–22.

15 D. W. Rollason, *Cuthbert Saint and Patron* (Durham, 1987), 45–49; A. J. Piper, 'The First Generations of Durham Monks and the Cult of St Cuthbert', in Gerald Bonner, David Rollason and Clare Stancliff (eds), *St Cuthbert, His Cult and His Community to AD 1200* (Woodbridge, 1989), 437–46 [hereafter: Piper, 'First Generations of Durham Monks'].

16 Ted Johnson South (ed.), *Historia De Sancto Cuthberto* (Cambridge, 2002), 11, and at 35–36 [hereafter: Johnson, *Sancto Cuthberto*].

Et hic est Lindisfarnensis terrae terminus: a fluuio Tweoda usque ad Warnedmuthe, et inde superius ad illum locum ubi haec aqua quae uocatur Warned oritur iuxta montem Hybberndune, et ab illo monte usque ad fluuium qui uocatur Bromic, et inde usque ad fluuium qui uocatur Till, et tota terra quae iacet ex utraque parte ipsius fluminis Bromic usque ad illum locum ubi oritur. Et illa terra ultra Tweoda ab illo loco ubi oritur fluuius Edre ab aquilone usque ad illum locum ubi cadet in Tweoda, et tota terra quae iacet inter istum fluuium Edre et alterum fluuium qui oucatur Leder uersus occidentem, et tota terra quae iacet ab orientali parte istius aquae quae uocatur Leder usque ad illum locum ubi cadet in fluuium Tweoda uersus austrum, et tota terra quae pertinet ad monasterium sancti Balthere, quod uocatur Tinningaham, a Lombormore usque ad Esce muthe.

And this is the boundary of the territory of Lindisfarne: from the River Tweed as far as the mouth of Warren Beck, and from there upwards as far as the place where Warren Beck rises next to Hepburn Hill, and from that hill as far as the river that is called Beamish, and from there as far as the river that is called the Till, and all the land that lies on both sides of the same River Beamish up to the place where it rises. And that land beyond the Tweed from the place where the River Blackadder rises in the north as far as the place where it flows into the Tweed, and all the land that lies between that River Blackadder and another that is called the Leader towards the west, and all the land that lies on the east side of that water that is called the Leader as far as the place where it flows into the Tweed toward the south, and all the land that pertains to the monastery of St Balthere, which is called Tynningham, from the Lammermuir Hills as far as the mouth of the Esk.[17]

Leaving the geographic details to one side for the moment, the important figure amid these claims is St Balthere (now known as St Baldred). Another medieval text, written by Symeon of Durham, adds the detail that St Baldred of Tyninghame was an Anglo-Saxon who died in AD 756.[18] Symeon of Durham, who joined the monastic community there *c*.1090, would have witnessed first-hand the translation of St Cuthbert's coffin to

17 Ibid., 46–47.
18 *SAEC*, 56.

Durham in 1104.[19] Since Durham would have had an interest at that time in controlling the lands and revenues that would have belonged to the cult of Cuthbert while it was successively resident at Lindisfarne, Norham, and Chester-le-Street, Symeon's attention to Baldred is understandable. The Cuthbertine community had already claimed possession of St Baldred's monastic lands in *Historia De Sancto Cuthberto*, so the final resting place of Cuthbert's body, Durham, could also legitimately lay a later claim to those same lands and revenues.

We will, however, probably never precisely know when and how the cult of Cuthbert at Lindisfarne came to assume superiority over the lands of the Baldred community at Tynningham. Part of the problem here is that we have no chronology for the conquest of the Lothian plain by the Northumbrians. Perry, for example, has recently asserted that the *obsessio Etin*, recorded in the *Annals of Ulster* in AD 638, completed the Northumbrian conquest of Lothian and presumably the people called *Y Gododdin*.[20] Yet, this is not what the annal states. In fact, the reduction of *Etin* in AD 638 could have been undertaken by any number of different war-bands from north Britain.

Matters become a little clearer during the following sixty years. According to Eddius Stephanus, an eighth-century hagiographer, Bishop Wilfred was imprisoned at Dunbar in 680.[21] A further piece of information was added by Bede when, following the Battle of Nechtanesmere in 685, he stated that the Northumbrian Bishop Trumwine abandoned his episcopal seat at Abercorn on the Forth.[22] Taken together, these pieces of evidence point to a complete Northumbrian takeover of Lothian before the end of the seventh century, to a point at which new episcopal sees were being formed. This conquest had subsequently been reversed to some extent by the Pictish king of Fortriu, Brude mac Bili. There is no record of either Bishop Trumwine or any subsequent Northumbrian bishop ever returning to Abercorn, but it cannot be assumed that after Nechtanesmere the Picts were able to establish effective overlordship in this area since there are later eighth-century records of Pictish-Northumbrian armed clashes some-where in the Plain of Manau around the Firth of Forth.[23] Unfortunately, it

19 Piper, 'First Generations of Durham Monks', 437–46.
20 David R. Perry, *Castle Park, Dunbar: Two Thousand Years on a Fortified Headland* (Edinburgh, 2000), 7; John T. Koch, *The Gododdín of Aneírín* (Cardiff, 1997).
21 Beltram Colgrave (ed), *Vita Sancti Wilfridi Episcopi Eboracensis* (Cambridge, 1985), 72.
22 D. H. Farmer (ed), *Ecclesiastic History of the English People*, rev. edn (London, 1990), 255.
23 *Ann. Ulster*, 710.3.

is unknown whether these were either Pictish war-bands attacking other areas under Northumbrian overlordship or Picts defending territory they had previously conquered from subsequent Northumbrian attempts at reconquest.

It is against this political backdrop that the mission of St Baldred into Lothian must be viewed. Clearly, he cannot have been a part of the initial Anglo-Saxon advance northwards into Lothian, since seventy years separated the abandonment of Abercorn by Bishop Trumwine and Baldred's death. It would be easier to interpret this evidence if the geographic extent of the original Northumbrian diocese of Abercorn were known, but it now appears impossible to resurrect these boundaries precisely. Matters are further complicated by the fact that parts of the Lothian plain, consisting of the detached parishes of Abercorn, Cramond, Preston and Bunkle, belonged to the medieval diocese of Dunkeld, whereas the remainder of Lothian belonged to the diocese of St Andrews. Accordingly, it seems unlikely that the boundaries of these medieval Scottish dioceses were based upon earlier Northumbrian ecclesiastic patterns.[24]

This leaves the eleventh-century perambulation of the lands of Lindisfarne between the River Tweed and the River Esk in *Historia De Sancto Cuthberto* as the sole piece of evidence, even though almost 400 years separate this description from the original creation of the see of Abercorn. Nevertheless, it is worth asking whether these Lothian lands claimed by the see of Lindisfarne in the eleventh century represented what had always been an entirely separate see, or whether they had once formed part of a larger and earlier Northumbrian see based at Abercorn.

One clue to answering this question lies in the *Historia Regum Anglorum*, an early-twelfth-century text attributed to Symeon of Durham, which incorporates earlier Northumbrian material compiled by Byrhtferth of Ramsey *c.*1000 and a possible lost Pictish source:

Anno.DCCCLIV., natiuitatis Regis Elfredi .vi., Wlfere, regnante rege Osberto super Northimbros, suscepto pallio confirmatus est in archiepiscopatum Eboracensem, et Eardulf suscepit episcopatum Lindisfarnensem. Quo pertinebant Lugubalia, id est Luel, nunc dicitur Carliel, et Northam, quae antiquitus Vbbanford dicebatur. Omnes quoque ecclesiae ab aqua quae uocatur Tweda usque Tinam australem, et ultra

---

desertum ad occidentem, pertinebant illo tempore ad praefatam eccle-
siam, et hae mansions, Carnam et Culterham, et duae Geddewrd ad
australem plagam Teinetae quas Ecgredus episcopus conditit: et Mailros,
et Tigbrethingham, et Eoriercorn ad occidentalem partem, Edwinesburch,
et Pefferham, et Aldham, et Tinnigaham, et Coldingham, et Tillmuthe, et
Northam supradictam.

In the year 854, in the sixth year after the birth of King Alfred, in the
reign of King Osbert over the Northumbrians, Wulfhere received the
pallium, and was confirmed in the archbishopric of York, and
Eardwulf received the bishopric of Lindisfarne; to which pertained:
Lugobalia, that is *Luel*, now called Carlisle, and Norham, that was
anciently called Ubbanford. And also all of those churches between
the river called Tweed and the southern Tyne, and beyond the desert
to the west, pertained at this time to the aforesaid church, and these
estates, Carnam and Culterham and the two Jedworths and the south
side of Teviot which Bishop Ecgred donated: and Melrose, and
Tighbrethingham, and Abercorn to the western extent, Edinburgh,
and Pefferham, and Aldham, and Tyninghame, and Coldingham, and
Tillmouth, and Norham, as said above.[25]

This text clearly indicates that at one point in time the see of Lindisfarne
claimed to possess jurisdiction over the whole of Lothian to a boundary
somewhere to the west of Abercorn. Its possessions are listed in a circuit
going down the Tweed to Melrose, then up through the unlocated
Tighbrethingham to Abercorn, then down the Lothian coast to Coldingham
and Tillmouth. The differences between this list of Lindisfarne possessions
preserved in *Historia Regum Anglorum* and the later list contained in the
eleventh-century *Historia De Sancto Cuthberto* can perhaps be explained
by the conquest of much of the Lothian plain by kings of Alba during the
intervening period. However, unfortunately, there is still a period of over
150 years between the abandonment of the see of Abercorn and the list
preserved in *Historia Regum Anglorum* (assuming that it is accurately

---

25 Johnson, *Sancto Cuthberto*, 119; Katherine Forsyth, 'Evidence of a Lost Pictish Source in the
Historia Regum Anglorum of Symeon of Durham', in Simon Taylor (ed), *Kings, Clerics and
Chronicles in Scotland, 500–1297* (Bodmin, 2000), 19–34. It seems likely that Pefferburn could
refer to the village now called Aberlady since Anglo-Saxon material has been excavated from
there too.

dated).[26] In theory this means that the see of Lindisfarne could have absorbed the possessions of the see of Abercorn after the retreat of Bishop Trumwine southwards to Whitby in 685.

The important point in all of this is that in the second half of the eleventh century the see of Durham, as the new cult centre of St Cuthbert, could legitimately claim ecclesiastic jurisdiction over a territory that included large swathes of the kingdom of Alba south of the Forth. Therefore, how King Máel Coluim mac Donnchada interacted with the community during his personal reign should have been of paramount importance to those monks. In addition, Barrow has noted the claim in a Durham source that Queen Margaret held the cult of Cuthbert in special reverence, and it is also well known that the queen's confessor, and later bishop of St Andrews, Turgot, had been a prior of Durham.[27]

Since King Máel Coluim mac Donnchada is the first king of Alba on record (in 1093) to have displayed any veneration towards St Cuthbert, Barrow also suggested that this behaviour could have been due to the influence of Queen Margaret.[28] Such an argument appears entirely logical since Queen Margaret's royal Anglo-Saxon ancestors had displayed great interest in the cult of St Cuthbert. King Æthelstan, for example, gave a gospel book to the community of Cuthbert while it was resident at Chester-le-Street and created a collection of material honouring the saint in Wessex. Even King Ælfred the Great is supposed to have been visited by St Cuthbert in a vision.[29] A scenario whereby King Máel Coluim surrendered to the influence of his queen and became a devotee of St Cuthbert, however, seems far less likely with the realisation that he must either have ignored or rejected Queen Margaret's alleged long-term interest in the cult of Cuthbert for over twenty years of marriage, only to perform a sudden *volte face* on 11 August 1093.

On that day King Máel Coluim mac Donnchada was the only layman permitted to take part in laying the new foundation stones of Durham

---

26 It has been noted that the list begins and ends at Norham, where the Cuthbertine community was based *c*.850, so this text may well be contemporary, Johnson, *Sancto Cuthberto*, 84–85; Woolf, *Pictland to Alba*, 82–84.

27 G. W. S. Barrow, 'The Kings of Scotland and Durham', in Gerald Bonner, David Rollason and Clare Stancliff (eds), *St Cuthbert, His Cult and His Community to AD 1200* (Woodbridge, 1989), 311–23.

28 Ibid., 313.

29 Alan Thacker, 'Dynastic Monasteries and Family Cults, Edward the Elder's Sainted Kindred', in N. J. Higham and D. H. Hill (eds), *Edward the Elder, 899–924* (Suffolk, 2001), 248–63, at 255.

Cathedral. Barrow has argued that it was surely around this date that a bond of confraternity was agreed between the Durham Benedictines and the royal kindred of Scotia:

Hæc est conventio quam conventus Sancti Cuthberti Malcolmo regi Scottorum et Margaritæ reginæ filiisque eorum et filiabus se perpetuo servare promisit. Scilicet, ut pro rege et regina dum vivunt unum cotidie pauperum nutriant, et duo item pauperes in Coena Domini ad commune mandatum pro eis habeantur, et una collecta ad letanias et ad missam habeatur. Sed utrimque in hac et post hanc vitam tam illi quam filii et filiæ eorum participes sint omnium quæ fiant ad servitium Dei in monasterio Sancti Cuthberti, missarum videlicet, psalmorum, elemosinarum, vigiliarum, orationum, et quicquid est hujusmodi. Singulariter vero pro rege et regina a die obitus sui in conventu triginta plenaria officia mortuorum et cotidie Verba mea fiant. Unusquisque autem sacerdos triginta missas, ceterorum unusquisque x. psalteria cantet. Anniversariusque eorum festive, sicut regis Ethelstani, singulis annis celebretur.

This is the covenant which the convent of Saint Cuthbert has promised to Malcolm, king of Scots, and to Queen Margaret, and to their sons and daughters, to keep forever. Namely that, on behalf of the king and queen, while they are alive, one poor man shall be nourished daily, and likewise two poor men shall be maintained for them on Thursday in Holy Week at the common maundy, and a collect said at the litanies and at mass. Further, that they both, in this life and after, and their sons and daughters, shall be partakers in all things that be to the service of God in the monastery of St Cuthbert, that is to say in masses, in psalms and alms, in vigils and prayers and in all things that are of this kind. And for the king and queen individually, from the day of their death there shall be thirty full offices of the dead in the convent, and *Verba mea* shall be done every day, and each priest shall sing thirty masses and each of the rest ten psalters; and their anniversary shall be celebrated as an annual festival like that of King Athelstan.[30]

30 J. Stevenson (ed.), *Liber Vitæ Ecclesiæ Dunelmensis; nec non obituaria duo ejusdem ecclesiæ* (Edinburgh, 1841), 73 [hereafter: Stevenson, *Liber Vitæ Ecclesiæ Dunelmensis*]. Translation from: G. W. S. Barrow, 'The Kings of Scotland and Durham', in Gerald Bonner, David Rollason and Clare Stancliff (eds), *St Cuthbert, His Cult and His Community to AD 1200* (Woodbridge, 1989), 311–23, at 314, and at 332–33.

It may even have been on this occasion that the name of King Máel Coluim mac Donnchada's first wife Queen Ingibjorg, *Ingeberga comitissa*, was also commemorated by the community.[31]

Once the influence of Queen Margaret is dropped from this equation there are two main options left. Quite simply, the attempted alignment of interests between the Cuthbertine community at Durham and King Máel Coluim mac Donnchada could have been initiated by the Benedictines for two reasons. First, to try to preserve their long-term property interests north of the River Tweed: it must have seemed increasingly likely to many in the 1090s, and particularly after the annexation of Strathclyde/Cumbria south of the Solway by King William Rufus in 1092, that in the east the ancient kingdom of Northumbria would be divided into Lothian and Northumbria, separated by a formalised and increasingly fortified border between Scotia and England. Second, through Queen Margaret and her children the Cuthbertine community could maintain their long-standing links with the Anglo-Saxon Wessex dynasty.[32]

An alternative scenario is that it was King Máel Coluim mac Donnchada who initiated the bond between the Cuthbertine community and his family as an alternate route through which he might exploit his foreign policy goals in relation to Northumbria. In fact, this arrangement between the Scottish Crown and Durham was probably mutually beneficial, at least at first, and successive kings of Scots actively continued to uphold the interests of the Cuthbertine community north of the border. But whatever immediate plans King Máel Coluim mac Donnchada had for Durham must have been shelved by his murder in November 1093.

31 Stevenson, *Liber Vitæ Ecclesiæ Dunelmensis*, 141.
32 Valerie Wall, 'Malcolm III and the Foundation of Durham Cathedral', in Gerald Bonner, David Rollason and Clare Stancliff (eds), *St Cuthbert, His Cult and His Community to AD 1200* (Woodbridge, 1989), 325–37.

CHAPTER FIVE

Civil War within Clann Custantín Meic Cináeda, 1093–1097

Writing in 1876, W. F. Skene was in little doubt that the death of King Máel Coluim mac Donnchada in 1093 also initiated the passing of the Celtic kingdom of Scotia and its replacement by the feudal kingdom of the Scots.[1] While it is now considered *passé* to use the f-word (it has been replaced by 'Europeanisation'), there is little doubt that the Scots must have experienced some sense of dislocation from the simultaneous deaths of both Máel Coluim and Margaret, together with their eldest son, Edward. Unfortunately, it is not known how quickly Domnall bán mac Donnchada was inaugurated after the death of King Máel Coluim, as that might have provided some indication of the scale of disruption.

One English source *Historia Regum*, claims that Edward mac Máel Coluim was the designated heir of King Máel Coluim, but this perhaps ignores the inconvenient fact that Donnchad mac Máel Coluim was actually the king's eldest son by his first marriage to Ingibjorg. Duncan, however, has recently demonstrated that the claim made in *Historia Regum* about the succession could have been true and he provided the example of how King William I of England had divided his posessions of Normandy and England between his elder son Robert (Normandy) and his favoured younger son, William (England). According to Duncan, Donnchad's long absence from Scotland, first as a hostage and thereafter voluntarily, meant that he had 'gone over' to the Norman monarchy and King William II Rufus, with whom King Máel Coluim mac Donnchada had quarrelled, making Donnchad somehow less acceptable to be recognised as king of Scotia.[2] Nevertheless, it is clear that even if Donnchad mac Máel Coluim had wished to actively push his claim to be inaugurated, his physical absence from Scotland at the time of his parents' deaths would have made it easier for his uncle, Domnall bán mac Donnchada, to take power.

It might also be questioned whether there was, despite the claims made in *Historia Regum*, a straightforward succession in Scotland. King Máel

1 Skene, *Celtic Scotland*, i, 433.
2 Duncan, *Kingship*, 54.

Coluim mac Donnchada had left behind two groups of male heirs by two different women and, while the sons of Ingibjorg perhaps represented the senior branch of the direct descendants of Máel Coluim mac Donnchada, they did not possess a claim to the kingship of the Anglo-Saxons. That claim was only vested in the second clutch of sons and daughters, fathered by the king with Margaret. It is a great shame that we know so little about the foreign policy aims and aspirations of the Scottish Crown at this time and into the twelfth century. We should, however, consider it likely that the claim possessed by that second group of children would have been a significant long-term factor in deciding between future claimants of the kingship of Scotia.

The sons and grandsons of Ingibjorg

The only descendant of Ingibjorg with whom most people are familiar is King Donnchad mac Máel Coluim, who reigned for approximately six months as king of Scotia in 1094 and who latterly gained much infamy as the progenitor of the MacWilliams. There is also a strong probability that Donnchad was not the only product of Máel Coluim's marriage to Ingibjorg. In 1085, the *Annals of Ulster* record the death of an important person in Scotland:

> *Murchadh H. Maeldoraidh ri Ceniuil Conaill, Domnall m. Maelcoluim ri Alban, Muiredach m. Ruaidri H. Ruadhacan, hUalgarc H. Ruairc ridomna Conacht, Oenghus H. Caindelban ri Loeguiri suam uitam infeliciter finierunt.*

> Murchad ua Maeldoraid, king of Cenél Conaill, Domnall son of Mael Coluim, king of Scotland, Muiredach son of Ruaidrí ua Ruadacán, Ualgarc ua Ruairc, heir designate of Connacht, Aengus us Caíndelbáin, king of Loegaire, ended their life unhappily.[3]

This entry seems to straightforwardly record the death of a son of King Máel Coluim mac Donnchada and, since there is no record of Máel Coluim and Margaret ever producing a son by that name, Domnall must have been a son of Máel Coluim and Ingibjorg, unless he was born out of wedlock.

---

3 *Ann. Ulster*, 1085.2.

However, the phrase '*ri Alban*' is a marginal interpolation into the main text in an unidentified and undated hand that may not be contemporary with the main text. So while Domnall could easily have been a son of King Máel Coluim mac Donnchada and Ingibjorg there is an equal chance that a later interpolator added the phrase '*ri Alban*' to the obit of someone who was not related to the royal kindred of Scotia, purely on the basis that the most famous person called Máel Coluim in Scotland in 1085 was King Máel Coluim mac Donnchada.

The appearance of the name Domnall mac Máel Coluim in 1085 can also be linked to a slightly later obit in the same source, which might help clarify matters. In 1116, the *Annals of Ulster* state:

> *Ladhmunn m. Domnaill H. righ Alban do mharbadh do feraibh Moraib.*

> Ladhmann son of Domnall, grandson of the king of Scotia, was killed by the men of Moray.[4]

If the Domnall referred to here is the same person whose obit was recorded in 1085 then the latter reference seems to offer unassailable evidence that both Domnall and his son Ladhmann were closely related to the ruling kindred, respectively being the son and grandson of Queen Ingibjorg. What is unknown about Ladhmann's death are the reasons behind his demise. Indeed, the involvement of the men of Moray in his death cannot be taken as meaning that the Moravians were challenging King Alexander mac Máel Coluim; they could just have easily been defending the king against Ladhmann if the latter had got fed up waiting and decided to exercise his right to challenge for the kingship of Scotia.

There may have been a third son produced by King Máel Coluim mac Donnchada and Queen Ingibjorg. The earliest surviving Scottish charter belongs to the reign of King Donnchadh mac Máel Coluim (1094) and in this he granted St Cuthbert and the saint's servants at Durham various things including the lands of Tyninghame, Auldhame, Scoughall, Knowes, Hedderwick, and Broxmouth. Donnchadh's named brothers *Eadgari* (Edgar) and *Malcolumb* (Máel Coluim), among others, witnessed the undated grant.[5]

---

4 Ibid., 1116.6.
5 A. A. M. Duncan, 'Yes, the Earliest Scottish Charters', *SHR*, 78, 1:205, 1999, 1–38, at 8 [hereafter: Duncan, 'Earliest Scottish Charters'].

Sir Archibald Lawrie had doubts about the authenticity of this charter but reasoned that, if it was genuine, it must have been granted when Donnchadh was at Durham in May 1094 and looking for aid before travelling north to seize the kingship of Scotia from King Domnall bán mac Donnchada. For Lawrie, the biggest sticking point in confirming the authenticity of this document was the presence of *Malcolumb* (Máel Coluim) in the witness list, since a brother by that name is not otherwise attested in any other surviving source.[6]

Duncan, writing in 1999, agreed with Lawrie. Duncan also pointed out that in a later charter King Edgar mac Máel Coluim named his dead brothers as Duncan and Edward. There was no mention of a brother called Máel Coluim. This absence led Duncan to suggest that if *Malcolumb* (Máel Coluim) was a member of the royal kindred, he could have been an otherwise unattested illegitimate son of King Máel Coluim mac Donnchada.[7]

Both these points can be countered. First, the King Edgar mac Máel Coluim charter also did not mention the Domnall mac Máel Coluim who had died in 1085 and who had probably also been a half brother to Edgar. As such, the absence of any mention of Máel Coluim in the Edgar charter becomes less important. Second, there is absolutely no reason for Duncan to have described Máel Coluim as an unattested illegitimate son as he could easily just have been a third son of the marriage of King Máel Coluim mac Donnchada and Ingibjorg.

There is one further name to consider. In the same King Edgar charter discussed above, the name Eyluerti filii Doncani (Gylnerti mac Donnchada) occurs on the witness list. A. A. M. Duncan suggested that Gylnerti could represent the Scandinavian personal name Kilvert, possibly bearing Gylnerti's position as a grandson of the Orcadian Queen Ingibjorg in mind.[8] If correct, this would mean that two of Ingibjorg's grandsons, Gylnerti and Ladhmann, bore Scandinavian personal names.

All of this provides us with the probable names of three sons and three grandsons of King Máel Coluim's marriage to Ingibjorg. If they have been identified correctly, all of these men would have possessed a claim to be considered for the kingship of Scotia. In this respect it is quite telling that, as far as we know from the sources, none of them ever pushed (or were

6 *ESC*, 241.
7 Duncan, 'Earliest Scottish Charters', 14, n. 52.
8 Ibid., 23; *ESC*, 12–13.

permitted to push) that claim of right as members of Clann Custantín meic Cináeda to be inaugurated. We also do not know their exact order of birth. Though it can be assumed with some certainty that Donnchad mac Máel Coluim was older than his brother Máel Coluim, it is impossible to tell whether Donnchad was also older than Domnall mac Máel Coluim. Domnall's death nine years before Donnchad mac Máel Coluim took the throne in 1094 precludes any discussion of this.

The wicked uncle? King Domnall bán mac Donnchada, November 1093–May 1094

Domnall bán mac Donnchada belongs to a very small group of kings in north Britain (and probably elsewhere) whose reigns covered two distinct periods. In Domnall bán's case his overall reign ran from 1093 to 1097 except for a *circa* six-month period in 1094 when Donnchadh mac Máel Coluim reigned. This hiatus in the reign of Domnall bán is very interesting in terms of the early constitutional history of Scotia for a number of reasons, not all of which can be adequately explained. First, were there two inaugurated kings in Scotia between May and November 1094 or did Domnall bán automatically lose the kingship when he was (presumably) defeated in battle by his nephew and dynastic rival Donnchadh mac Máel Coluim? If Domnall bán did lose the kingship, did this mean that he had to be re-inaugurated when he finally managed to recover his kingship in November that same year or was inauguration something that lasted for the lifetime of a person? Unfortunately, we do not yet know enough about the 'rules' of inauguration in Scotia. Yet another oddity is that the descendants of his daughter Bethòc never seem to have advanced a claim to the throne.

English sources present the inauguration of Domnall bán as a straightforward and logical event, stating that the Scots themselves had chosen him. However, the situation was clearly more complicated, since those same sources also state that all the English who had been with King Máel Coluim mac Donnchada were driven out of Scotia.[9] While we do not know the exact circumstances surrounding this enforced exodus, it does seem to indicate that there was lingering bitterness in Scotia in relation to people who had either arrived in Scotia along with Margaret or been attracted to Scotia after Margaret became queen. Alternatively, and perhaps more

9 *SAEC*, 117–18.

pragmatically, this event could also be explained by King Domnall bán removing from Alba an established power-base which could have supported his various nephews' claims to be inaugurated.

The Scottish sources provide more information. One of our earliest surviving sources, *Gesta Annalia* I, dated to the thirteenth century, relates that Domnall bán invaded the kingdom (perhaps implying that he was outwith Scotia when his brother was killed) and besieged Edinburgh Castle where the body of Queen Margaret still lay and where he knew King Máel Coluim mac Donnchada's heirs were staying. The story then describes how Margaret's body and the 'rightful' heirs escaped from the clutches of Domnall bán because of a miracle. As the royal party escaped from a postern gate, a miraculous mist arose which shielded the family from being seen by the enemy until they safely arrived at Dunfermline, where the queen was subsequently buried. Thereafter, Edgar Ætheling, brother of Margaret, removed both himself and all the children of Máel Coluim and Margaret secretly to England.[10]

This story is repeated by Bower with one main difference: this is that Domnall bán received help from the king of Norway to invade Scotland.[11] The editors of the volume of Bower's work speculated that there could have been some truth in this statement because Bower had earlier stated that, after the inauguration of MacBethad mac Findlaích in 1040, Domnall bán had fled to the Western Isles, then under the control of Norway.[12] There is perhaps another possibility. If there is any truth to the story that Domnall bán received Norwegian aid to invade Scotland in 1093, it could also be explained by reference to the kin of Queen Ingibjorg from the Northern Isles. Orkney was also under the control of Norway and supporting Domnall bán might have been a way of ensuring that the sons of King Máel Coluim mac Donnchada and Margaret did not immediately gain primacy in Scotia to the detriment of Ingibjorg's sons and grandsons.

---

10 W. F. Skene (ed.), *Johannis de Fordun Chronica Gentis Scotorum* (Edinburgh, 1871), 422–23. The text of *Chronica Gentis Scotorum* has recently been re-examined by Dauvit Broun [Broun, 'Gesta Annalia']. In this article Broun convincingly demonstrates that the text of the work known as *Chronica Gentis Scotorum* also preserves two earlier texts that Broun called *Gesta Annalia* I (completed before April 1285 but probably based on an earlier Dunfermline work) and *Gesta Annalia* II (completed by 1363). Accordingly, only the first five books, together with the unfinished sixth book, of *Chronica Gentis Scotorum*, are likely to have been Fordun's work, completed sometime between 1371 and the mid-1380s.

11 *Chron. Bower* (Watt), iii, 77–79.

12 Ibid., ii, 426–27; iii, 221–22.

In contrast to the latter two sources, Wyntoun obviously either did not know about or chose to ignore the *Gesta Annalia* account of a siege of Edinburgh Castle. He simply stated that Domnall bán took the kingship of Scotia and immediately banished three of his brother's sons, Edgar, Alexander and David.[13] Unfortunately, the lack of any corroborating evidence from outside Scotland in relation to a siege of Edinburgh Castle in the winter of 1093 must raise some doubts about the veracity of the story, particularly as it involves a miracle and St Margaret. The possibility that this story was invented in order to enhance the saintly reputation of the ex-queen during the thirteenth-century campaign to canonise her cannot be entirely rejected.

English sources are also quite clear that at some point between Domnall bán mac Donnchada seizing the kingship in November 1093 and May 1094, Donnchadh mac Máel Coluim had approached, asked for, and received his father's kingdom and military aid from William II Rufus with the aim of deposing Domnall bán and seeking inauguration for himself. In return for this aid, English sources inform us that Donnchadh performed homage to the king of England.[14] Surviving Scottish sources are silent on this detail but this is perhaps not surprising since many of them post-date the wars of independence when the subject of Scottish homage was something of a recurring issue.

King Donnchad mac Máel Coluim, May/June to November 1094

Quhen Malcom the kynge was dede,
His brothir Donalde than his stede,
Fandit to wyn and tak; than he
Banyst his brethir barnys thre,
Edgar, Alexander and Dawy,
That flede for thar emys fellony.

Thai had a brothir of purchas,
That Malcomys bastarde son than was,
Duncan callit, and was duellande
Withe Wilyam Rede, that of Inglande,

---

13 *Chron. Wyntoun*, iv, 350–52.
14 P. McGurk (ed.), *The Chronicle of John of Worcester: The Annals from 1067 to 1140 with the Gloucester Interpolations and the Continuation to 1141*, (Oxford, 1998), iii, 66–67.

As kynge that tyme bare the crowne,
And herde of this presumpsion,
That his eme than tuk on hande.

In to the kynrik of Scotlande,
He coyme withe powar of this kynge,
That Inglande hade in gouernynge.
His eme than he chassit swa,
That the flicht he gert hym ta,
And fra hym qwhit wan the lande,
And was a yhere in it wonnande,
And ane halfe. The erl than
Off the Meryrnnys, a manly man,
Agayne Duncane with his power,
Rasse with Donalde in to were,
And slew this Duncan son to dede,
His eme restoryt in his stede,
That befor as kynge hade he.
The state he helde as yheris thre.[15]

Though we have no idea about his date of birth, except that it must have occurred before King Máel Coluim mac Donnchada's marriage to Margaret *c*.1070, it is clear that Donnchadh mac Máel Coluim spent many of his formative years in England, since he was handed over as a hostage to William the Conqueror in 1070 after the agreement made at Abernethy. Because of this agreement, it is frequently suggested that Donnchadh was King Máel Coluim's eldest surviving son and heir at that time. Little is known about Donnchadh's enforced sojourn abroad but he is recorded as having been honoured with military arms (knighted) by William the Conqueror upon his release in 1087. Thereafter, there is no sign of Donnchadh returning north to Scotland, and it may be that by 1087 he was already married to Octreda, daughter of Earl Cospatrick of the House of Bamburgh, and settled in north England. It is in this marriage that many of the puzzles surrounding the descendants of Donnchadh lie.

In his only surviving charter, dated to 1094, Donnchadh referred to his wife and children (plural): . . . *et pro uxore mea et pro infantibus meis* . . .[16]

---

15 *Chron. Wytoun*, iv, 353.
16 *ESC*, 10.

This statement would appear to be correct. Gylnerti mac Donnchada has already been discussed, but Donnchadh's infinitely more famous male child was William fitz Duncan. He was a prominent noble during the reign of King David I (1124–1153), probable earl of Moray, and progenitor of the MacWilliam kindred who were eventually deliberately exterminated by King Alexander II.[17]

But this single charter is important for another reason. In it Donnchadh is described as *Rex Scotie* and on his seal as *Regis Scottorum*.[18] Duncan has argued that this concept had been directly borrowed from the English style *Rex Anglorum*.[19]

Even if it had, Donnchadh was still effectively being cast as the king of a people (the Scots) rather than as the king of a realm (*rí Alban*), as Irish Gaelic chronicle sources were wont to do. This is an important distinction.

However, because this document is only the earliest surviving Scottish charter, there is a very good chance that the concept may be older. The *Anglo-Saxon Chronicle*, for example, refers to *Scottas* in the 920s, but it is unknown whether this was a term the Scots used to describe themselves or whether it had been coined by the Anglo-Saxons to describe a people living in north Britain, much in the same way as they used the term *Wealhas* (foreigners) to describe the peoples living to the west to them (now Wales). What is clear is that by 1094 the kings of north Britain preferred to view themselves as the rulers of a people rather than the rulers of a country. Unfortunately, there is no way of telling whether the majority of 'Scots' who were then being ruled by these men had bought into this message.

It may seem strange that Donnchadh did not return north to Scotland after his release in 1087, particularly since he was the eldest surviving son of King Máel Coluim mac Donnchada. However, this may just seem peculiar to us as we are now accustomed to primogeniture in royal succession. In the later 1080s, there would have been no certainty that Donnchadh either would or could have automatically succeeded his father as king of Scotia. Despite this lack of certainty, there is some evidence in Donnchadh's only surviving charter that he clearly had no qualms about the legitimacy of his

17 For a reappraisal of the MacWilliams see: Ross, 'Moray, Ulster, and the MacWilliams', 24–44.
18 Duncan, 'Earliest Scottish Charters', 12.
19 Duncan, *Kingship*, 4.

own claim. In this document Donnchadh described himself both as *Ego Dunecanus filius Regis Malcolumb constans hereditary rex Scociei* (son of King Máel Coluim, hereditably certain king of Scotland) and in the witness list as *Signum Dunecani Regis* (King Duncan).[20] Furthermore, Edgar's witnessing of this charter might indicate that he had no problem with his half-brother describing himself in such terms.[21] Yet, Donnchadh is, along with King MacBethad mac Findláich, a king of Scotia whose reputation has been deliberately and universally trashed.

The excerpt above from Wyntoun's Chronicle is a good example of this slander: Donnchadh is described as 'Malcomys bastarde son'. Wyntoun was by no means the first, nor was he the last, chronicler and historian to describe Donnchadh in such terms. For example, recent work by Dauvit Broun has examined two Scottish king-lists written during the thirteenth century, the first around December 1214, the second between 1198 and 1214.

The first list, now known as the *Verse Chronicle* (W. F. Skene's *Chronicon Elegiacum*), begins with the reign of King Cináed mac Ailpín and is written in Latin elegiac couplets inserted into the margins of the *Chronicle of Melrose*. It continues until the reign of King William I in 1214, and the couplets typically include details of each king's death and provide reign lengths.[22]

A version of the *Verse Chronicle* was included in Bower's *Scotichronicon*, and Broun has shown that there were significant differences between the way Moravians were portrayed in the original in the Melrose Chronicle and how they were regarded in the *Scotichronicon* edition. The former states that two kings of Alba, King Máel Coluim mac Domnaill (d. 954) and King Dub mac Máel Coluim (d. 966) died in Moray. There is a slight hint that some treachery was employed in the death of the former.

The latter, in contrast, displays a much greater degree of antipathy towards Moravians. In relation to the death of King Máel Coluim mac Domnaill it states:

Huic rex Malcolmus successit ter tribus annis.
Regis Dovenaldi filius iste fuit.
Tortores regum fuerant qui Moraviensis
Hunc extinxerunt ense doloque suo.

---

20 Duncan, 'Earliest Scottish Charters', 8.
21 Duncan, *Kingship*, 55.
22 Broun, 'Contemporary Perspectives', 79–98.

He was succeeded by King Malcolm for thrice three years.
He was the son of King Donald.
Men of Moray were the regicides who killed him
With their treachery and their sword.[23]

Describing the death of King Dub mac Máel Coluim, *Scotichronicon* states:

Quatuor et semis rex Duff regnavit aristis,
Malcolmo natus, Regis jura gerens.
Hunc interfecit gens perfida Moraviensis,
Cuius erat gladiis cesus in urbe Fores.
Sol abdit radios, ipso sub ponte latente,
Quo fuit absconsus usque repertus erat.

King Duf reigned for four and a half years.
He was the son of Malcolm, administering royal justice,
He was killed by the treacherous people of Moray,
by whose swords he was slain in the city of Forres.
The sun hid its rays while his body lay hid under the bridge,
Where it lay hidden until it was found.[24]

Of course, in fact, only one of these kings was actually killed in Moray by
Moravians, King Dub mac Máel Coluim. Broun has argued that the reason
behind this systematic slandering of Moravians was that the descendants of
King Donnchadh mac Máel Coluim, the MacWilliams, were active in
Moray from where they consistently challenged the kingships of both King
William I and King Alexander II before 1230. Accordingly, this explains
why King Donnchadh mac Máel Coluim is described as a 'bastard
king' and the statement that 'because he lived badly, the whole populace
crushed him'.[25]

The second king-list examined by Broun was inserted into the *Chronicle
of Melrose* during the lifetime of Alexander II. It begins with the start of the
reign of King Máel Coluim mac Donnchada in 1056 and ends upon the
birth of Alexander II in 1198. Broun has dated the original to 1198 x 1214.
According to Broun, the fact that this king-list began with King Máel
Coluim mac Donnchada was no accident but instead a conscious attempt

23 *Chron. Bower* (Watt), ii, 348.
24 Ibid., 352–54.
25 Anderson, *ESSH*, ii, 90–91.

to emphasise the legitimacy of the descendants of King Máel Coluim mac Donnchada and Queen Margaret by focusing on primogeniture.

The king-list states that King Máel Coluim mac Donnchada became king by hereditary right and that King Domnall bán mac Donnchada (1093–1097) had usurped the kingship, forcing the legitimate heirs into exile. King Donnchadh mac Máel Coluim was again labelled as *nothus* (illegitimate).[26] Two later Scottish sources, *Gesta Annalia I* and *Scotichronicon*, repeat the same claim. They justified their denigration of the MacWilliam claims by asserting that the progenitor of the MacWilliam kindred, King Donnchad mac Máel Coluim, was a 'bastard son', and that it was therefore absurd that any of his descendants should have considered themselves suitable candidates for the kingship of Scotia.[27]

While these two king-lists examined by Broun may be the earliest surviving Scottish sources to slander the reputation of King Donnchadh mac Máel Coluim by turning him into a 'bastard king', they were not the first sources to do so. In fact, this description (*nothus*) of King Donnchadh mac Máel Coluim first appeared in an English source almost contemporary with his reign, William of Malmesbury's *Gesta Regum Anglorum*, written c.1126.[28] This creates something of a conundrum because, as far as we know, neither William fitz Duncan nor any other direct descendants of King Donnchadh mac Máel Coluim challenged King David I for the kingship of Scotland during the period between 1124 and 1140. This would indicate that William of Malmesbury had another reason for deliberately slandering the reputation of King Donnchadh.

The reason behind this sudden description of King Donnchad mac Máel Coluim as *nothus* after c.1126 in an English source may have everything to do with the fact that he was not a son of King Máel Coluim mac Donnchada and Queen Margaret, but a scion of King Máel Coluim mac Donnchada's first marriage to Ingibjorg of Orkney. Given the continued English interest in and military support for the sons of Máel Coluim and Margaret, as well as the marriage of King Henry I to Edith (Matilda), this slandering of King Donnchad is perhaps hardly surprising and should probably be regarded as English-driven propaganda to ensure and advance the claims of just one segment of the royal kindred of Scotia, the one descended from Queen Margaret. It is also probably no coincidence that

---

26 Broun, 'Contemporary Perspectives', 92–94.
27 For example: *Chron. Fordun (GA 1)*, 268.
28 Mynors and Thomson, *Gesta Regum Anglorum*, i, 725.

the claim regarding the bastard ancestry of King Donnchad mac Máel Coluim appeared around the time of the inauguration of David I in 1124, when David's right to be inaugurated was challenged by Máel Coluim, son of King Alexander I, who was described in the same terms.[29]

It is also noticeable, however, that this English propaganda (if that is indeed what it amounts to) is not repeated in royal charters in Scotland. For example, a probable 1128 confirmation from King David I for Dunfermline Abbey simply refers to '*Duncani fratris mei*' (Duncan, my brother).[30]

Heir today, gone tomorrow

While both Scottish and English sources are clear that Donnchad mac Máel Coluim succeeded in forcing his uncle to demit the office of kingship, only the English sources claim that Donnchad's short reign was unstable. The *Anglo-Saxon Chronicle*, for example, informs us that, after Donnchad had presumably been inaugurated, the Scots slew most of his followers. This possibly refers to the military aid that King Donnchad had received from King William II Rufus. The consequence was that Donnchadh agreed never again to introduce either English or Norman-French into Scotia and the two sides were reconciled.[31] This was the second occasion in under a year that anti-English/Norman-French sentiment in Scotia was recorded in the sources.

Having survived one conspiracy, King Donnchad mac Máel Coluim quickly fell victim to a second, and it might be questioned whether he was ever given the chance to settle into his new role as king of Scotia. Indeed, in this respect *Gesta Annalia I* notes that King Donnchad mac Máel Coluim had often defeated King Domnall bán mac Donnchada in battle, implying that the conflict between the two men was drawn out over a period of time.[32] In any event, the second conspiracy against him was successful and some of the broad details of it have survived in the sources. *Gesta Annalia* I, Fordun, Bower, and Wyntoun are united in naming and shaming a mormaer of the

29 For a re-evaluation of the career of Máel Coluim, son of King Alexander I, see: Alasdair Ross, 'The Identity of the "Prisoner of Roxburgh": Malcolm Son of Alexander or Malcolm Macheth?', in S. Arbuthnot and K. Hollo (eds), *Fil súil nglais – A Grey Eye Looks Back: A Festschrift in Honour of Colm Ó Baoill* (Ceann Drochaid, 2007), 269–82 [hereafter: Ross, 'Prisoner of Roxburgh'].

30 Barrow, *Chrs. David I*, 70–71.

31 *SAEC*, 118.

32 *Chron. Fordun*, 426.

Mearns called Maol Peadair (servant of [St] Peter), ably assisted by the trickery of King Domnall bán, as the murderer of King Donnchad at Mondynes in the Mearns on 12 November 1094.[33] No other conspirator is named. Local tradition in the Mearns has identified the site of the murder as the so-called 'Court stane' in Fordun parish, which may have been the judgement seat for the barony of Mondynes. However, there seems to be no evidence earlier than the nineteenth century to directly link this standing stone to the scene of the crime.[34]

It is left to a contemporary English source to name a third party to this conspiracy: Edmund mac Máel Coluim, third son of King Máel Coluim mac Donnchada and Margaret. William of Malmesbury states that Edmund was deeply involved in the death of his half-brother (without going into details) and had bargained for half of the kingdom as the price of his support:

> *Solus fuit Edmundus Margaretae filius a bone degener, qui, Duuenaldi patrui nequitiae particeps, fraternae non inscius necis fuerit, pactus scilicet regni dimidium; sed captus et perpetuis compedibus detentus ingenue penituit, et ad mortem ueniens cum ipsis uinculis se tumulari mandauit, professus se plexum merito pro fratficidii delicto.*

Edmund was the only son of Margaret who sank from this high standard: his uncle Donald's partner in crime, he cannot be held innocent of his brother's death, for he bargained that he should receive half the kingdom. Being taken, however, and imprisoned for life, he frankly repented, and on his deathbed gave instructions that his fetters should be buried with him, admitting that he was rightly punished for the crime of his brother's murder.[35]

There is now no way of telling exactly which part of the kingdom Edmund wanted, but one might wonder whether the division envisaged in November 1094 was identical to that agreed between King Edgar mac Máel Coluim, Alexander mac Máel Coluim, and their younger brother David before 1107, whereby David eventually received an appanage that stretched from the Lennox to the Solway and included Teviotdale.[36]

33 For example: *Chron. Bower* (Watt), iii, 85.
34 http://canmore.rcahms.gov.uk/en/site/36385/details/court+stane
35 Mynors and Thomson, *Gesta Regum Anglorum*, i, 727.
36 Duncan, *Kingship*, 61.

This agreement between uncle and nephew is also interesting because Edmund was not the oldest surviving son of King Máel Coluim mac Donnchada and Margaret at that time. His elder brother Edgar was still alive. This might indicate that besides the civil war within the wider kindred of Clann Custantín meic Cináeda there must also have been robust debates amongst the sons of Máel Coluim and Margaret about which of them was better suited to claim the kingship of Scotia in the late Autumn of 1094. The debate may not have been confined just to this group of royal males.

Even after the death of King Donnchad mac Máel Coluim, the males of the royal kindred who were eligible to be considered for inauguration consisted of four sons from King Máel Coluim mac Donnchada's marriage to Queen Margaret, various sons and grandsons of King Máel Coluim mac Donnchada's first marriage to Queen Ingibjorg, and the progeny of King Lulach mac Gilla Comgáin in Moray. Even though our sources for the royal kindreds of Scotia before 1100 are relatively sparse, this seems like an extraordinary amount of eligible royal male heirs, many of whom would have been following different political agendas. Perhaps the closest parallel to this would be the various situations King Robert II had to manage among his clutch of sons in the fourteenth century.

The return of the king(s): King Domnall bán mac Donnchada and Edmund, 1094–1097

Unfortunately, Scottish sources reveal little about King Domnall bán's second period of kingship. We do not even know if the kingdom was in fact divided between himself and his nephew Edmund, or whether Edmund was just officially recognised as his heir. English sources are equally silent about this period and the sole overall assessment of Domnall bán's reign is found in the problematic text called the *Prophecy of Berchán*:

Íarsin nos géabha Domnall
uch mo craoidh aga rádhadh
is fria ré tíagaid anall
fir Alban dochum nÉirenn.

Ceithre rígh is fhichid sin
ón gcédrígh ghéabhus Albain
go Domhnall Bán dháiles graig
fagbhas Albain do Geinntibh.

After that Domnall will take sovereignty,
alas my heart when I say it;
in his time the men of Alba will go yonder, to Ireland.

Twenty-four kings then,
from the first king who will take Alba
to Domnall Bán who distributes horses,
who leaves Alba to Vikings.[37]

Clearly, this is a fairly damning indictment of Domnall bán's reign and the last sentence is particularly interesting in light of the gains made by King Magnus Barelegs, king of Norway, in the Irish Sea Zone after 1097.

The establishment of Scottish overlordship from the 1070s onwards across most of the territories that once comprised the Brittonic kingdom of Strathclyde was important. It gave the kings of Alba direct access to the Firth of Clyde and the Irish Sea, probably for the first time, and it is difficult to assess the degree to which this new presence might have either stressed or destabilised the existing web of power in that area. At that time the Isle of Man and its king Gofraid Crobán were at the centre of this web, and he was the founder of a dynasty that held the kingship of Man until the mid-thirteenth century. Not only was Gofraid king of Man, but he also extended his overlordship across the Hebrides before he died on Islay in 1095.[38]

It is likely that Gofraid extended his kingship in an attempt to seize complete control of the extensive west-coast trade routes that led from Dublin to the Baltic Sea and beyond. To this end, he took the kingship of Dublin in 1091. This only lasted for about three years before he was driven out of Dublin by Muirchertach uí Briain, king of Munster. After his death in 1095 Gofraid was suceeded by his son Lagmann. The *Chronicle of Man* assigns Lagmann a reign of seven years before his death on crusade, allegedly while doing penance for blinding and castrating his brother Harald.[39] The *Chronicle of Man* relates that after Lagmann's departure the chief men of the Isles invited Muirchertach uí Briain to send someone to rule over them until Lagmann's younger brother, Óláfr son of Gofraid, came of age. Muirchertach chose Domnall mac Taidc, but Domnall's reign

---

37 Hudson, *Berchán*, 55–56, 92. Amended translation by A. Ross.
38 http://www.isle-of-man.com/manxnotebook/manxsoc/msvol22/p044.htm Accessed 9 January 2010.
39 Ibid.

seems only to have resulted in further bloodshed and discontent, leading to a civil war between the Manxmen and the eventual permanent return of Domnall to Ireland. However, Domnall may not have been the sole cause of this unrest in Man and the Isles: Magnus Barelegs, according to the *Chronicle of Man*, had sent one of his deputies, Ingimundr, to seize the Manx kingdom.[40]

Though the chiefs of the Isles successfully managed to burn alive Ingimundr and his followers in a house in Skye, according to the *Chronicle of Man*, the following year (1098) Magnus Barelegs appeared in person and chose Man as his new base of power.[41] There is, however, some uncertainty about this chronology. According to *Fagrskinna* (fair parchment), Magnus first landed in Orkney before sailing to Lewis and Skye. After Skye he proceeded to Tiree and North Uist, and from there to Iona, accepting tribute as he went. He then burned Islay and captured King Lagmann of Man before taking possession of that island.[42] This Norse account directly links the two kings, so it is possible that Lagmann's departure on crusade was a direct consequence of his capture by King Magnus rather than any filial regret. In this account it is also stated that Magnus raided the shore of Scotland, 'doing great deeds', and this is discussed more fully in the next chapter. If true, this may be why the *Prophecy of Berchán* accused King Domnall bán of leaving Alba to Vikings.

The depth of the familial ructions caused by the murder of King Donnchadh mac Máel Coluim can perhaps be best measured by the response of Edgar mac Máel Coluim, the eldest surviving son of the marriage between King Máel Coluim mac Donnchada and Margaret. On 29 August 1095, nine months after the death of his half-brother, Edgar granted a charter to St Cuthbert, giving Durham the two estates of Coldinghamshire and Berwickshire. While the original grant has not survived, the wording can be resurrected from later fifteenth-century copies, and two writs issued by King William II Rufus confirm the authenticity of the original. In this document Edgar carefully described himself as possessing the whole land of Lothian and the kingship of Scotland, respectively by the gift of King William II Rufus and by paternal heritage. This charter must have been issued after Edgar had conquered Lothian, as he

40 Ibid.
41 Ibid.
42 Alison Finlay, *Fagrskinna, a Catalogue of the Kings of Norway* (Leiden, 2004), 247 [hereafter: Finlay, *Fagrskinna*].

restored those properties to Durham and the cult of Cuthbert that they had previously held there. Edgar signed the document, *Signum Edgari regis*.[43]

Duncan has argued that since Edgar had almost certainly not travelled to Scotia for inauguration, he had become a king through recognition by King William II Rufus and by the gift of Lothian, followed by a symbolic investiture. Moreover, Duncan also demonstrated that such an act was not unusual in a European context, and listed similar contemporary or near-contemporary recognitions in Poland, Bohemia and Denmark. The investiture ceremony may also have involved William II Rufus crowning Edgar, as the latter's 1095 seal depicts him as a crowned king with sceptre and sword and shows some similarity to the seal of Edgar's ancestor, Edward the Confessor.[44]

What is very interesting about this charter is that it was also witnessed by *Constantini filii Magdufe*. It seems likely that this was the person referred to as both Earl Constantine of Fife and chief *judex* in Scotia during the reign of King David I before c.1130.[45] His presence alongside Edgar in England in 1095, if Wyntoun was correct to state that the head of the Fife kindred became the senior inaugural official during the reign of King Máel Coluim mac Donnchada, would perhaps indicate that some very significant people in Scotia did not support King Domnall bán mac Donnchada and may even have been actively plotting to remove him from power.

Two years later, in October 1097, William II Rufus sent an army into Scotland under the command of Edgar Ætheling, accompanied by his nephew, and they succeeded in forcing King Domnall bán mac Donnchada to abdicate his office. Edmund is not mentioned in the sources that describe the expedition, so his involvement in these events is unknown. A short account of this conflict appears in *Gesta Annalia* I where the triumph of Edgar Ætheling and Edgar mac Máel Coluim is closely linked to the prowess of St Cuthbert and the raising of his battle banner in front of the army belonging to King Domnall bán mac Donnchada. The Scottish fighting champions were promptly killed and King Domnall bán's army chose to flee rather than fight and suffer the wrath of St Cuthbert. According to the account, King Edgar mac Máel Coluim then entered the kingdom that was his by right and was joyfully accepted by the people.[46]

43 Duncan, 'Earliest Scottish Charters', 16–17; Duncan, *Kingship*, 56–57.
44 Duncan, *Kingship*, 57.
45 *ESC*, 66–67.
46 *Chron. Fordun*, 426–27.

A near-contemporary English chronicle adds one very interesting piece of information. William of Malmesbury states:

Sed eo patrui Duuenaldi fraude interempto, Edgarum in regnum promouit, prefato Duuenaldo astutia Dauid iunioris et uiribus Willelmi extincto.

When Duncan was treacherously killed by his uncle Donald, he [William Rufus] advanced Edgar to the throne, Donald having been done to death by the intrigue of the younger David with William's powerful aid.[47]

This is the first reference to the future King David I (1124–1153) taking an active role in the politics of Scotia. It is very curious that Malmesbury is the only source who places the teenage and obviously precocious David at the centre of the scheme to force regime change in Scotia in the 1090s. One potential problem with this extract is that King Domnall bán mac Donnchada was not killed in 1097 but instead imprisoned. He was still alive in 1099 when he seems to have been involved in another plot and subsequently mutilated, so it should be questioned whether Malmesbury conflated two or more separate events in the above extract. Whatever the case, it is unknown if David primarily became involved in these murderous intrigues to support his brothers but the future king could just as easily have calculated that by ridding Scotia of King Domnall bán and Edgar, he advanced one step closer to claiming the kingship for himself.

Mutilation, banishment, repentance, and death

Both Domnall bán mac Donnchada and Edmund survived their defeat by the two Edgars, though we cannot be sure that Edmund had not previously been captured after Edgar mac Máel Coluim had taken Lothian in 1095. As far as Domnall bán mac Donnchada is concerned, an insertion in the *Chronicle of Melrose* states that Edgar condemned him to perpetual imprisonment in Roscobie.[48] No date of death is ever provided for Domnall

---

47 Mynors and Thomson, *Gesta Regum Anglorum*, i, 725.
48 Dauvit Broun and Julian Harrison, *The Chronicle of Melrose Abbey, a Stratigraphic Edition* (Chippenham, 2007), Faustina B. IX, fo. 14r.

bán but we are told that he was originally buried at Dunkeld before his bones were subsequently removed and taken to Iona.

This would make Domnall bán mac Donnchada the last king of Scotia to be interred on Iona though we have no clues about the precise date of his final burial there. There is some indication why he was disinterred from Dunkeld and his bones taken to Iona, but part of the problem is that we know little about the relative strength of the cult of St Colum Cille in Scotia at this time. King Alexander I certainly showed enough interest in the cult to have a copy of Adomnan's Life of Colum Cille made for himself.[49]

On the assumption that Domnall bán died in or near the same place that he had been imprisoned, the choice of Roscobie as the place of his incarceration is also initially puzzling. There are two Roscobie place-names in eastern Scotland, one in Angus and the second near Dunfermline in Fife. It is the former that has become the favourite candidate as the site in Angus of Domnall bán's imprisonment in historical writings since at least 1862.[50] While it is not recorded as a royal possession or medieval stronghold, which would have been an obvious choice in which to imprison Domnall bán, there is strong evidence of an early high-status Christian site at nearby Restenneth. Some of the surviving stonework there has been dated, using the context of English examples, to the late tenth or early eleventh century.[51] Accordingly, this pre-1100 religious centre, with its church dedicated to St Peter, might have been an obvious choice to place Domnall bán so that he might repent of his sins.

There is some evidence to indicate that the ex-king may not have accepted his incarceration at Roscobie/Restenneth gracefully. In 1099, the *Annals of Tigernach* record that, *Domnall mac Donnchada, rí Alban, do dallad da brathair* (Domnall bán mac Donnchada was blinded by his brother).[52] It may just be a coincidence, but it is known that King Edgar was absent from Scotia for a period of time between Easter and the end of May 1099, when he was commanded to attend upon King William II

49 A. O. Anderson and M. O. Anderson (eds), *Adomnan's Life of Columba* (Edinburgh, 1961), 10 [hereafter: Anderson and Anderson, *Life of Columba*].

50 Robertson, *Early Kings*, i, 159.

51 N. Cameron, 'St Rule's Church, St Andrews, and Early Stone-built Churches in Scotland', *PSAS*, 124, 1994, 367–78; *MRHS*, 95–96.

52 http://www.ucc.ie/celt/published/G100002/index.html Brother, if taken literally, must be a mistake for nephew.

Rufus upon the latter's return from Normandy. This may have provided Domnall bán with an opportunity to create mischief. If the entry in the *Annals of Tigernach* is accurate, it may suggest that Domnall bán had been plotting to remove yet another of his nephews from the kingship of Scotia and was deliberately mutilated as punishment when the plot was discovered. Such mutilation would prevent Domnall bán from ever claiming the kingship again and it is surely possible that his death was a direct consequence of this mutilation. Interestingly, this is the first recorded instance of the brutality that the descendants of King Máel Coluim mac Donnchada and Margaret consistently displayed towards their dynastic rivals for over 130 years until, with the death of the last MacWilliam in 1230, a female infant whose brains were battered out against the market cross in Forfar, such rivals had all been exterminated. The path that led to the unchallenged inauguration of Alexander III in 1249 was both vicious and bloody.

The decisions surrounding the eventual fate of Domnall bán's co-conspirator Edmund are equally mysterious. Almost all we know of his life post-1097 comes from the writings of William of Malmesbury: Edmund is said to have repented of having committed fratricide by plotting the death of his half-brother King Donnchad mac Máel Coluim, and Edmund was directed to wear iron fetters for the remainder of his life. We are also informed that he decided to be buried in those same chains.[53] But Edmund was not allowed to remain in Scotland.

Gesta Annalia I, the Poppleton manuscript (and Bower) are the only witnesses to the fact that Edmund spent the remainder of his life at the Cluniac priory of Montacute in Somerset:

> *Edmundus autem, vir strenuissimus, et in dei servitio dum vitam ageret presentem valde devotus, in Anglia, apud Montem Acutum, ubi post mortem matris morabatur, vitam finiens, in quadam cellula, videlicet, Cluniacensi, ibidem [fundata] requiescit humatus.*

> Edmund however, a very forceful man who was greatly devoted to god's service while he was alive, died in Anglia, by Montacute, where he remained after his mother's death, and is buried in a certain cell, namely, of the Cluniacs, which was founded there.[54]

---

53 Mynors and Thomson, *Gesta Regum Anglorum*, i, 727.
54 *Chron. Fordun*, 426.

King Edgar mac Máel Coluim and his uncle Edgar Ætheling seem to have been determined to place as much distance as possible between the two co-conspirators and Montacute was at that time a relatively new foundation. In fact, there seems to be some dispute about the date of foundation. English Heritage argue for a date of *c*.1078 x 1104. This inexact date is unfortunate as it means that the founder of the priory could either have been Count Robert de Mortain, half-brother of William the Conqueror, or Robert's son Count William.[55] In one sense it does not really matter which Count was the founder since both were closely linked, at least before 1104, to an Anglo-Norman monarchy that was actively supporting the kingships of Edgar mac Máel Coluim and Alexander mac Máel Coluim in Scotia.

After the Battle of Tinchebray in Normandy in 1106, Count William de Mortain was captured, imprisoned, and never really forgiven by King Henry I. What exactly happened at Montacute Priory during the period after Count William de Mortain was stripped of his lands is unknown, but King Henry I was a strong believer in the Cluniac ideals and there is some indication that he may have been considering endowing Montacute himself.[56] He certainly confirmed grants to the priory after 1107 and also granted the Cluniac monks at Montacute some lands that had previously been held by Count William de Mortain.[57]

For Edmund this meant that he was under constant supervision by Cluniac monks who were dependent upon the family of the Anglo-Norman rulers of England for patronage. Perhaps more intriguingly, the priory church at Montacute originally seems to have been dedicated to St Peter. If the argument that Domnall bán was imprisoned in an ecclesiatic establishment in Scotland dedicated to the same saint is correct, this seems to be rather more than a coincidence. Not only was St Peter the brother of St Andrew, he was also the keeper of the keys to heaven, and this belief may have been used to remind both uncle and nephew of the scale of repentance required for fratricide.

There was perhaps one other casualty of this civil war conducted by the wider family of King Máel Coluim mac Donnchada between 1093 and 1097. This is the mormaer of the Mearns, Maol Peadair, who was named as a co-conspirator in the death of King Donnchadh mac Máel Coluim. Recent

---

55 http://pastscape.english-heritage.org.uk

56 Judith A. Green, *Henry I, King of England and Duke of Normandy* (Cambridge, 2006), 278 [hereafter: Green, *Henry I*].

57 *Two Cartularies of the Augustinian Priory of Brunton and the Cluniac Priory of Montacute in the County of Somerset* (Somerset, 1894), 119–22.

research has demonstrated the importance of the Mearns in the pre-900 Pictish period. For one, the Mearns seems to have been the home territory of one of the most powerful kings of Pictland, Onuist son of Wrguist (728–761) and it may have maintained some kind of special relationship with royal authority after his demise. In addition, the name Mearns in Gaelic is *An Mhaoirne* 'the stewartry', but this name is British rather than Gaelic in origin, and of course it denotes an area under the authority of a maer or steward.[58]

So during the period 1094–97 the mormaer Maol Peadair controlled an area known as 'the stewartry' yet his was the only pre-1100 mormaerdom not to reappear in the twelfth century reinvented as an earldom (or as any other large block of secular lands or non-Crown authority). This surely implies that something catastrophic occurred to what was probably the top layer of secular authority below the Crown in the Mearns post-1094. If, for the sake of argument, Maol Peadair had been the only surviving member of his kindred and died childless, we might assume that the Crown would have appointed someone new to this important position. Yet, it very much looks as though the mormaership of the Mearns was dismantled post-1094, though the Mearns survived as a judicial province.[59] Nothing further is ever heard either about the office of mormaer in the Mearns or the family of Maol Peadair. One final point to make is this: there is a rather delicious irony in the fact that Maol Peadair's (servant of [St] Peter) two co-conspirators in the plot to murder King Donnchad mac Máel Coluim were each separately jailed in religious establishments dedicated to St Peter.

58 Fraser, *Caledonia to Pictland*, 290, 357–58.
59 Barrow, *Kingdom of the Scots*, 62.

CHAPTER SIX

The Beginnings of a New Order, 1097–1124?

King Edgar mac Máel Coluim, 1097–8 January 1107

As far as can be ascertained, King Edgar was not challenged for the kingship of Scotia by any of the men descended from King Máel Coluim mac Donnchada's first marriage to Ingibjorg. On the whole, Edgar seems to have left a positive impression in both English and Scottish chronicles, even though they provide remarkably little detailed information about his reign.[1] This absence of information may, however, conceal some ugly truths.

But the accession of King Edgar mac Máel Coluim is crucially important for another reason in the history of Scottish kingship. He was the first of three brothers to hold the kingship in the first straight line royal succession since Cinaed mac Ailpín became king of the Picts in the 840s. This domination of the kingship by one sub-branch of the royal kindred is an extraordinary development in the history of Scottish kingship. It is made even more unusual by the fact that there were other candidates that should also have been considered for inauguration. However, Kings Edgar mac Máel Coluim, Alexander mac Máel Coluim, and David mac Máel Coluim shared three things in common: they were the sons of Queen Margaret, they shared a brother-in-law in King Henry I of England, and they each possessed a claim to the kingship of England.

Coping with Norwegian aggression

It appears as though late-1097 to 1099 could have been a very difficult period for King Edgar mac Máel Coluim. A possible plot against him, led by his uncle Domnall bán mac Donnchada when Edgar left Scotia to attend upon King William II Rufus between Easter and May 1099, has already been discussed. The timing of this plot is interesting for another

---

1 *SAEC*, 128; *Chron. Bower* (Watt), iii, 88–89.

reason: 1097–99 was also a period when the actions of Magnus Barelegs, king of Norway, destabilised the entire western seaboard of Britain.

As we have already seen, this reassertion of Norwegian power in the west began in late-1097 when King Magnus Barelegs sent a man called Ingimundr to assume kingship in the Western Isles. The Hebrideans rose against Ingimundr and killed him and as a result King Magnus personally led an army into the western islands and the Irish Sea zone where he chose the Isle of Man as his new base of operations. His intention seems to have been the firm establishment of Norwegian overlordship over the Western Isles and perhaps even parts of mainland Britain.[2]

Norwegian accounts of this expedition from both *Heimskringla* (Chronicle of the Kings of Norway) and *Fagrskinna* (fair parchment) provide details of King Magnus's steady progress southwards through the islands of the Hebrides to Islay and mainland Kintyre, receiving submissions and taking plunder as he went, before he and his forces reached the Isle of Man. Scottish sources are largely silent about the consequences of this expedition, so we are forced to rely upon the dramatic praise-poetry of the sagas to gauge the effects of this warfare upon the Hebrideans:

The branch-scorcher played greedily up into the sky, in Lewis;
There was far and wide an eager going into flight.
Flame spouted from the houses.
The active king ravaged Uist with fire.
The king made red the ray of battle.
The farmers lost life and wealth.

The diminisher of the battle-gosling's hunger caused Skye to be
    plundered:
The glad wolf reddened tooth in many a mortal wound, within Tiree.
The Scot's expeller went mightily; the people of Mull ran to
    exhaustion.
Greenland's king caused maids to weep, south in the islands.[3]

---

2 http://www.isle-of-man.com/manxnotebook/manxsoc/msvol22/p044.htm Accessed 9 January 2010.
3 Ibid., 106.

From there, Galloway, Ulster, mainland Wales and Anglesey were also raided and the Norman earl of Shrewsbury, Hugh de Montgomery, together with Robert lord of Rhuddlan, were killed in battle.[4] By any stretch of the imagination, Magnus's expedition during 1098 had been a huge success, but it is unlikely that, as king of Norway, he could realistically afford to spend much more time away from his kingdom. This may be why, in an attempt to consolidate his new gains, he entered into a treaty with King Edgar of Scotia.

According to the Norwegian evidence, it was King Edgar who first approached King Magnus Barelegs offering messages of reconciliation. It is this same body of evidence that describes the otherwise unsubstantiated proposal from Edgar to Magnus:

> Then messages of reconciliation came from the king of Scots, proposing that if he did not raid in his kingdom the king would give him as his share all the islands that were so far off Scotland that he could pass in a ship with a steering-oar attached to it between them and the mainland. Then King Magnus appointed his own men to govern them and laid a tribute on this domain, and when he turned back northwards he sailed towards the isthmus of Kintyre and had a small boat dragged over it, and he himself sat by the steering-oar on the afterdeck, and when the boat was hauled over to the sea on the northern side he laid claim to the whole on Kintyre ... which is a large piece of land.[5]

If true, these actions confirmed all of King Magnus's gains: permanent Norwegian possession of the Western Isles, and perhaps even parts of mainland Scotia, would effectively have become a reality until that situation was reversed by the Treaty of Perth in 1266. From 1098 there was a new power in western Britain, one that had seized control of parts of Scotia, one that had fought against and defeated some of William II Rufus's Norman lords in Wales, and one that had effectively checked any hope of Irish Gaelic expansion into the Western Isles. King Magnus Barelegs posed a danger to many different people and there is little doubt that the Norman kings of England would also have felt threatened by his presence, not the

---

4 Green, *Henry I*, 69.
5 Finlay, *Fagrskinna*, 247.

least as he was the grandson of Harald Harðráði who had attempted to seize the English throne in 1066.

In summer 1099, King Magnus Barelegs returned to Norway and remained there for three years. When he returned to the seas off the western coast of Britain in 1102 it seems that Ireland and Muirchertach uí Briain, king of Munster, were his chosen targets. Having taken Dublin, Magnus effectively forced Muirchertach to reach an accommodation via a marriage treaty between Magnus's son Sigurðr and Muirchertach's daughter Bláthmín. However, while on his return to Norway in spring 1103, Magnus raided Ulster and was killed. His death meant that his plans for the western seaboard of Scotia and Ireland were abandoned as Sigurðr repudiated Bláthmín and returned home to ensure a share of his father's Norwegian kingdom. Thereafter, King Magnus's western sea kingdom was gradually broken up into individual territories of competing and ambitious warlords, including one Sumarliði mac Gofraid.

In all of this upheaval no record survives of King Edgar mac Máel Coluim opposing King Magnus Barelegs militarily, and it should be questioned whether he ever possessed or commanded sufficient resources to challenge the Norwegian king. Though it is difficult not to sound like an apologist for King Edgar, the fact that the people of Scotia had inaugurated three different kings and been subject to four reigns between the death of King Máel Coluim mac Donnchada in 1093 and the inauguration of Edgar in 1097 cannot have helped 'national unity', if indeed there was such a concept in eleventh-century Scotia. What had in effect been a short but vicious civil war within the ruling kindred of Scotia must have had a debilitating effect, not just upon the fighting resources of the country, but also upon morale. This picture of depleted resources might also explain why there is also no record of King Edgar attempting to recover those parts of the western mainland and the Hebrides for Scotia after the death of Magnus in 1103.

But how accurate is this picture of Norwegian supremacy over Edgar in 1098? Though the evidence from both *Heimskringla* and *Fagrskinna* seems unequivocal, they are the only witnesses to the treaty of 1098 and, even more importantly, these texts were not contemporary to the events they purport to describe. In fact, both *Heimskringla* and *Fagrskinna* belong to a category of writings called *konungasögur* (king's sagas) which were composed to record Norwegian dynastic history, and the genre seems to have evolved out of twelfth-century Icelandic works referred to as *konunga ævi* (lives of kings).[6]

Morkinskinna (rotten parchment), written in Iceland c.1220, is reckoned to be the first of these king's sagas to tackle the reigns of the twelfth-century Norwegian kings in more depth. It is now known that both *Heimskringla* and *Fagrskinna* make extensive and frequent use of a version of *Morkinskinna* and must post-date it, though the actual textual relationships are complicated.[7] The most recent editor of *Fagrskinna* has argued that *Fagrskinna* was written in Norway, perhaps by an Icelander living and working there, a few years before *Heimskringla* was written. *Heimskringla*, on the other hand, was composed in Iceland, probably by Snorri Sturluson writing 1225 x 35. This dating would place the writing of *Fagrskinna* c.1220 x 35.[8] What is crucially important about both these datings, and the events of 1098 in the Hebrides that both texts purport to describe, is that these works were composed during the reign of the Norwegian king Håkon Håkonarson (1217–1263).

During his reign King Håkon Håkonarson came under sustained pressure from both King Alexander II (1214–1249) and King Alexander III (1249–1286) to relinquish control of the western Highlands and Islands to Scotland. Murray has clearly shown that after 1214 King Alexander II, building upon policies intiated by his father William I, began to expand Scottish royal authority in the region of the Firth of Clyde which was key to controlling Argyll and the southern Hebrides. This was followed by expeditions in 1221 (aborted because of bad weather) and 1222 to subdue Kintyre, where the local Mac Raonaill lords were expelled and a new royal castle was built at Tarbert. These actions seem to have convinced the southern Hebridean Mac Dubhgaill lords to consider switching allegiance from Norway to Scotland. A Norwegian fleet under the command of Uspak Håkon was dispatched to Scotland in 1230 and attacked Bute but achieved little else. Uspak was killed.[9]

Encouraged by this success and the failure of the Mac Dubhgaills to support Uspak in 1230, King Alexander II then turned to the Steward and

---

6 Ibid., 2–3.
7 Ibid., 11–12.
8 Ibid., 17.
9 Noel Murray, 'Swerving from the Path of Justice: Alexander II's Relations with Argyll and the Western Isles, 1214–49', in R. D. Oram (ed.), *The Reign of Alexander II, 1214–49* (Leiden, 2005), 285–305, at 285–93.

Comyn families for help in extending Scottish royal authority in the west, using them to conquer south-west Argyll. These actions were so successful that by 1241 the Stewards had brought the Cowal peninsula under firm Scottish control and further extended Scottish overlordship into mid-Argyll. Further north, the territories of Comyn lords of Badenoch and Lochaber marched alongside the Mac Dubhgaill lordship of Argyll and the Mac Raonaill lordship of Garmoran. Next, King Alexander II made offers to King Håkon Håkonarson in 1244 and 1248 to purchase the Isles from Norway. Both overtures were refused and Alexander II died at Kerrera on 8 July 1249 on his final expedition westwards.[10]

King Alexander III tried to build upon his father's policies and initiated diplomatic contact with Norway by sending an envoy to Bergen. When this failed, the Scots, led by the earl of Ross, raided Skye in 1262. King Håkon Håkonarson interpreted this action as Scottish aggression and, in 1263, assembled a naval expedition to attack the Scots. The outcomes of this expedition, the skirmish at Largs, the death of King Håkon in the Northern Isles, and the eventual signing of the Treaty of Perth in 1266 whereby Norway sold the Western Isles and Man to the Scots for 4,000 merks are well known.[11]

It is against this backdrop of sustained Scottish military and diplomatic efforts to regain control of Argyll and the Western Isles from Norway between 1214 and 1263 that the writings in *Morkinskinna, Heimskringla*, and *Fagrskinna* should be viewed. Adding the fact that the supposed earlier treaty is not referred to in the text of the Treaty of Perth, it is entirely possible that the claims made about King Edgar mac Máel Coluim having ceded a part of Argyll and the Hebrides to King Magnus Barelegs by international treaty in 1098 were a blatantly fraudulent thirteenth-century Norwegian attempt to establish formal rights to those same lands, and to any compensation should they later abandon their alleged rights to those lands to the Scots.

The Church

Writing in 1975, A. A. M. Duncan labelled the history of the Church during the reign of King Edgar mac Máel Coluim 'unremarkable'. As Duncan

---

10 Ibid., 294–305.
11 Duncan, *Kingdom*, 577–82.

stated, the see of St Andrews was not filled after the death of Bishop Fothad *ardespoc Alban* (chief bishop of Alba) in 1093,[12] the king founded no religious houses, and his great 1095 endowment to Durham and the cult of St Cuthbert of the shires of Coldingham and Berwick was diminished when he later clawed back Berwickshire. Despite this latter act, as far as Duncan was concerned, King Edgar was only concerned with the Church of Lothian and St Cuthbert and he cared little for Scotia.[13]

To a certain extent Duncan's comments are correct. After all, the reign of King Edgar mac Máel Coluim coincided with a spiritual revival throughout western Christendom, yet other than making some small grants to existing institutions, the king appears to have done very little to encourage Christianity in Scotia north of the Forth during his lifetime.[14] Durham, on the other hand, was another matter altogether and it seems clear that King Edgar maintained royal Scottish interest in the cult of Cuthbert in a series of grants that were later confirmed by King David I.[15]

A saintly sister and the return of the House of Wessex to power in England

If events to the west of Scotland had diminished Edgar's kingship of Scotia, what happened in England following the sudden murder of King William II Rufus on 2 August 1100 while hunting in the New Forest provided a new opportunity. Rufus's death was quickly followed by the accession of King Henry I and his subsequent quick marriage to Edgar's sister, Princess Edith (Matilda). This must have seemed like a huge reversal in fortune for the king of Scotia once Henry had secured his position as king.

Princess Edith is not a prominent figure in the sources prior to her marriage, possibly a result of her upbringing. Born in 1080, Edith was the eldest daughter of King Máel Coluim mac Donnchada and Queen Margaret and, like many of her siblings, she was given an Anglo-Saxon name. She was probably named after Edith, the wife of King Edward the Confessor (reigned 1042–1066) though St Edith, daughter of King Edgar (d. 975) and his concubine Wulfthryth, is another option. Edith's recent

---

12 *Ann. Ulster*, 1093.2. When this title appears in an Irish Gaelic context, Etchingham translates *ardescop* as 'archbishop' [Etchingham, *Church Organisation in Ireland*, 180–83.

13 Duncan, *Kingdom*, 127.

14 Dunfermline Registrum, no. 1.

15 Barrow, *Chrs. David I*, nos 9, 10 and 11.

biographer has suggested that the young princess accompanied her maternal aunt Christine when she travelled south into England to become a Benedictine nun at Romsey Abbey in 1086. This was an entirely appropriate choice for her parents to make as Romsey was one of the wealthiest pre-1066 nunneries in England and had been frequently patronised by Queen Margaret's Anglo-Saxon forebears.[16]

Life at Romsey does seem to have been a particularly happy time for Edith and sometime before 1093 she moved to the nearby (also Benedictine) Wilton Abbey. This would again have been an appropriate choice for the young princess, as by that time Wilton was the major cult centre of St Edith, patron saint of the abbey, and the *Vita Edithe* (Life of St Edith) had been written *c.*1080. In addition, in the 1090s, Wilton was still a renowned centre for female learning and literary culture.

Edith was removed from Wilton Abbey by her father and taken back to Scotland in the summer of 1093. The chain of events that led up to this are still unclear but seem to have involved one (or possibly two) marriage offers, a visit by King William II Rufus to Wilton where he saw Edith wearing a nun's veil and promptly left, and a visit by King Máel Coluim mac Donnchada to England where King William II Rufus refused to see him.[17] The outcome of these intrigues was that Edith ended up back in Scotland. Then she was almost immediately deprived of her parents in separate but linked incidents in the autumn of that year. Thereafter Edith's whereabouts become mysterious until she reappears in sources again in 1100 upon her marriage to King Henry I, by which time she had changed her name to Matilda. The reasons for this change are still unknown.[18]

Commentators argue that there were a number of reasons for the two to get married. According to a near-contemporary source, William of Malmesbury, they had known each other for some time. Henry was in love and he did not want a rich dowry. All were well aware that if they had children, those offspring would unite the houses of the current and past kings of England.[19] Of course, King Henry I was not entirely secure in his kingdom and, as a younger son, first had to negotiate a settlement with his brother Duke Robert of Normandy over the English throne. The Treaty of Alton, agreed in 1101, sorted these matters. King Henry I surrendered

16 Lois L. Huneycutt, *Matilda of Scotland* (Woodbridge, 2003), 17.
17 Ibid., 22–24.
18 Ibid., 26.
19 Mynors and Thomson, *Gesta Regum Anglorum*, i, 715.

almost all of his land in Normandy to Duke Robert and promised to pay him a pension that may have amounted to as much as £3,000 per annum. In return, Duke Robert formally accepted Henry as king of England. Each man agreed to forgive those who had supported the opposite side and it was also agreed that King Henry and Duke Robert were to be each other's heir.[20]

Unfortunately, the surviving sources are quiet about King Edgar's views on the seizure of the English throne by Henry and his subsequent marriage to Edith. If these events brought him pleasure, this must have been tempered by a stark reality. Edgar had only gained support from King William II Rufus after a form of overlordship had been established between the two men for the lands of Lothian in the charter of 29 August 1095 and an accompanying investiture ceremony that may have involved William II Rufus crowning Edgar. In addition, on 29 May 1099, King Edgar had carried the sword of state for King William II Rufus at Westminster, establishing his position as a great *fideles* for Lothian.[21] As far as we know, however, King Edgar was never again called upon to perform English service during the remainder of his lifetime and in this we may see the mitigating influence of Queen Edith.

For his part, like King Edward the Confessor, King Henry I certainly wore an imperial crown and he was not averse to reminding Queen Edith's other brothers of the *realpolitik* in medieval Britain. But, whereas he made two military expeditions in 1114 and 1121 into Wales, there is no sign that King Henry I ever contemplated extending the boundaries of his overlordship in Britain northwards into Scotia proper. King Henry I was, nevertheless, concerned with the security of the porous northern frontier between Scotia and England and English control of the Cumbrian region was tightened. His brother King William II Rufus had previously driven out Dolfin, the local ruler there, in 1092 and built a castle at Carlisle.[22] During King Henry's reign, and after the death of Ivo Taillebois, Carlisle was granted to Ranulf Meschin, one of the king's most loyal supporters. As lord, Green has demonstrated that Meschin was responsible for the establishment of a number of new lordships in the area at Burgh by Sands, Kirklinton, and Liddel, some of which were created for native families rather than for Normans. These lordships together formed the core of a new military

---

20 Green, *Henry I*, 64–65.
21 Duncan, *Kingship*, 58.
22 Green, *Henry I*, 34.

organisation in Cumberland and Westmoreland that strengthed King Henry's control over both the lands bordering Scotia and along the western sea-flank of Cumberland that bordered upon the Irish Sea zone.[23]

Sources are silent on whether King Edgar viewed these developments with suspicion or equanimity though, as far as we know, there were no similar developments on the Scottish side of the frontier zone. If we knew more about Edgar's character, it would be easier to predict how he might have responded to these developments, but given the paucity of sources for his reign it is difficult to arrive at any real measure of the man. Perhaps the only glimpse into his personal life comes from a brief entry in the Irish *Annals of Innisfallen* under the year-date 1105:

> *Isin bliadain sin tucad in camall, quod est animal mírae magnitudinis,*
> *o ríg Alban do Muircertach U Briain.*

> In the above year [1105] a camel, an animal of remarkable size, was brought from the king of Alba to Muirchertach Ua Briain.[24]

This is the earliest reference we have to the presence of exotic animals in Scotia, but the gift of unusual specimens to kings or between royal families was common in medieval Europe. King Edgar's brother-in-law King Henry I, for example, kept a royal menagerie at Woodstock, including lions, lynxes, camels and a porcupine, which was only later moved to the Tower of London.[25] This makes it possible that King Edgar had purchased this animal from King Henry I for onward shipping to Ireland, though there is no good reason to reject the notion that King Edgar, like later kings of Scots, could have possessed his own menagerie of exotic animals.

An heir and the spares

Like his elder brothers Edward, Edmund, and Ethelred, Edgar never married and there is no sign in the sources of any illegitimate offspring. This left his two youger brothers, Alexander and David, together with any

23 Judith Green, 'King Henry I and Northern England', *Transactions of the Royal Historical Society*, 17, 2007, 35–55.

24 S. Mac Airt (ed.), *The Annals of Inisfallen (MS. Rawlinson B. 503)* (Dublin, 1988), 1105.7.

25 Green, *Henry I*, 294; H. O'Regan, A. Turner, and R. Sabin, 'Medieval Big Cat Remains from the Royal Menagerie at the Tower of London', *International Journal of Osteoarchaeology*, 16, 2006, 385–94.

descendants of King Máel Coluim mac Donnchada's first marriage to Ingibjorg and the descendants of King Lulach mac Gilla Comgáin as potential contestants for inauguration. The former group included William fitz Duncan, son of King Donnchadh mac Máel Coluim, who according to primogeniture represented the senior branch of the royal kindred.

Next to nothing is known about the claimants descended from Queen Ingibjorg during this period, what their aims and aspirations were, whether they ever challenged for the right to be inaugurated and, perhaps even more importantly, whether anyone in Scotia actually supported their claims. Fortunately, a little more is known about Alexander and David. It appears that Alexander remained in Scotia during Edgar's reign and may even have been granted an earldom since one English source refers to him as *comes* in 1104 when he travelled south to witness the translation of St Cuthbert.[26] If this source contains a correct reflection of political circumstances, it is the earliest surviving reference to a *comes* in Scotia.

Deciding what was meant by this title is another matter altogether. The Latin word *comes* was the equivalent given to the Anglo-Saxon word *eorl*, and described those who formed an aristocratic elite of seven earls in England before 1135. Was, then, the English source that described Alexander mac Máel Coluim merely ascribing him a title to which it was felt he was due as a direct descendant of Anglo-Saxon royalty or had Alexander been granted this title by his brother, so formally joining the aristocratic elite of Britain? In England, the *comes* was entitled to a third of the profits of the county court and the royal burghs in each county under his jurisdiction.[27] The same kind of function was also the preserve of the *vice-comes* (sheriff), a royal official who undertook a range of judicial and financial duties on behalf of the Crown.

David, on the other hand, seems to have spent less time in Scotia and this is perhaps understandable if the account of his upbringing in the writings of Orderic Vitalis is correct. There, it is written that David was brought up at the court of King Henry I and was knighted by the king.[28] It is certainly known that he was in England in 1108, but he then disappears from the historical record for five years. It is often assumed that he was in Scotia during this period, but Duncan has suggested that he could have

26 Duncan, *Kingship*, 59.
27 Robert Bartlett, *England under the Norman and Angevin Kings, 1075–1225* (Padstow, 2000), 208–9.
28 Chibnall, *Orderic Vitalis*, 274–75.

been in France, visiting the monks of Tiron and exercising lordship on the Cotentin peninsula.[29]

Whatever the case, it is clear that although King Edgar had designated Alexander as his heir, their youngest brother David was provided with an appanage that seems to have been equal in extent to the older kingdom of Strathclyde, last heard of in the 1070s. This appenage included all the lands between the Lennox and the Solway, including Teviotdale, and David was later sometimes referred to as *princeps et dux, Cumbrensis regionis princeps* (prince and leader of the Cumbrian region/kingdom), or *princeps Cumbrensis* (prince of the Cumbrians). This cannot have been a satisfactory arrangement, at least for King Alexander, and it has been argued that King Henry I had to lead an expedition to Scotland soon after his return from France in July 1113 to force King Alexander mac Máel Coluim to hand over David's inheritance. At that time Tweeddale and Berwickshire also passed into David's control. This was a personal triumph for David, but a surviving fragment of poetry, 'A Verse on David Son of Mael Coluim', suggests that resentment towards Earl David's greed for forcing this issue was more widespread and the division of Scotia was disliked by some amongst the Gaelic elite of southern Scotland:

It's bad what Mael Coluim's son has done,
dividing us from Alexander;
he causes, like each king's son before,
the plunder of stable Alba.[30]

Throughout all of this manoeuvring the descendants of Ingibjorg are conspicuous by their silent absence. This has led to speculation that they were too young to effectively press a claim, but, at the very least, their perfectly legitimate claims to be considered for inauguration might reasonably have been expected to have warranted some kind of compensation from Edgar in return for being sidelined from the succession, much the same as Prince David.

Trying to decide why the descendants of Ingibjorg were not (as far as we are aware) considered as suitable candidates for inauguration in 1097, 1107, and 1124 is very difficult. It might help if we knew what the aims and

29 Duncan, *Kingship*, 63.
30 T. O. Clancy (ed.), *The Triumph Tree* (Edinburgh, 1998), 184.

aspirations of the senior kindreds and mormáir of Scotia were in terms of foreign policy. For example, the claims of the children of King Máel Coluim mac Donnchada and Margaret might have been favoured over Ingibjorg's descendants just because the former possessed a clear descent from the House of Wessex and Edward the Confessor. This must have been a tremendously important factor to take into account when choosing a new king of Scotia, yet the sources are silent on this matter.

Other factors that should also be taken into account were the foreign policy aims of King Henry I, and it might be asked whether he consciously favoured the descendants of Margaret over the descendants of Ingibjorg. Judging by the fact that *c*.1125 the English chronicler William of Malmesbury labelled King Donnchadh mac Máel Coluim as *nothus* (bastard), there may well have been English-driven propaganda created to ensure and advance the claims of the royal Scotian segment descended from Queen Margaret.[31]

King Alexander mac Máel Coluim, 1107–1124

King Edgar mac Máel Coluim died at Edinburgh on 8 January 1107. According to one source, the recognition of Alexander as heir and his succession, like those of his two brothers Donnchad and Edgar, had been previously approved by King Henry I. It is, however, difficult to ascertain exactly what the *Anglo-Saxon Chronicle* meant by this phrase, as other English chroniclers are silent on the matter. One answer may be found in the succession itself. Alexander inherited only Scotia north of the Forth, since his younger brother David had been provided for with his own appanage in Edgar's settlement. Though there is no record of the negotiations surrounding it, this deal must have been approved by King Henry I since it fundamentally affected the security of his northern frontier region.

Alexander also clearly inherited pressing ecclesiastic concerns in his kingdom. The evidence indicates that soon after he was inaugurated in 1107 he asked King Henry I's permission for Prior Turgot of Durham to be elevated to the see of St Andrews.[32] This request was granted, though Turgot's consecration was delayed by the continuing controversy between Canterbury and York over metropolitan supremacy. Essentially, Anselm,

---

31 Mynors and Thomson, *Gesta Regum Anglorum*, i, 725.
32 *SAEC*, 129.

the archbishop of Canterbury, wanted the new archbishop of York to profess obedience to him and, until he did so, Archbishop Anselm actively prevented any other bishops from consecrating Turgot. This situation was only resolved when Anslem died in April 1109, after which King Alexander received his new bishop of St Andrews.[33]

Brothers in arms?

As the youngest of six sons of King Máel Coluim mac Donnchada's second marriage to Queen Margaret, it is perhaps unlikely that David mac Máel Coluim would have begun his adult life with any great expectations that he might one day become king of Scots. This may be why he chose service at the court of King Henry I, calculating that it was an obvious route by which an ambitious younger son might gain social and political advancement. He was right because King Henry I showed him great favour.

After his return from France in the summer of 1113, King Henry I seems to have forced King Alexander mac Máel Coluim to hand over the appanage that David had been previously granted by King Edgar mac Máel Coluim. Following this, sometime around Christmas Day 1113, King Henry gave his permission for the marriage between David and Matilda de Senlis, widow of Simon de Senlis. This was an extraordinary concession. Not only was Matilda one of the richest heiresses in England, the union also meant that David became earl of Northampton in right of his wife. Matilda de Senlis also carried a claim to the earldom of Northumberland. Until the children of Matilda and her first husband Simon de Senlis came of age, David effectively controlled their vast inheritance in England.[34] When these lands are added to the area of his appanage, with two strokes David mac Máel Coluim had become one of the most powerful men in north Britain. What King Alexander mac Máel Coluim personally thought about these two developments has either been lost or was never recorded, which is a great shame.

It is also greatly unfortunate that the reactions of that segment of the royal family descended from King Máel Coluim mac Donnchada's first marriage to Ingibjorg to these events are unknown. For example, might they have viewed their inability to attract the patronage of a great man,

33 Duncan, *Kingship*, 84.
34 Green, *Henry I*, 128–29.

thereby gaining lands and power, as a terminal disadvantage to their undoubted claims to be considered for inauguration? If it were even known where they were physically located and which titles (if any) they held during this period, it would be easier to determine which political bonds they were trying to forge. Underpinning all of this uncertainty was the question about who would eventually succeed King Alexander mac Máel Coluim.

Historians are divided on this question. For some, David mac Máel Coluim was already the heir-presumptive to the throne of Scotia by 1113.[35] Others, like Duncan, have argued that David mac Máel Coluim cannot have been recognised as heir until late in Alexander mac Máel Coluim's reign, at least not until after the death of Queen Sibylla on 12 July 1122.[36] To support this notion Duncan advanced two key statements. The first of these was testimony from Version B of the foundation legend of St Andrews, in which it was stated that Earl David was the designated heir and successor to King Alexander mac Máel Coluim. The second came from the writings of Orderic Vitalis and essentially stated the same fact: Alexander had bequeathed his kingdom to David.[37]

The fact that both Scottish and English sources could independently agree that David was the approved successor to King Alexander mac Máel Coluim is indeed remarkable. However, such testimony cannot be wholly accepted without qualification. For example, Prior Robert, the first head of the Augustinian priory of St Andrews, wrote version B of the foundation legend of St Andrews before 1153.[38] Importantly, this priory was a royal foundation of King David I's and, perhaps unsurprisingly, King David had intervened in a dispute between the priory and the bishop of St Andrews and found in favour of the priory. Given these circumstances, one might ask how likely it would have been for the prior to criticise the founder of his priory. It should also never be forgotten that this commentator was writing with the benefit of hindsight and perhaps trying to explain the hijacking of the kingship of Scotia by a single branch of the royal dynasty.

35 Ibid., 129.
36 Duncan, *Kingship*, 65.
37 Ibid.
38 Simon Taylor, 'The Coming of the Augustinians to St Andrews and Version B of the St Andrews Foundation Legend', in Simon Taylor (ed.), *King, Clerics and Chronicles in Scotland, 500–1297* (Bodmin, 2000), 115–23.

Quite simply, version B of the St Andrews foundation legend could contain pro-Crown propaganda designed to add legitimacy to and explain King David mac Máel Coluim's inauguration back in 1124.

As there is no surviving contemporary description of the processes that occurred between Alexander's death and David's inauguration, it might be better to view the events leading up to the latter's eventual inauguration as 'unclear' and accept that David may not actually have been the first choice of some people living in Scotia. After all, King Alexander mac Máel Coluim had an adult son, Máel Coluim mac Alexandair. No source gives any indication about the identity of Máel Coluim mac Alexandair's mother or whether King Alexander had been married before his marriage to Sibylla. The possibility that a previous wife was repudiated in favour of a royal princess cannot be discounted given Alexander's immediate family history.

The sins of the father

Although the inauguration of King David mac Máel Coluim in 1124 is almost universally presented as a foregone conclusion, there is a strong hint that it was not so. There actually were a number of different candidates who could have been inaugurated following the death of King Alexander mac Máel Coluim, including the late king's own adult son, Máel Coluim mac Alexandair.[39] Another associated problem is that the exact time period between Alexander's death and David's inauguration is not known. Barrow has suggested that it was immediate, but this is perhaps wishful thinking.[40]

Under the year-date 1124 Orderic Vitalis stated:

Anno ab incarnatione Domine MCXXV Alexander rex Scottorum uita exuit, et Dauid frater eius regni gubernacula suscepit. Melcofus autem nothus Alexandri filius regnum patruo preripere affectauit, eique duo bella satis acerrima instaurauit; sed Dauid qui sensu et potentia diuitiisque sullimior erat illium cum suis superauit.

39 *Chron. Holyrood*, 124–25; Ross, 'Prisoner of Roxburgh', 269–82. My thanks to the publisher of this book, Clann Tuirc, for permission to reproduce parts of the original article.

40 Barrow, *Chrs. David I*, 62. See comments by Richard Oram, *David I, the King Who Made Scotland* (Stroud, 2004), 231, fn. 4 [hereafter: Oram, *David I*].

In the year of our Lord 1125 [*recte* 1124] Alexander, king of Scotland, died, and his brother David took up the government of the kingdom. Malcolm, a bastard son of Alexander, made a bid for his father's kingdom, and instigated two bitter wars against him; but David, being wiser, more powerful and wealthier, defeated him and his supporters.[41]

This passage clearly describes a man known as Máel Coluim mac Alexandair and seems to differentiate between Máel Coluim pushing his right as the son of a king to be inaugurated in 1124 and the two wars that he later initiated against King David. Orderic Vitalis refers to a man by the same name again in 1130:

> *Anno ab incarnatione Domine MCXXX dum Dauid rex in curia Henrici regis caute iudicium indagaret, et de reatu perfidiae quam Goisfredus de Clintonia ut dicunt contra regem agitauerat diligenter discuteret; Aragois comes Morafiae cum Melcolfo et quinque milibus armatorum Scotiam intrauit, totamque regionem sibi subigere studuit. Porro Eduardus Siwardi filius qui sub Eduardo rege tribunus Merciorum fuit, princeps militiae et consobrinus Dauid regis exercitum aggregauit; et hostili repente exercitui obuiauit. Tandem facta congressione Aragois consulem occidit; eiusque turmas prostrauit, cepit atque fugauit. Deinde cum cohortibus suis iam triumpho elatis fugientes auide insecutus est; et Morafiam defensore dominoque uacantem ingressus est, totumque regionis spaciosae ductatem Deo auxiliante nactus est. Sic Dauid aucta potestate super antecessores suos exaltus est; studioque eius religionis et eruditis personis regio Scottorum decorata est. En causa Scottorum qui ab antiquis temporibus adheserunt catholicae fidei, et christianae gratanter seruierunt simplicitati; inceptam epanalempsim aliquantulum protelaui, sed nune ad propositum nitor opus de nostris regredi.*

In the year of our Lord 1130, while King David was carefully investigating a case in the court of King Henry, and meticulously examining a charge of treason which Geoffrey of Clinton was said to have committed against the king, Angus earl of Moray and Malcolm entered Scotland with five thousand armed men, attempting to gain

---

41 Chibnall, *Orderic Vitalis*, iv, 276.

control of the kingdom. Then Edward, son of Siward who had been a thane of Mercia in King Edward's time, himself a constable and a kinsman of King David, mustered the army and fell without warning on the enemy forces. In the course of the conflict he killed the earl of Moray and shattered his troops, killing some and putting the rest to flight. He and his forces, triumphant at their victory, hotly pursued the fugitives into the territory of Moray which no longer had a lord and defender, and with God's aid conquered the whole of that extensive duchy. In this way David grew more powerful than his predecessors, and the kingdom of Scotland became famous for its religious zeal and learning. This is why I have somewhat prolonged this digression on the Scots, who have adhered to the Catholic faith from ancient times, and have had great regard for the Christian religion. Now however I propose to return to my intended work on our own people.[42]

Robert de Torigni, abbot of Mont Saint-Michel between 1154 and 1186, also gave a version of the events of 1130 in his continuation to the *World Chronicle*:

Eodem anno Aragois, comes Morafiae, cum Melcolmo notho filio Alexandri fratris regis David, qui ante eum regnaverat, et cum quinque milibus armatorum, Scotiam intravit, totamque regionem sibi subjicere voluit. David rex tunc curiae regis Anglorum intererat; sed Edwardus, consobrinus ejus et princeps militiae, cum exercitu illis obviavit, et Aragois consulem occidit, ejusque turmas prostravit, cepit, atque fugavit. Deinde Morafiam defensore dominoque vacantem ingressus est, totiusque regionis spatiosae ducatus, Deo auxiliante, per Edwardum extunc David regi religioso subditus est.

In the same year, Angus, earl of Moray, with Malcolm, illegitimate son of Alexander, who was brother of King David and had reigned before him, and with five thousand armed men entered Scotland, and wished to reduce the whole region to himself. At that time David was present in the court of the king of the English; but Edward, his kinsman and leader of his knighthood, went against them with an

---

42 Ibid., 276–78.

army and slew Angus, and overthrew, captured and routed his troops. Then he entered Moray, which lacked a defender and a lord; and control of the whole spacious region was, with God's help, through Edward made subject thenceforth to the religious King David.[43]

Until recently it has been common to identify this Máel Coluim, who was politically active between 1124 and 1134, as Malcolm MacHeth. However, this identification, as we have seen, is not supported by the primary source evidence. Máel Coluim MacHeth was an earl of Ross who died in 1168 and annalists clearly included his patronymic to distinguish him from the earlier Máel Coluim mac Alexandair.[44]

There might, however, be a further problem with the identification of the Máel Coluim of 1124 and 1130 with Máel Coluim mac Alexandair. Orderic Vitalis also stated:

Vltor itaque et successor fratris aliquot annis Alexander regnauit, et filiam Henrici regis Anglorum ex concubina uxorem duxit, moriensque sine liberis Dauid fratri suo regnum dimisit.

Alexander reigned for some years, the successor and avenger of his brother; he married a natural daughter of King Henry of England and, dying without children, left the kingdom to his brother David.[45]

This second passage by Orderic Vitalis is fairly unequivocal in stating that King Alexander mac Máel Coluim did not have any children. This is something of a problem because Orderic Vitalis has contradicted himself. A solution to this contradiction may lie in the suggestion that Vitalis had miscopied his information about King Alexander's lack of progeny from an earlier work by William of Malmesbury (*c*.1095–1143). William stated that:

Edgaro fatali sorte occumbente, Alexandrum successorem Henricus affinitate detinuit, data ei in coniugium filia notha, de qua ille uiua nec sobolem, quod scian, tulit.

---

43 R. Howlett, *Chronicles of the Reigns of Stephen, Henry II, and Richard I*, 4 vols (London, 1884–89), iv, 118 [hereafter: Howlett, *Chronicles of the Reigns*].
44 Duncan, *Kingship*, 71–72.
45 Chibnall, *Orderic Vitalis*, iv, 274–75.

Edgar in his turn having died, Henry bound his successor Alexander by ties of relationship, giving him his own illegitimate daughter in marriage, during her lifetime, however, he had no children by her.[46]

This last statement is a far cry from the assertion that King Alexander mac Máel Coluim had no children. However, even if Orderic Vitalis did not borrow his information from William of Malmesbury, it is still possible that his passage has been slightly mistranslated by previous historians. The key lies in the use of the noun *liberi* ('children'). Although *liberi* has been correctly translated by the most recent editor of Vitalis, it also carries a strong connotation of legitimacy. Consequently, Orderic Vitalis may well have been referring to King Alexander's lack of legitimate children with Queen Sybilla when he said that the king died *sine liberis* (without children).

So, the contemporary evidence strongly indicates that the Máel Coluim of 1124 and 1130 was a son of King Alexander mac Máel Coluim. This perception is surely strengthened by the timing of Máel Coluim's bid to be inaugurated in 1124 after his father had died. It is thus possible that David I's accession to the kingship of Scotia in that year was challenged by another member of the royal kindred, his nephew Máel Coluim mac Alexandair. In order to challenge for the kingship of Scotia, Máel Coluim presumably possessed the necessary resources and support to mount his own bid for inauguration. Máel Coluim was at large to challenge the king again in 1130, alongside Oengus of Moray.

It also seems fairly clear that Máel Coluim mac Alexandair was not captured in the aftermath of the battle of Stracathro in 1130. In the entry for 1134, the *Chronicle of Melrose* states: *Melcolmus capitur et in arcta ponitur in turre rokesburg custodia* (Malcolm was taken, and placed in close custody in the keep of Roxburgh).[47] This is a frustratingly brief statement. Fortunately, Ailred of Rievaulx in his work *Relatio de Standardo*, probably written between 1155 and 1157, provided more detail:

> *Recole præterito anno cum adversus Malcolmum, paterni odii et persecu-*
> *tionis hæredem, Anglorum auxilium flagitares, quam læti, quam alaxres,*
> *quam ad auxilium prompti, quam proni ad periculum Walterus Espec*
> *aliique quamplures Anglorum proceres tibi apud Carleolum occurrerint,*

---

46 Mynors and Thomson, *Gesta Regum Anglorum*, i, 725–27.
47 *Chron. Melrose*, 33.

quot paraverint naves, quæ arma intulerint, qua juventute munierint, quomodo omnes tuos terruerint hostes, donec ipsum Malcolmum proditum caperent, captum vincirent, vinctum traderent. Ita terror noster ipsius quidem membra, sed magis Scottorum animos, vinxit, omnique spe præficiendi frustrata, audaciam abstulit rebellandi.

Remember when in a previous year you asked for the help of the English against Malcolm, the heir of his father's hatred and persecution, how joyful, how eager, how willing to help, how ready for danger Walter Espec and many other English nobles hastened to meet you at Carlisle, how many ships they prepared, how they waged war, how they built defences, how they terrified all your enemies until they captured Malcolm himself betrayed; captured, they bound him; bound, they delivered him. Thus the fear of us bound his limbs, but bound even more the courage of the Scots, and having quenched all hope of success, removed the audacity to rebel.[48]

Even though this passage belongs to a dramatic speech allegedly made by Robert de Brus before the Battle of the Standard in 1138, it is possible that the sheer scale of the military expedition outlined in the passage above against Máel Coluim mac Alexandair is accurate. There are hints in another source that the campaign of 1130 and the Battle of Stracathro were not as decisive a victory for David I as is sometimes imagined. The *Annals of Ulster*, for example, recorded that 1,000 men of Alba fell in a counter-attack after the battle.[49] It is extremely difficult to reconcile this information with the statement by Orderic Vitalis that the victorious Edward son of Siward rushed into Moray immediately after the battle and took it for King David.[50]

If the *Annals of Ulster* are correct, it would seem that Máel Coluim mac Alexandair still possessed considerable resources and support from somewhere either within, or close to, Scotia in order to press the fight against his uncle for four years after the Battle of Stracathro. Interestingly, according to both the skeleton itinerary of David I and his surviving charters, there is no indication of the king travelling north of the Forth–Clyde line, or even being in Scotland, between 1130 and 1134.[51] Accordingly, it is possible that

48 Howlett, *Chronicles of the Reigns*, iii, 193.
49 *Ann. Ulster*, 1030.4.
50 Chibnall, *Orderic Vitalis*, iv, 276–78.
51 Barrow, *Chrs. David I*, 33–38.

the Battle of Stracathro in 1130 was not a decisive victory for King David I and that it took a further four years, together with a second major military campaign, at least part of which was conducted in the western sea, for Máel Coluim mac Alexandair to be betrayed and captured by his own supporters before they handed him over to King David's forces.

It is also interesting that Walter Espec is specifically named in this account, particularly since Ailred of Rievaulx knew both men.[52] Espec was a man who was a loyal English royal servant who had been favoured by King Henry I and received grants of lands in Wark (Northumberland) and Helmsley (Yorkshire) in return for service.[53] As such, he and David, the latter acting as *princeps Cumbrensis* (prince of the Cumbrians), must surely have cooperated in running the area now comprising the north of England and southern Scotland before 1124. Accordingly, Espec's presence in David's expedition against Máel Coluim mac Alexandair might suggest official English royal aid to help King David I secure Scotia in the 1130s, particularly as Ailred also specifically states that King David had to ask for help in defeating his nephew. The image of the powerful and all-conquering 'good King David' conjured up by Professor Barrow is persuasive and has swayed many subsequent commentators, but it is by no means the only interpretation of the early part of King David's reign.

Even this second campaign against Máel Coluim mac Alexandair cannot have been straightforward. The reference to the king's forces making defences before 1134 implies that they either expected, or were subjected to, counter-attacks. This would again suggest that between 1130 and 1134 a number of people still thought that Máel Coluim mac Alexandair had a better right to be king than King David I and, importantly, they were prepared to support the alternative claimant. We now know where some of that support may have come from. Máel Coluim mac Alexandair was married to a sister (unnamed) of Sumarliði mac Gillebrigte (Somerled), ruler of Argyll. Like the MacWilliams, Máel Coluim mac Alexandair and his descendants never relinquished their right to be considered for

52 David N. Bell, 'Ailred of Rievaulx (1110–1167)', *Oxford Dictionary of National Biography* (Oxford University Press, 2004) [http://www.oxforddnb.com/view/article/8916 Accessed 9 January 2010]

53 Paul Dalton, 'Espec, Walter (d.1147x58)', *Oxford Dictionary of National Biography* (Oxford University Press, 2004) [http://www.oxforddnb.com/view/article/8885 Accessed 9 January 2010]

inauguration until their line was extinguished at Coupar Angus monastery in 1186.[54]

However, Máel Coluim mac Alexandair was not the only grandson of King Máel Coluim mac Donnchada who could have claimed a right to be considered for inauguration in 1124. William fitz Duncan also possessed a strong claim and in fact represented the senior branch of the family, descended as he was from King Máel Coluim mac Donnchada's first marriage to Ingibjorg of Orkney. There is, nevertheless, no surviving record of William fitz Duncan opposing the inauguration of David mac Máel Coluim in 1124, and this conundrum has led historians to speculate that perhaps his claim was bought off in return for being named as David's *tanaiste*.[55] On the face of it such an explanation seems plausible, but only until the political activities of William fitz Duncan's descendants, the MacWilliams, are evaluated. Clearly, until their deliberate extermination by King Alexander II in 1230, consecutive generations of that kindred refused to abandon their claim to be inaugurated as kings of Scotia. Thus it seems very unlikely that their progenitor William fitz Duncan would have done so in 1124 when his only reward for acquiescing to David's inauguration was to be named as potential heir, knowing that David already had a ten-year-old son.

There is perhaps one further character who should be considered as a possible kingship claimant in 1124. This is the man to whom we only have a single reference, in the witness list of King Alexander mac Máel Coluim's diploma to Scone Abbey *c*.1120: *Alexander nepos regis Alexandri* (Alexander nephew of King Alexander).[56] The identity of this man has been discussed by Duncan who came to the conclusion that the fifteenth-century scribe who transcribed this document was guilty of dittography and had in fact miscopied the name *Willelmus nepos regis Alexandri* (William [fitz Duncan] nephew of King Alexander).[57]

This suggestion is entirely possible, but Duncan made the assumption that this second Alexander had been named in recognition of the ruling king of Scots, thereby implying that the former Alexander had been born in or around 1107. In turn, Duncan then discussed why *Alexander nepos*

---

54 *Chron. Holyrood*, 170–71.
55 Oram, *David I*, 74.
56 *ESC*, no. 36.
57 Duncan, *Kingship*, 59–60.

regis Alexandri cannot have been the son of either King Donnchadh mac Máel Coluim, Edward mac Máel Coluim, Edmund mac Máel Coluim, or David mac Máel Coluim.

However, Duncan did not discuss the possibility that *Alexander nepos regis Alexandri* could have been either a son (or grandson?) of one of the other sons of King Máel Coluim mac Donnchada and Ingibjorg. As discussed earlier, we know that other descendants of King Máel Coluim mac Donnchada's first marriage were present in Scotia during the reign of King Alexander mac Máel Coluim; and the Latin word *nepos* can mean either nephew or kinsman. Bearing this in mind it seems rather rash to completely reject the possibility that *Alexander nepos regis Alexandri* actually existed.

Scotia post-1113: politics and the Church

Nowadays we can only imagine the awfully grim reality that faced King Alexander mac Máel Coluim in December 1113. He was ruler of a kingdom much reduced in size from that controlled by his father King Máel Coluim mac Donnchada. The Western Isles and Argyll had been lost to the Norwegian Crown during King Edgar's reign. His younger brother David, who now effectively ruled over parts of Lothian and a large part of the old kingdom of Strathclyde, was referring to himself as prince of Cumbria, and clearly had the favour of King Henry I. Perhaps more importantly, the lands that King Alexander had been forced to hand over to David were economically important and their loss must have placed even more strain upon his kingship.

To make matters worse, in 1114 King Alexander was called upon to perform armed service for King Henry I in Wales. Norman lordship in that country was destabilising native Welsh lordship and Gruffud ap Cynan, king of Gwynedd, was held responsible for attacks upon property owned by Norman lords in north Wales. The army that King Henry I sent into Wales was composed of three separate divisions led by the king himself, Gilbert FitzRichard, lord of Ceredigion, and King Alexander mac Máel Coluim. Henry's armed threat worked. The Welsh rulers treated for peace and King Henry continued to encourage Norman and Breton families to settle along the Welsh Marches and in Wales itself.[58]

---

58 Green, *Henry I*, 132–33.

In agreeing to perform this armed service King Alexander was openly acknowledging King Henry's overlordship. Whether he was forced into performing service as punishment over his refusal to grant David mac Máel Coluim his appanage does not really matter. Much of the cult of kingship is about external perception and, after the events of 1113 in combination with the Welsh campaign of 1114, Alexander's contemporaries would surely have been left in no doubt about his position in relation to both King Henry I and to David mac Máel Coluim.

It has been suggested that it was in the aftermath of this Wales expedition that King Alexander mac Máel Coluim married Sibylla, illegitimate daughter of King Henry I.[59] This is possible, but, if truth be told, it is impossible to decide exactly when this marriage might have taken place.

Perhaps the key to understanding the relationship between the two brothers (and King Henry I) after 1114 lies in deciding what David's plans for his new appanage lands were. Not only did he control Cumbria as far north as the Lennox by 1114, his sway also extended across northern Britain into Berwickshire in the east. By right of his wife, he also possessed a claim to the old earldom of Northumbria which had included the whole of Lothian. However, while he may have held Cumbria as a prince, David does not seem to have possessed the same powers in Lower Tweeddale or Berwickshire. In those districts King Alexander and Earl David seem to have acted in concert to protect the monks of Durham.[60]

Once in this position of power David evidently moved quickly to begin to reorganise the economy of the region. One of his first acts in 1113 was to establish a Tironensian monastery at Selkirk (Plate 6). This new establishment was founded directly from Tiron and Earl David had probably become an admirer of the order when he was in England since King Henry I was a patron and benefactor of the founder of the Tironensians, Bernard of Tiron.[61] David's personal chaplain John was also a Tironensian, and he was later elevated to the bishopric of Glasgow c.1116, being consecrated in 1119.[62] There are also architectural links between Glasgow and Jedburgh and it has been argued that the earlier of the two structures,

59 Oram, *David I*, 67.
60 Duncan, *Kingship*, 61.
61 Barrow, *Kingdom of the Scots*, 180–81.
62 Duncan, *Kingship*, 63 and at 89.

Glasgow Cathedral, provided a template for the building design of Jedburgh Abbey.[63]

John's predecessor as bishop of Glasgow was Michael, possibly a Briton, who had been consecrated by Archbishop Thomas II of York around 1109 and thereafter acted as one of the bishopric of York's suffragans.[64] Unfortunately, however, the archbishops of Canterbury also claimed that the bishops of Glasgow belonged to their province and, in 1119, the see of Glasgow became caught up in the struggle for metropolitan supremacy in Britain when Archbishop Ralph of Canterbury wrote to Pope Calixtus II attacking the claim made by Archbishop Thurstan of York that York did not owe obedience to Canterbury.[65]

There is little doubt that the diocese of Glasgow, arguably the equivalent of the old kingdom of Strathclyde,[66] benefited from Earl David's new status as *princeps Cumbrensis*, though his claim that he was saving it from barbarism, shamelessness, and wickedness was perhaps slightly exaggerated.[67] Although the exact date of his famous inquest to establish the extent of the see of Glasgow's property rights is unknown (Barrow dates it to either 1120 x 21 or 1123 x 24),[68] it is clear the see gained Teviotdale – possibly from St Andrews – during David's period of lordship there.[69]

David's inquest, and the preamble that accompanied it, are interesting for a number of reasons. For example, it is stated in the document that Cumbria was the *regio* (realm) between England and Scotia, thereby providing a historical precedent for David's new lordship that also stretched across north Britain from west to east, but that David's new realm had been limited in extent: *non enim toti Cumbrensi regioni dominabatur* (because he did not rule over the whole of the Cumbrian realm).[70] This latter statement reflects the conquest of southern Cumbria to the Esk and Solway by King William II Rufus in 1092, after which he established Ranulf

---

63 Ralph Mentel, 'The Twelfth-Century Predecessors of Glasgow Cathedral and their Relationship with Jedburgh Abbey', in Richard Fawcett (ed.), *Medieval Art and Architecture in the Diocese of Glasgow* (Leeds, 1998), 42–49.

64 Shead, 'Origins of Glasgow', 220–25.

65 Broun, 'Welsh Identity', 119.

66 Ibid., 141–42.

67 *ESC*, 44–46.

68 Barrow, *Chrs. David I*, 60–61.

69 Shead, 'Origins of Glasgow', 223. See also the discussion about this in: Broun 'Welsh Identity', 139, fn. 117.

70 *ESC*, 44–46.

Meschin at Carlisle. Annandale sat on the northern boundary of these lands and this border also marked the division between the sees of Carlisle and Glasgow, as well as the later border between England and Scotland.[71]

From the perspective of King Alexander mac Máel Coluim post-1114 it must have seemed unlikely that Scotia north of the Forth would ever be reunited with David's new realm of Cumbria. While it is true that David did not have any direct heirs at this time, he was married to a woman who had already borne children and who was still clearly capable of bearing more. Even if David died suddenly by an accident or by natural causes, it must have occurred to King Alexander that King Henry I could just replace David with someone else loyal to the English Crown. Moreover, the new lands David had been granted were economically important and the decision to establish a community of reformed monks at Selkirk in 1113 was likely, in the longer term, to provide an economic boost for David's territories. King Alexander, in contrast to his brother, already had a male heir, but not by Queen Sibylla, and there were the other segments of the royal dynasty to keep happy. It might also have been of concern to King Alexander that David's appanage of Cumbria effectively created a greater buffer zone between Scotia north of the Forth and the centre of the cult of Cuthbert located at Durham.

Getting back to basics? King Alexander, the cult of Colum Cille, and the invention of tradition

It is probably not a coincidence that only one year after David established a Tironensian community at Selkirk, King Alexander established an Augustinian community at Scone sometime between Christmas 1114 and March 1115. The foundation of the Augustinians at Scone can probably be directly linked to King Alexander being forced to relinquish the valuable lands of David's appanage, plus Lower Tweeddale and Berwickshire. The loss of these rich lands south of the Forth must surely have forced a massive economic retrenchment within Scotia proper given the huge expansion of arable that is thought to have occurred south of the Forth during the Medieval Warm Epoch. By attracting Augustinian canons into Scotia the king was effectively planning the diversification of the fiscal portfolio of his

---

71 Barrow, *Kingdom of the Scots*, 116.

realm by plugging it into a monastic economic network that stretched across western Christendom.[72]

The six Augustinian canons who formed the new Scone community came from the church of St Oswald in Nostell (Yorkshire). Duncan has established that the secular clergy of Nostell had accepted the Augustinian Rule before February 1114. He also suggested that the military service performed by King Alexander in Wales during the summer of 1114 could have seen him visit Nostell during his travels.[73] Both Veitch and Duncan further argued that in making this foundation at Scone, literally adjacent to the inauguration site, King Alexander was perhaps consciously remodelling the ritual landscape of Scone to mirror that found at Westminster Abbey.[74]

His plans for the Augustinian order in Scotia did not end there. King Alexander also planned Augustinian priories at St Andrews, Loch Tay, and at Inchcolm, but he died before these could be completed. At Inchcolm, for example, the earliest surviving charter for that priory records that King David mac Máel Coluim had given Bishop Gregory of Dunkeld custody of the properties and income previously granted (presumably by Alexander) to the priory until the new community was ready to begin operations.[75] Less is known about the Augustinian priory on Loch Tay that Alexander intended to establish for remembering the souls of both Queen Sibylla and himself. Much of the land around the loch was clearly part of an important royal estate from an early date (Bower claims that Queen Sibylla died there) and the island, now called Priory Island, may originally have been a crannog, as it is at least partly of artificial construction.[76] There now appear to be no remains of an early priory, but a fire was recorded on the island in 1509, after which major rebuilding work was undertaken.[77]

1115 was also the year in which Bishop Turgot of St Andrews died on 31 August at Durham and King Alexander was faced with the twin

---

72 This is an under-researched topic in a Scottish context, but some discussion can be found in: Richard D. Oram, 'A Fit and Ample Endowment? The Balmerino Estate, 1228–1603', in R. Oram, *Life on the Edge. The Cistercian Abbey of Balmerino, Fife (Scotland)* (Forges-Chimay, 2008), 61–80, at 70.

73 Duncan, *Kingship*, 85.

74 Kenneth Veitch, ' "Replanting Paradise": Alexander I and the Reform of Religious Life in Scotland', *Innes Review*, 52, no. 2, 2001, 136–66, at 141–42 [hereafter: Veitch, 'Replanting Paradise']; Duncan, *Kingship*, 82–83.

75 D. E. Easson and Angus Macdonald (eds), *Charters of the Abbey of Inchcolm* (Edinburgh, 1938), 1.

76 *Chron. Bower* (Watt), iii, 125.

77 T. N. Dixon, 'A Survey of Crannogs in Loch Tay', *PSAS*, 112, 1982, 17–38.

problems of first choosing a successor and then getting that person consecrated. The choice was clearly crucial because of the claims of supremacy
made by York, and the search for a suitable candidate appears to have taken
five years. These ecclesiastic squabbles might also explain why King
Alexander chose a Canterbury monk, Eadmer, to be the next bishop of St
Andrews. Veitch has clearly demonstrated that the new bishop took a pro-
active role in refuting the claims of York.[78] But Eadmer and King Alexander
appear to have quarrelled, possibly about the new bishop's insistence that
he should be consecrated by the archbishop of Canterbury. By early 1121
Eadmer had resigned his position and returned to England. King
Alexander then turned to Robert, prior of Scone, to fill the position of
bishop of St Andrews, and he was officially consecrated in July 1127.[79]

As if these problems associated with filling the diocese of St Andrews
were not bad enough, King Alexander was faced with other pressing ecclesiastic issues during his reign, many of them not his fault. For example, he
had inherited what had perhaps been intended to be a brand new royal
mausoleum at Dunfermline following the burial there of Queen Margaret.
Possibly a more urgent inherited problem was the island of Iona: by earlier
surrendering the Western Isles to King Magnus Barelegs, King Edgar
mac Máel Coluim had effectively abandoned (as far as we know without
a fight) what has been traditionally regarded as the royal Scottish
mausoleum on Iona.

Indeed, the striking image presented in the sagas of King Magnus effectively closing down Iona in 1098 by barring the church was seemingly a
propaganda coup of the highest order, designed to strike at the heart of a
royal Scottish dynasty that prided itself on presenting a continuation of
tradition from Pictish times:

> King Magnus came with his host to the holy island, and gave there
> quarter and peace to all men, and to the household of all men. Men say
> this, that he wished to open the small church of Columcille; and the
> king did not go in, but closed the door again immediately, and imme-
> diately locked it, and said that none should be so daring thenceforward
> as to go into that church; and thenceforward it has been so done.[80]

78 Veitch, 'Replanting Paradise', 149.
79 D. E. R. Watt and A. L. Murray, *Fasti Ecclesiae Scoticanae Medii Aevi Ad Annum 1638* (Bristol,
    2003), 377–78.
80 *ES*, ii, 107–08; Finlay, *Fagrskinna*, 246.

Nowadays we can only hazard an estimate of the loss of prestige that such a loss of the traditional royal mausoleum must have entailed, and how damaging it could be, particularly to a branch of the royal kindred that was not entirely secure in their kingship. It surely would have been viewed as a sign of divine displeasure.

There does not seem to have been an obvious mainland site that could have acted as an alternative to the royal mausoleum on Iona after this point in time. While Queen Margaret had been buried at Dunfermline in 1093, to be joined by her son Edgar in 1107, she was only later joined there by King Máel Coluim mac Donnchada's bones since his body had originally had been buried at Tynemouth Abbey. There is no indication that King Máel Coluim mac Donnchada had originally intended to be buried at Dunfermline. In contrast to these burials, King Domnall bán mac Donnchada was interred at Dunkeld Cathedral and in 1130 Queen Matilda was buried at Scone by her husband.[81] During his reign King Alexander must have been faced with the stark choice of either continuing to develop Dunfermline as a royal mausoleum or finding a new site to inter members of the royal dynasty. Alexander's determination to reunite the remains of his mother and father at Dunfermline may just have been formed out of his respect for his parents rather than being part of a grander dynastic commemorative plan. Only six of the ten kings of Scots who had reigned between 1090 and 1300 were buried at Dunfermline and the remains of one of them, King Máel Coluim mac Donnchada, had been moved there from elsewhere. If Dunfermline had originally been intended as a royal mausoleum, it seems that an unusually high percentage of kings of Scots actually preferred to be buried elsewhere.

King Alexander was also faced with a dilemma over saintly cults. It is well known that he had been the only layman present to witness the translation of St Cuthbert (along with the head of St Oswald) on 30 August 1104.[82] This honour seems to give some indication of the depth of his devotion to a saintly cult to which his immediate family had abruptly decided to provide patronage in August 1093,[83] but it might also measure the determination of Durham to stay in the good graces of the king of Scotia, to preserve their property portfolio north of the Tweed.

81 *ES*, ii, 90, fn. 3; *Chron. Bower* (Watt), iii, 135.
82 Duncan, *Kingship*, 84.
83 Veitch, 'Replanting Paradise', 136–66.

However, if King Alexander was distanced from the cult centre of Cuthbert at Durham by his brother David's new appanage, it is maybe surprising that Alexander did not turn to the cult of St Andrew as a new focus of foyal interest. The cathedral in Fife might have been an obvious choice around which to base a new royal mausoleum, particularly since St Andrews also seems to have had much earlier royal connections. However, if the problems between 1115 and 1124 in obtaining a consecrated bishop for that see were not off-putting, then perhaps the unresolved issue of York's primacy over St Andrews might have made the seat of any Scottish see a less appealing choice for a royal mausoleum. In addition, it also appears that during this same period the intended establishment of a community of Augustinian canons at St Andrews by King Alexander had foundered. This may be why the king temporarily withdrew his gift of the Boar's Raik.[84]

There was a third option. According to Abbot Walter Bower of Inchcolm, King Alexander personally experienced a miracle towards the end of his reign:

> . . . *et circa annum domini m^m centisimum vicesimum tercium, non minus mirifice quam miraculose, fundatum est monasterium Sancti Columbe de Insula Emonia juxta Edenburgh. Nam cum nobilis et Christianissimus rex dominius Alexander primus hoc nomine ob certa negocia regni passagium facaret trans Portum Regine, subito exorta est tempestas valida, flante africo, et ratem cum naucleris, vix vita comite, compulit applicare ad Insulam Emoniam, ubi tunc degebat quidam heremita insulanus qui servicio Sancti Columbe deditus ad quamdam inibi capellulam, tenui victu, utpote lacte unius vacce et conchis ac pisciculis marinis collectis, contentatus, sedule se dedit. De cuius quidem tali annona rex cum suis commilitonibus admodum non paucis per tres dies continuos, impellente vento, vitam gratulanter transigebat. Sed cum pridie in maximo maris periculo et tempestatis rabie quassatus, de vita desperaret, votum fecit sancto ut si eum cum suis ad insulam incolumem perduceret, ad eius laudem in ipsa insula talem memoriam relinqueret, quod navigantibus et naufragis ad asilum cederet et solamen. Hac itaque occasione actum est, ut fundaret ibidem monasterium canonicorum, sicut inpresenciarum cernitur. Tum eciam*

---

84 A. A. M. Duncan, 'The Foundation of St Andrews Cathedral Priory, 1140', *SHR*, 84:1 (April 2005), 1–37.

quia Sanctum Columbam semper et a juventute speciali venerabatur honore. Tum insuper quia parentes ipsius per aliquot annos infecundi, sobolis solacio erant destituti, donec devocione supplici Sanctum Columbam implorantes, gloriose consequti sunt quod tam hanelo desiderio diu quesierunt.

. . . and about the year 1123 the monastery of St Columba on the island of Inchcolm near Edinburgh was founded in a way that was as remarkable as it was miraculous. For when the noble and most Christian lord king Alexander the first of his name was making the crossing at Queensferry in pursuit of some business of the kingdom, a violent storm suddenly arose as wind blew from the south-west, and compelled the ship with its crew scarcely clinging to life to put in at the island of Inchcolm, where a certain island hermit lived at that time. He was dedicated to the service of St Columba, and earnestly devoted himself to it at a certain little chapel on the island, content with a meagre diet consisting of the milk of one cow, shells and a little fish that he gathered from the sea. The king with his very large number of fellow soldiers gratefully lived on this food for three days on end under compulsion from the wind. But on the previous day when he was giving up hope of surviving, as he was being buffeted by the very great danger of the sea and the madness of the storm, he made a vow to the saint that if he brought him safely to the island along with his men, he would leave on the island such a memorial to his glory as would serve for asylum and solace to sailors and victims of shipwreck. This is how it came about that he founded a monastery of canons in that same place, just as it can be seen at the present day. There was also the fact that he had always even from his youth revered St Columba with particular honour. There was moreover the fact that his parents had been infertile and deprived of the comfort of children for some years, until they implored St Columba with suppliant devotion, and gloriously achieved what they had long sought with eager desire.[85]

Of course, as a fifteenth-century abbot of Inchcolm, Bower would have been keen to promote the cult of Colum Cille at any opportunity, and the

---

85 *Chron. Bower* (Watt), iii, 110–11.

Scotichronicon certainly provided him with the means to do so. Indeed, the story related above is not the only miracle in the *Scotichronicon* linked to the saint and his island in the middle of the Forth, nor is it the most dramatic. For example, in 1336, the power of the saint is said to have prevented some thieving English pirates from escaping with fine woodwork from Dollar church by sinking their ship as it passed Inchcolm (Plate 7).[86]

It is, however, difficult to be completely cynical about the whole of the miracle related by Bower in connection to the original foundation of Inchcolm. This is because there is independent evidence which demonstrates that during his lifetime King Alexander commissioned a new transcription of the *Life of Colum Cille* and it is known that this text was written by a scribe called William at a location called *insula pontificum*, possibly St Serf's island on Loch Leven.[87]

At face value there seems to be nothing odd about either King Alexander's foundation on Inchcolm or his commissioning of a new *Life*. After all, many Scots would still feel an intimate connection to Colum Cille. In 848/9 half of his relics were transferred from Kells in Ireland to a new church at Dunkeld and these relics may have included both the *Breacbennach* (possibly the Monymusk reliquary) and the *Cathbuaid* (battle-triumph, most likely a crozier), both of which were used by the Scots in battle. The latter is first attested in 918:

> As beag nach insa laithibh si ro chuirsead Foirtreannaigh agus
> Lochlannaig cath. As cruaidh imorro ro cuirsiot Fir Alban an cath so,
> úair baoí Coluim Cille ag congnamh leó, úair ra ghuidhsiod go diochra
> é, úair ba he a n-apstol é, agus as tríd ro ghabhsad creideamh. Úair
> feacht oile, an uair ro bhaoí Imar Conung 'na ghilla óg, agus tainig d'in-
> radh Alban, trí catha móra a líon, as eadh do ronsad Fir Alban eider
> láoch agus chléireach bheith go maidin i n-áoine agus a n-iornáidhe ra
> Día, agus ra Colam Cille, agus éighmhe móra do dhenamh risin
> Choimdhidh, agus almsana iomdha bídh agus édaigh do thabhairt
> dona h-eagalsaibh agus dona bochtaibh, agus Corp an Choimdheadh
> do chaitheamh a Ilamhuibh a sagart, agus gealladh gach maithiusa do
> ghénamh amhail as fearr nó ioralfaidís a cclerigh forra, agus comadh
> eadh be meirge dhóibh i gceann gach catha Bachall Cholaim Cille;

86 *Chron. Bower* (Watt), vii, 119–21.
87 Anderson and Anderson, *Life of Columba*, 10.

gonadh aire sin adberar cathbhuaidh fría ó sin alle; agus ba h-ainm cóir, úair is minic rugsad-somh búaidh a ccathaibh le, amhail do rónsad iaram an tan sin, dola a muinnighin Cholaim Cille.

Almost at the same time the men of Fortriu and the Norwegians fought a battle. The men of Alba fought this battle steadfastly, moreover, because Colum Cille was assisting them, for they had prayed fervently to him, since he was their apostle, and it was through him that they received faith. For on another occasion, when Imar Conung was a young lad and he came to plunder Alba with three large troops, the men of Alba, lay and clergy alike, fasted and prayed to God and Colum Cille until morning, and beseeched the Lord, and gave profuse alms of food and clothing to the churches and to the poor, and received the body of the Lord from the hands of their priests, and promised to do every good thing as their clergy would best urge them, and that their battle-standard in the van of every battle would be the crozier of Colum Cille – and it is on that account that it is called the *Cathbuaid* from then onwards; and the name is fitting for they have often won victory in battle with it, as they did at that time, relying on Colum Cille.[88]

In 2005, Hall discussed a thirteenth-century Dunkeld seal matrix that displayed both a house-shaped reliquary and a crozier.[89] However, while there is every possibility that the crozier displayed on the matrix was the *Cathbuaid*, it would be more difficult to justify that the house-shaped reliquary image was the *Breacbennach* because the seal is dated to *c*.1221, and it is known that King William I had granted custody of the *Breacbennach* to his abbey at Arbroath before 1211.[90] This, of course, assumes that the *Breacbennach* of Colum Cille and the Monymusk reliquary now held by National Museums Scotland are one and the same. This is not entirely clear.[91]

This is where a major problem appears in relation to royal burials in Pictland/Alba. Because the relics of Colum Cille had been split between

88 Radner, *Fragmentary Annals*, 168–71.

89 M. A. Hall, 'Of Holy Men and Heroes: The Cult of Saints in Medieval Perthshire', *The Innes Review*, 56:1, 2005, 61–88.

90 Gilbert Márkus, 'Dewars and Relics in Scotland: Some Clarifications and Questions', *The Innes Review*, 60:2, 2009, 95–144.

91 David H. Caldwell, 'The Monymusk Reliquary: the *Breccbennach* of St Columba?', *PSAS*, 131, 2001, 267–82.

Armagh and Dunkeld *c.*848, why would the kings of Pictland and Alba from Cináed mac Ailpín onwards continue to insist that they should be buried on Iona, an island bereft of saintly relics and (presumably) much prestige? Surely Dunkeld with its half-share of Columban relics would have been a more logical (and much closer) site for royal interment if the kings of Alba continued to hold St Colum Cille in such high regard.

Almost thirty years ago, Cowan discussed this exact problem when he noted that one group of king-lists was the sole source of information that kings of Alba were buried on Iona. This group, using Anderson's notations, comprised the D, F, I, K, and N king-lists, although they occasionally differed about which kings had been buried on Iona and which had not.[92] A couple of kings were clearly left out because other independent sources stated that they had either been killed in a foreign kingdom or buried elsewhere. As Cowan noted, the only information this group of king-lists had in common was the statement that the bones of King Domnall bán mac Donnchada had been removed from Dunkeld and taken for re-interment on Iona. Because that king was still alive in 1099 the archetype of this group of king-lists cannot be older than that date.[93]

One common factor shared by this group of king-lists is that they all make Cináed mac Ailpín the historical horizon of royal burials on Iona. This commonality should instantly raise suspicions about the veracity of these claims since Cináed mac Ailpín was used by these same medieval authors as the alleged founder of the (then current) Scottish dynasty, the heirs of *Clann Cinaeda meic Ailpín*, and the man who had (allegedly) destroyed the Picts.[94]

Work by Broun on this group of king-lists has posited an archetype in which remarkably accurate reign lengths were given for Kings Edgar, Alexander, and David mac Máel Coluim. Because the date of Edgar's inauguration is not known there is currently no way of telling whether the reign length provided for him is accurate, but the other two are both precise. This means that the archetype of this group of king-lists must have been updated at some point shortly after each king's death and, if the reign-length given for Edgar is also accurate, then the archetype must have been first updated during the reign of King Alexander. Essentially, Broun has

92 Anderson, *Kings and Kingship*.
93 Edward J. Cowan, 'The Scottish Chronicle in the Poppleton Manuscript', *The Innes Review*, 32, 1981, 3–21 [hereafter: Cowan, 'The Scottish Chronicle'].
94 Broun, *Irish Identity*, 172–73.

pushed the dating of the common ancestor of this group of king-lists back to 1034 x 40, with the additional notes on the deaths and burials of Scottish kings being added *c.*1124 (or presumably almost two decades earlier if Edgar's reign length is also precise).[95] All of which means that it could have been King Alexander himself, with his obvious interest in and patronage of the cult of St Colum Cille, who was the inventor of the 'tradition' that the vast majority of his royal ancestors had been buried on Iona since the mid-ninth century.

Cowan suggested a reason why King Alexander might want to do this, namely that it constituted a reassertion of Scottish sovereignty over Iona and the other Western Isles that had been lost to King Magnus Barelegs in 1097/98.[96] This theory is entirely possible and it is unfortunate that the exact date of the translation of King Domnall bán mac Donnchada's bones from Dunkeld to Iona, which is present in all versions of the king-lists, is not known. Such an event is unusual enough in a Scottish context to actually be true.[97] Presumably, the translation must have occurred some time after the death of King Magnus Barelegs in 1103 and so King Alexander, with his obvious interest in the cult of Colum Cille, is probably the most likely royal candidate to take responsibility for this event.

However, even if Cowan's suggestion is correct, this translation has more subtle layers to it. The movement of royal remains from one of the two new St Colum Cille cult centres back to the original home of the cult on Iona must have had a resonance in the minds of people even if no saintly relics appear to have travelled back to the island with King Domnall bán mac Donnchada's bones, or at least not permanently. There is one other factor to take into consideration at this point. This is the marriage of King Alexander's son, Máel Coluim mac Alexandair, to an unnamed sister of Sumarliði mac Gillebrigte, *rí Indsi Gall & Cind Tíre* (king of the Isles of the Strangers and Kintyre), whose territories included Iona.[98]

95 Ibid., 153–74.
96 Cowan, 'The Scottish Chronicle', 7.
97 Ibid. It is difficult to decipher the statement in Bower [*Chron. Bower* (Watt), ii, 427] that Domnall bán had entered voluntary exile in the Hebrides during the reign of King MacBethad mac Findlaích. While it may well be based upon fact, Bower later describes Domnall bán as a murdering usurper. Given the relationship between the Lords of the Isles and the Scottish Crown in the fifteenth century at the time Bower was writing, the association he makes between Domnall bán and the Western Isles may have been a device employed by the author to emphasise to his readership just how bad a man King Domnall bán really was.
98 http://www.ucc.ie/celt/published/G100002/index.html Accessed 23 November 2009.

All of this evidence allows us to conclude that the marriage between Máel Coluim mac Alexandair and the unnamed sister of Sumarliði mac Gillebrigte was a pragmatic diplomatic solution to the loss of the Western Isles that could have occurred during the reign of King Edgar mac Máel Coluim. Since it was unlikely that Sumarliði mac Gillebrigte would have voluntarily surrendered his new power base and authority to a king of Alba, this dynastic marriage drew the two kindreds together. Viewed in this context, the reopening of Iona, the translation of Domnall bán's bones, and the invention of a myth that every king of 'Scots' since Cináed mac Ailpín had been buried there was perhaps a diplomatic way by which Sumarliði mac Gillebrigte could tacitly acknowledge Scottish overlordship of the Western Isles and Kintyre without having to formally concede power to a 'foreign' king.

But whatever long-term plans King Alexander had for his son and the Western Isles, they were brought to a close on 24 April 1124 when the king seems to have suddenly died at Stirling, 'while not yet old'. He chose to be buried before the high altar at Dunfermline, close to his father. As William of Malmesbury commented, King Alexander may well have held his kingdom *laboriosissime* (with great effort), but it is frequently forgotten that it took his infinitely more famous brother and successor, David mac Máel Coluim, eleven years and at least two civil wars to finally secure the kingship of the Scots for himself.

Conclusion

No single book can hope to answer all of the outstanding questions that remain about the kingdom of the Scots during the eleventh and twelfth centuries. Our surviving written sources are just too sparse and too ambiguous for historians ever to reach a consensus. But that should not preclude us from trying to exploit new lines of enquiry as they open. For the period c.1000 to 1130 this means increasingly utilising other sources of potential information like proxy climate data, palaeoecology, and historical geography. Though palaeoecology may be site-specific, pollen diagrams with a long chronology provide glimpses into what was growing and being cultivated at sites for which we often have no detailed historical records until the seventeenth or eighteenth century, and so they help to inform historical discussion.

Historical geography can be even more useful. For example, it allows us to demonstrate that during the eleventh century Alba was a highly organised kingdom that had already been divided up into distinct units of land assessment, just like many other precocious kingdoms in Europe. These units of land assessment were designed to efficiently exploit the available natural resources for the twin purposes of resource allocation between areas of settlement and tax assessment. It has been argued here that the commonest of these units in north Britain, the davoch, was pre-900 or Pictish in origin, but the evidence base upon which this argument has been constructed is extremely narrow. The date at which davochs first appear in a written source is c.1030 in the *Book of Deer*.

What is undeniable is that the davoch and other similar units of land assessment in north Britain underpin and so must pre-date the medieval parochial system. It is just a shame that neither the different individual units of land assessment nor the process of parochial creation can currently be precisely dated because this would allow historians to begin to construct a chronology of state development. While it is dangerous to argue from negative evidence, if the latter process had occurred during the relatively well documented reign of King David I (1124–1153), it is astonishing that no record has survived of what must have been an extraordinary burst of activity as davochs and other units of land assessment were organised into distinct groups so that they might form parishes. While investigation into this process of organisation is only beginning, it also might be considered surprising that there are also no records of any challenges from the people who inhabited these particular units of land assessment to the process of parish formation.

One consequence of this process of land assessment is that everyone living in Alba during the eleventh century must have known exactly how much and to whom they were expected to render in taxation and services on a yearly basis. These renders of taxation and other services also surely indicate that Alba possessed a form of local government that had made provision for the efficient collection and utilisation of those same taxes and services. Here, we should perhaps be looking to the dochasser, to the maer, and to the thane as people who were actively involved in such processes.

The surviving evidence strongly suggests that Alba was a stratified kin-based society, but next to nothing is known about the vast majority of people who lived and died in north Britain during the eleventh century and how they coped with the challenges they must have faced on a regular basis, given the vagaries of a north British climate. A sustained campaign of paleoecological investigation may begin to answer some of these questions but will never provide all the answers. Indeed, if it were not for a few entries in Irish Annals, English chronicles, and the land grants preserved in the *Book of Deer*, we would also know very little about officers like the mormaer who appear to have occupied the upper level of society below the royal kindreds of Alba. If there were familiar links between mormaír, Clann Áeda meic Cináeda, and Clann Custantín meic Cináeda, these are now largely lost to us. Mormaír themselves disappear from the historical record by 1130 and, though it is often assumed that their office transmuted into the title of *comes* (earl), this is not certain. The office of mormaer could just as easily have been made redundant by the physical expansion of Alba during the eleventh century as by changing cultural mores.

Within this expansion of overlordship driven by Clann Custantín meic Cináeda after *c*.1000, there are clear differences in the reactions of those being (re)conquered. Writing in 1996 about the absorption of minority cultures and western 'barbarian warrior' aristocracies into the European mainstream, Patrick Wormald remarked that he had never yet encountered one that rolled over and died of osmosis.[1] Yet, in eleventh-century north Britain the different reactions of the peoples of Strathclyde and Moray to the lordship established over them by the ruling segment of Clann

---

1 Patrick Wormald, 'The Emergence of the *Regnum Scottorum*: a Carolingian Hegemony?', in Barbara E. Crawford (ed.), *Scotland in Dark Age Britain* (St Andrews, 1996), 131–60, at 133–34.

Custantín meic Cináeda are quite remarkable. If ever there was a candidate for a western kingdom dying of osmosis, it is Strathclyde.

No Scottish source records precisely how the kings of Alba established their overlordship across Strathclyde or when the inhabitants of that region finally accepted their cultural rebranding as Scots. In addition, apart from a very brief appearance by a member of the ruling Strathclyde kindred in the 1050s, there is no record of any leaders from Strathclyde leading a native resistance against the process of absorption. Was Strathclyde then a kingdom that had already been decimated by Northumbrians and others before 1050 and glad of the protection that the kings of Alba could offer it, or has a large chunk of history that documented the final years of Strathclyde just simply been lost? The latter might be the favoured option if we were just talking about Scottish sources, but English, Welsh, and Irish sources also fail to record any prolonged war of attrition between Alba and Strathclyde during the eleventh century. Whatever happened, the absorption of Strathclyde into Alba allowed the kings of Alba direct access to the Firth of Clyde and the Irish Sea Zone and would also have added very valuable exploitable natural resources, like the Solway Firth, to the economic portfolio of Alba.

To all intents and purposes the addition of Strathclyde to Alba stands in complete contrast to the fate of Moray. It has been argued in this book that Moray was not an independent kingdom at any point during the eleventh century and that the only reason why Moravians entered into conflict with the ruling royal kindred of Alba was because an important female from Clann Custantín meic Cináeda had married into a leading Moravian kindred. This was the marriage of Gruoch, daughter of Boite mac Cináeda, to the mormaer of Moray, Gilla Comgáin mac Máel Brigte. Through processes that are still unclear, this marriage began a chain of events that allowed two Moravians to successfully and successively claim the kingship of Alba, MacBethad mac Findláich and Lulach mac Gilla Comgáin. Their subsequent murders at the hands of Máel Coluim mac Donnchada ushered in a period of unrest in northern Scotland that was not brought to an end until the death of Oengus of Moray by forces loyal to King David I in 1130. From this viewpoint, the ructions in northern Scotland between c.1000 and 1130 were a product of disputes about which males within or connected to the royal kindred of Clann Custantín meic Cináeda had the better right to be inaugurated.

With the benefit of hindsight it is now clear that the second marriage of Máel Coluim mac Donnchada to Margaret brought about a decisive shift in this inter-kindred rivalry. Though King Máel Coluim mac Donnchada and his first wife Queen Ingibjorg seem to have had three sons (and three grandsons), only one of these assorted offspring, Donnchadh mac Máel Coluim, ever attained the kingship of Alba. Instead it was the sons produced by Máel Coluim mac Donnchada and Margaret who came to the fore to dominate the kingship of Scotia for the next two centuries or so. The descendants of King Donnchadh mac Máel Coluim (the MacWilliams) clearly regarded this monopolisation of the kingship by their cousins as unfair and campaigned on this basis until the last MacWilliam representative was deliberately exterminated in Forfar in 1230. But what differentiated the offspring of King Máel Coluim mac Donnchada and Queen Margaret from their cousins was that they inherited a claim to the Anglo-Saxon kingship of England from their mother.

It is a great shame that no Scottish source comments on this aspect of their inheritance because we now cannot tell what the rest of the Scots thought about this development. Might it, for example, have hindered other branches of the royal kindred from successfully prosecuting their claims to be inaugurated because that scenario would have resulted in Scots temporarily losing a key component that must have greatly influenced foreign policy?

In addition, it is during the reigns of the sons of King Máel Coluim mac Donnchada and Queen Margaret that Scotia begins to emerge as a unified and important power in north Britain, but we should never forget that this perception may just be in part a reflection of the survival of increasing amounts of written evidence from *c.*1100 onwards. Equally, the sons of Máel Coluim mac Donnchada and Margaret are allocated a huge amount of credit by historians for bringing communities of reformed monks to Scotia, thereby dragging the Church of Scotia into mainstream western Christendom. Nevertheless, it is interesting to note that King Alexander I was an equal opportunist who also chose to boost a much older saintly cult alongside his introduction of Augustinian canons, and his invention of tradition about royal burials on Iona was a masterpiece of diplomacy. Here was a king determined to maintain a balance of old and new.

Bibliography

Primary printed sources

F. J. Amours (ed.), *The Original Chronicle of Andrew of Wyntoun*, 6 vols (Edinburgh, 1908).

A. O. Anderson (ed.), *Scottish Annals from English Chroniclers* (London, 1908).

A. O. Anderson (ed.), *Early Sources of Scottish History, A.D. 500 to 1286*, 2 vols (Edinburgh, 1922).

A. O. Anderson and M. O. Anderson (eds), *The Chronicle of Melrose from the Cottoniam Manuscript, Faustina B ix in the British Museum: a complete and full-size facsimile in collotype* (London, 1936).

A. O. Anderson and M. O. Anderson (eds), *Adomnan's Life of Columba* (Edinburgh, 1961).

M. O. Anderson (ed.), *A Scottish Chronicle known as the Chronicle of Holyrood* (Edinburgh, 1938).

M. O. Anderson, *Kings and Kingship in Early Scotland*, rev. edn (Edinburgh, 1980).

Thomas Arnold (ed.), *Symeonis Monachi Opera et Collectanea* (Edinburgh, 1868).

Bannatyne Club, *Registrum Episcopatus Moraviensis* (Edinburgh, 1837).

Bannatyne Club, *Liber Sancte Marie de Melros*, 2 vols (Edinburgh, 1837).

Bannatyne Club, *Liber Cartarum Sancte Crucis* (Edinburgh, 1840).

Bannatyne Club, *Liber Cartarum Prioratus Sancti Andree* (Edinburgh, 1841).

Bannatyne Club, *Registrum de Dunfermelyn* (Edinburgh, 1842).

Bannatyne Club, *Registrum Episcopatus Glasguensis*, 2 vols (Edinburgh, 1843).

Bannatyne Club, *Liber Ecclesie de Scon* (Edinburgh, 1843).

Bannatyne Club, *Liber S. Marie de Calchou*, 2 vols (Edinburgh, 1846).

Bannatyne Club, *Registrum S. Marie de Neubotle* (Edinburgh, 1846).

Bannatyne Club, *Liber S. Marie de Dryburgh* (Edinburgh, 1847).

Bannatyne Club, *Registrum Episcopatus Brechinensis*, 2 vols (Aberdeen, 1856).

G. W. S. Barrow (ed.), *Regesta Regum Scottorum* i: *The Acts of Malcolm IV* (Edinburgh, 1960).

G. W. S. Barrow (ed.) with W. W. Scott, *Regesta Regum Scottorum* ii: *The Acts of William I* (Edinburgh, 1971).

G. W. S. Barrow (ed.), *The Charters of David I* (Woodbridge, 1999).

Robert Bartlett (ed. and trans.), *The Miracles of St Æbbe of Coldingham and St Margaret of Scotland* (Oxford, 2003).

Edward A. Bond (ed.), *Chronica Monasterii de Melsa*, 2 vols (London, 1867).

Dauvit Broun and Julian Harrison, *The Chronicle of Melrose Abbey, a Stratigraphic Edition* (Chippenham, 2007).

M. Chibnall (ed. and trans.), *The Ecclesiastical History of Orderic Vitalis*, 6 vols (Oxford, 1968–80).

Bertram Colgrave and R. A. B. Mynors (eds), *Bede's Ecclesiastical History of the English People* (Oxford, 1969).

Beltram Colgrave (ed.), *Vita Sancti Wilfridi Episcopi Eboracensis* (Cambridge, 1985)

Lord Cooper, *Regiam Majestatem and Quoniam Attachiamenta* (Edinburgh, 1947).

D. E. Easson and Angus Macdonald (eds), *Charters of the Abbey of Inchcolm* (Edinburgh, 1938).

Douglas Museum, *Chronica Regum Manniae et Insularum* (Oxford, 1924).

D. H. Farmer (ed.), *Ecclesiastic History of the English People*, rev. edn (London, 1990).

Alison Finlay, *Fagrskinna, a Catalogue of the Kings of Norway* (Leiden, 2004).

A. P. Forbes, *Kalendars of Scottish Saints* (Edinburgh, 1872).

J. France (ed.), *Historiarum Libri Quinque*, 2 vols (Oxford, 1989).

A. Martin Freeman (ed.), *The Annals of Connacht, 1224–1544* (Dublin, 1983).

G. N. Garmonsway (ed. and trans.), *The Anglo-Saxon Chronicle* (Guernsey, 1994).

William Hennessy (ed. and trans.), *Chronicon Scotorum. A Chronicle of Irish Affairs from the Earliest Times to A.D. 1135, with a Supplement, containing the Events from 1141 to 1150* (London, 1866).

William Hennessy (ed. and trans.), *The Annals of Loch Cé. A Chronicle of Irish Affairs from A.D. 1014 to A.D. 1590*, 2 vols (Dublin, 1871).

William Hennessy and B. MacCarthy (eds and trans.), *Annála Uladh: Annals of Ulster; otherwise Annála Senait, Annals of Senait; a Chronicle of Irish Affairs from A.D. 431 to A.D. 1540*, 4 vols (Dublin, 1887–1901).

R. Howlett, *Chronicles of the Reigns of Stephen, Henry II, and Richard I*, 4 vols (London, 1884–89).

B. T. Hudson, *Prophecy of Berchán* (Westport, 1996).

H. James (ed.), *Facsimiles of National Manuscripts of Scotland*, 3 vols (Edinburgh, 1870).

Dafydd Jenkins (ed.), *The Law of Hywel Dda* (Llandysul, 1986).

Fergus Kelly, *A Guide to Early Irish Law* (Dublin, 1988).

Fergus Kelly, *Early Irish Farming* (Dublin, 1998).

John T. Koch, *The Gododdin of Aneírín* (Cardiff, 1997).

Archibald C. Lawrie, *Early Scottish Charters prior to 1153* (Glasgow, 1905).

Henry R. Luard (ed.), *Flores Historiarum*, 3 vols (London, 1890).

Joseph R. Lumby (ed.), *Polychronicon Ranulphu Higden Monachi Cestrensis*, 8 vols (London, 1882).

Joseph R. Lumby (ed.), *Chronicon Henrici Knighton, Monachi Leycestrensis*, 2 vols (London, 1889).

S. Mac Airt and G. Mac Niocaill (eds), *The Annals of Ulster (To AD 1131)* (Dublin, 1983).

S. Mac Airt (ed.), *The Annals of Inisfallen (MS. Rawlinson B. 503)* (Dublin, 1988).

Maitland Club, *Cartularium Comitatus de Levenax ab initio seculi decimi tertii usque ad annum M.CCC.XCVIII* (Edinburgh, 1833).

P. McGurk (ed.), *The Chronicle of John of Worcester: The Annals from 1067 to 1140 with the Gloucester Interpolations and the Continuation to 1141*, iii (Oxford, 1998).

John Morris, *Nennius: British History and the Welsh Annals* (Chichester, 1980).

Kathleen Mulchrone (ed.), *The Book of Lecan. Leabhar Mór Mhic Fhir Bhisigh Leacain, with Descriptive Introduction and Indexes*, facsimile edn (Dublin, 1937).

Dennis Murphy (ed.), *The Annals of Clonmacnoise, being Annals of Ireland from the Earliest Period to A.D. 1408, translated into English by Conell Mageoghagan* facsimile edn (Llanerch, 1993).

R. A. B. Mynors and Rodney M. Thomson (eds), *Gesta Regum Anglorum*, 2 vols (Oxford, 1998 and 1999).

J. F. Niermeyer, *Mediae Latinitatis Lexicon Minus* (Leiden, 1976).

M. A. O'Brien (ed.), *Corpus Genealogiarum Hiberniae* i (Dublin, 1962).

John O'Donovan (ed.), *Annála Ríoghachta Éireann. Annals of the Kingdom of Ireland by the Four Masters, to the Year 1616*, 7 vols (Dublin, 1851).

D. Ó Murchadha, *The Annals of Tigernach, Index of Names* (Dublin, 1997).

Padraig O'Riain (ed.), *Corpus Genealogiarum Sanctorum Hiberniae* (Dublin, 1985).

Anne O'Sullivan (ed.), *The Book of Leinster, formerly Lebar na Núachongbála*, 7 vols (Dublin, 1983).

Hermann Pálsson and Paul Edwards (trans.), *Orkneyinga Saga* (London, 1978).

Georg Heinrich Pertz (ed.), *Monumenta Germaniae Historica Scriptores*, 5 vols (Hannover, 1872–).

Joan Newlon Radner, *Fragmentary Annals of Ireland* (Dublin, 1978).

Henry T. Riley (ed.), *Chronica Monasterii S. Albani Historia Anglicana*, 2 vols (London, 1863 and 1864).

Royal Irish Academy, *Dictionary of the Irish Language Based Mainly on Old and Middle Irish Materials* (Dublin, 1913–75).

Richard Sharpe (trans.), *Adomnan of Iona: Life of St Columba* (London, 1995).

Lachlan Shaw, *The History of the Province of Moray*, 3 vols (Edinburgh, 1775).

F. J. H. Skene (ed.), *Liber Pluscardensis*, 2 vols (Edinburgh, 1877–80).

W. F. Skene (ed.), *Collectanea de Rebus Albanicus* (Edinburgh, 1839).

W. F. Skene (ed.), *Chronicles of the Picts, Chronicles of the Scots and Other Memorials of Scottish History* (Edinburgh, 1867).

W. F. Skene (ed.), *Johannis de Fordun Chronica Gentis Scotorum* (Edinburgh, 1871).

J. Stevenson (ed.), *Liber Vitæ Ecclesiæ Dunelmensis; nec non obituaria duo ejusdem ecclesiæ* (Edinburgh, 1841).

Whitley Stokes (trans.), *The Annals of Tigernach*, 2 vols, facsimile edn (Felinfach, 1993).

Louise W. Stone and William Rothwell, *Anglo-Norman Dictionary*, 8 vols (London, 1977–1992).

E. L. G. Stones (ed.), *Anglo-Scottish Relations, 1174–1328* (Oxford, 1965).

J. Stuart (ed.), *The Book of Deer* (Edinburgh, 1869).

William Stubbs (ed.), *Gesta Regis Henrici Secundi Benedicti Abbatis*, 2 vols (London, 1867).

William Stubbs (ed.), *Chronica Magistri Rogeri de Houedene*, 4 vols (London, 1868–71).

William Stubbs (ed.), *Memoriale Fratris Walteri de Coventria*, 2 vols (London, 1872–73).

William Stubbs (ed.), *The Historical Works of Gervase of Canterbury*, 2 vols (London 1879–80).

Charles Sandford Terry, *A Catalogue of the Publications of Scottish Historical and Kindred Clubs and Societies, and of the Volumes Relative to Scottish History Issued by His Majesty's Stationery Office, 1780–1908* (Glasgow, 1909).

Augustinus Theiner, *Vetera Monumenta Hibernorum et Scotorum* (Rome, 1864).

Edward M. Thompson (ed.), *Adae Murimuth Continuatio Chronicarum* (London, 1889).

Lewis Thorpe (ed. and trans.), *The History of the Kings of Britain* (Middlesex, 1966).

Two Cartularies of the Augustinian Priory of Brunton and the Cluniac Priory of Montacute in the County of Somerset (Somerset, 1894).

Elisabeth M. C. Van Houts (ed. and trans.), *The Gesta Normannorum Ducum of William of Jumièges, Orderic Vitalis, and Robert of Torigni*, 2 vols (Oxford, 1992 and 1995).

D. E. R. Watt (general ed.), *Scotichronicon*, 9 vols (Aberdeen, 1987–98).

D. E. R. Watt and N. F. Shead (eds), *The Heads of Religious Houses in Scotland from Twelfth to Sixteenth Centuries* (Edinburgh, 2001).

D. E. R. Watt and A. L. Murray, *Fasti Ecclesiae Scoticanae Medii Aevi Ad Annum 1638* (Bristol, 2003).

J. Wilson (ed.), *The Register of the Priory of St Bees* (Durham, 1915).

Secondary printed sources

J. Aikman (trans.), *The History of Scotland*, 6 vols (Glasgow and Edinburgh, 1827–29).

Nick Aitchison, *Macbeth, Man and Myth* (Sparkford, 1999).

John Bannerman, *Studies in the History of Dalriada* (Edinburgh, 1974).

A. D. M. Barrell, *Medieval Scotland* (Cambridge, 2000).

G. W. S. Barrow, *Robert Bruce and the Community of the Realm of Scotland*, 3rd edn (Edinburgh, 1988).

G. W. S. Barrow, *The Kingdom of the Scots*, 2nd edn. (Chippenham, 2003).

G. W. S. Barrow, *The Anglo-Norman Era in Scottish History* (Oxford, 1980).

G. W. S. Barrow, *Kingship and Unity* (Edinburgh, 1981).

Robert Bartlett, *England under the Norman and Angevin Kings, 1075–1225* (Padstow, 2000).

John Blair, *The Church in Anglo-Saxon Society* (Oxford, 2005).

Peter Hunter Blair, *The World of Bede* (London, 1970).

Robert L. Bremner, *The Norsemen in Alban* (Glasgow, 1923).

Dauvit Broun, *The Irish Identity of the Kingdom of the Scots* (Woodbridge, 1999).

Dauvit Broun, *Scottish Independence and the Idea of Britain* (King's Lynn, 2007).

P. Hume Brown, *History of Scotland to the Present Time*, 3 vols (Cambridge, 1911).

J. H. Burton, *The History of Scotland*, 8 vols (Edinburgh, 1897).

Francis J. Byrne, *Irish Kings and High-Kings*, 2nd edn (Dublin, 2001).

Martin Carver, *Portmahomack: Monastery of the Picts* (Bodmin, 2008).

George Chalmers, *Caledonia: or a Historical and Topographical Account of North Britain*, 8 vols, new edn (Paisley, 1887).

Pierre Chaplais, *English Diplomatic Practice in the Middle Ages* (London, 2003).

T. Charles-Edwards, *Early Irish and Welsh Kingship* (Oxford, 1993).

T. O. Clancy (ed.), *The Triumph Tree* (Edinburgh, 1998).

Archibald Constable (trans. and ed.), *A History of Greater Britain as well England as Scotland* (Edinburgh, 1892).

Ian B. Cowan and David E. Easson, *Medieval Religious Houses (Scotland)*, 2nd edn (London, 1976).

Ian B. Cowan (ed. James Kirk), *The Medieval Church in Scotland* (Edinburgh, 1995).

Barbara Crawford, *Scandinavian Scotland* (Exeter, 1987).

Barbara Crawford, *Earl and Mormaer, Norse-Pictish relationships in Northern Scotland* (Rosemarkie, 1995).

David Crouch, *The Image of Aristocracy in Britain*, 1000–1300 (London, 1992).

David Dalrymple, *Annals of Scotland* (Edinburgh, 1776).

R. R. Davies, *The First English Empire* (Oxford, 2000).

Wendy Davies, *Patterns of Power in Early Wales* (Oxford, 1990).

Alastair Dawson, *So Foul and Fair a Day* (Glasgow, 2009).

W. Croft Dickinson, *Scotland from the Earliest Times to 1603* (Alva, 1961).

Robert A. Dodgshon, *Land and Society in Early Scotland* (Oxford, 1981).

Gordon Donaldson, *Scotland: The Shaping of the Nation* (Newton Abbot, 1974).

Gordon Donaldson, *Scottish Church History* (Edinburgh, 1985).

David N. Dumville, *The Churches of North Britain in the First Viking-Age* (Stranraer, 1997).

A. A. M. Duncan, *Scotland: The Making of the Kingdom* (Edinburgh, 1975).

A. A. M. Duncan, *The Kingship of the Scots, 842–1292* (Edinburgh, 2002).

Dorothy Dunnett, *King Hereafter* (London, 1982).

Edward Dwelly, *Illustrated Gaelic-English Dictionary* (new edition, Edinburgh, 2001).

Christopher Dyer, *Making a Living in the Middle Ages* (London, 2002).

Colmán Etchingham, *Church Organisation in Ireland AD650 to 1000* (Kildare, 1999).

Robin Frame, *The Political Development of the British Isles, 1100–1400* (Bristol, 1995).

James E. Fraser, *From Caledonia to Pictland, Scotland to 795* (Edinburgh, 2009).

Antonia Gransden, *Historical Writing in England, c.550–c.1307*, 2 vols (London, 1974 and 1982).

Judith A. Green, *Henry I, King of England and Duke of Normandy* (Cambridge, 2006).

D. M. Hadley, *The Northern Danelaw, Its Social Structure, c.800–1100* (Trowbridge, 2000).

D. M. Hadley, *The Vikings in England: Settlement, Society and Culture* (Manchester, 2006).

Della Hooke, *The Landscape of Anglo-Saxon England* (Wiltshire, 1998).

Benjamen T. Hudson, *Kings of Celtic Scotland* (Westport, 1994).

Lois L. Huneycutt, *Matilda of Scotland* (Woodbridge, 2003).

Nils Hybel and Bjørn Poulsen, *The Danish Resources, c.1000–1550* (Leiden, 2007).

Cosmo Innes, *Scotland in the Middle Ages* (Edinburgh, 1860).

Cosmo Innes, *Lectures on Scotch Legal Antiquities* (Edinburgh, 1872).

Thomas Innes, *A Critical Essay on the Ancient Inhabitants of the Northern Parts of Britain, or Scotland*, 2 vols (London, 1729).

Thomas Innes, *The Civil and Ecclesiastical History of Scotland* (Aberdeen, 1853).

Kenneth Jackson, *The Gaelic Notes in the Book of Deer* (Cambridge, 1972).

William E. Kapelle, *The Norman Conquest of the North. The Region and Its Transformation, 1000–1135* (London, 1979).

Andrew Lang, *A History of Scotland*, 4 vols (Edinburgh, 1900–07).

R. E. Latham, *Revised Medieval Latin Word-List* (London, 1965).

Charlton T. Lewis and Charles Short, *A Latin Dictionary* (London, 1966).

Philip Line, *Kingship and State Formation in Sweden, 1130–1290* (Leiden, 2007).

H. R. Loyn, *The Governance of Anglo-Saxon England 500–1087* (Suffolk, 1984).

Adam Lucas, *Wind, Water, Work: Ancient and Medieval Milling Technology* (Leiden, 2006).

Paul MacCotter, *Medieval Ireland: Territorial, Political and Economic Divisions* (Bodmin, 2008).

John Macintosh, *The History of Civilisation in Scotland*, 4 vols, new edn (Paisley, 1892).

F. W. Maitland, *Domesday Book and Beyond. Three Essays in the Early History of England* (Cambridge, 1907).

R. Andrew McDonald, *The Kingdom of the Isles* (East Linton, 1997).

R. Andrew McDonald, *Outlaws of Medieval Scotland* (East Linton, 2003).

Peter G. B. McNeil and Hector L. MacQueen (eds), *Atlas of Scottish History to 1707* (Edinburgh, 1996).

T. E. McNeill, *Anglo-Norman Ulster: The History and Archaeology of an Irish Barony, 1177–1400* (Edinburgh, 1980).

A. D. Morrison-Low (ed.), R. D. Connor and A. D. C. Simpson, *Weights and Measures in Scotland: A European Perspective* (East Linton, 2004).

Cynthia J. Neville, *Native Lordship in Anglo-Norman Scotland: The Earldoms of Strathearn and Lennox, 1170–1350* (Dublin, 2005).

W. F. H. Nicolaisen, *Scottish Place-Names* (London, 1976).

R. Nicholson, *Scotland, The Later Middle Ages* (Edinburgh, 1974).

Richard Oram, *The Lordship of Galloway* (Edinburgh, 2000).

Richard Oram, *David I, the King Who Made Scotland* (Stroud, 2004).

David R. Perry, *Castle Park, Dunbar: Two Thousand Years on a Fortified Headland* (Edinburgh, 2000).

John Pinkerton, *An Enquiry into the History of Scotland*, 2 vols, new edn (Edinburgh, 1814).

Charles Rampini, *History of Moray and Nairn* (Edinburgh, 1897).

Anna Ritchie (ed.), *Govan and its Early Medieval Sculpture* (Somerset, 1994).

R. L. G. Ritchie, *The Normans in Scotland* (Edinburgh, 1954).

E. William Robertson, *Scotland under her Early Kings*, 2 vols (Edinburgh, 1862).

Mairi Robinson, *The Concise Scots Dictionary* (Aberdeen, 1985).

D. W. Rollason, *Cuthbert Saint and Patron* (Durham, 1987).

W. D. H. Sellar (ed.), *Moray: Province and People* (Edinburgh, 1993).

John Shaw, *Water Power in Scotland, 1550–1870* (Edinburgh, 1984).

I. G. Simmons, *An Environmental History of Great Britain, from 10,000 Years Ago to the Present* (Edinburgh, 2001).

W. F. Skene, *Celtic Scotland: A History of Ancient Alban*, 3 vols (Edinburgh, 1876–80).

W. F. Skene, *The Highlanders of Scotland*, 2 vols (London, 1837).

T. C. Smout, Alan R. MacDonald and Fiona Watson, *A History of the Native Woodlands of Scotland, 1500–1920* (Trowbridge, 2005).

A. P. Smyth, *Warlords and Holy Men* (Edinburgh, 1984).

Frank Stenton, *Anglo-Saxon England*, 3rd edn (Oxford, 1971).

Richard Tipping, *Bowmont: An Environmental History of the Bowmont Valley and the Northern Cheviot Hills, 10000 BC–AD 2000* (Malta, 2010).

W. J. Watson, *The History of the Celtic Place-Names of Scotland* (Edinburgh, 1926).

W. J. Watson, *Bardachd Ghaidhlig: Specimens of Gaelic Poetry, 1550–1900*, 2nd edn (Stirling, 1932).

W. J. Watson, *Scottish Place-Name Papers* (London, 2002).

Bruce Webster, *Medieval Scotland, The Making of an Identity* (Hong Kong, 1997).

Chris Wickham, *Studies in Italian and European Social History, 400–1200* (London, 1994).

Alan J. Wilson, *St Margaret Queen of Scotland* (Bristol, 1993).

Angus J. Winchester, *Landscape and Society in Medieval Cumbria* (Edinburgh, 1987).

Alex Woolf, *From Pictland to Alba, 789–1070* (Edinburgh, 2007)

Articles and pamphlets

E. W. M. Balfour-Melville, 'A Northamptonshire Estate of Malcolm Canmore', *SHR*, 27, 1948, 101–02.

Malcolm Bangor-Jones, 'Land Assessments and Settlement History in Sutherland and Easter Ross', in John R. Baldwin (ed.), *Firthlands of Ross and Sutherland* (Edinburgh, 1986), 153–68.

Malcolm Bangor-Jones, 'Ouncelands and Pennylands in Sutherland and Caithness', in L. J. Macgregor and B. E. Crawford (eds), *Ouncelands and Pennylands* (St Andrews, 1987), 13–23.

J. Bannerman, 'MacDuff of Fife', in A. Grant and K. Stringer (eds), *Medieval Scotland* (Cambridge, 1993), 20–38.

J. Bannerman, 'The Scots Language and Kin-based Society', in Derick S. Thomson (ed.), *Gaelic and Scots in Harmony* (Glasgow, 1990), 1–19.

G. W. S. Barrow, 'The Beginnings of Feudalism in Scotland', *Bulletin of the Institute of Historical Research*, 29, 1956, 1–31.

G. W. S. Barrow, 'Rural Settlement in Central and Eastern Scotland: The Medieval Evidence', *Scottish Studies*, 6, 1962, 123–44.

G. W. S. Barrow, 'The Pattern of Lordship and Feudal Settlement in Cumbria', *Journal of Medieval History*, 1, 1975, 117–38.

G. W. S. Barrow, 'MacBeth and other Mormaers of Moray', in Loraine MacLean (ed.), *The Hub of the Highlands* (Lerwick, 1975), 109–23.

G. W. S. Barrow, 'Some problems in twelfth- and thirteenth-century Scottish history', *Scottish Genealogist*, 25, 1978, 99–100.

G. W. S. Barrow, 'The Sources for the History of the Highlands in the Middle Ages', in Loraine MacLean (ed.), *The Middle Ages in the Highlands* (Inverness, 1981), 11–22.

G. W. S. Barrow, 'The Childhood of Scottish Christianity: A Note on Some Place-name Evidence', *Scottish Studies*, 27, 1983, 1–15.

G. W. S. Barrow, 'David I of Scotland (1124–1153): the Balance of Old and New' (Stenton Lecture, 1984).

G. W. S. Barrow, 'Badenoch and Strathspey, 1130–1312: 1 Secular and political', *Northern Scotland*, 8, 1988, 1–16.

G. W. S. Barrow, 'Badenoch and Strathspey, 1130–1312: 2 The Church', *Northern Scotland*, 9, 1989, 1–16.

G. W. S. Barrow, 'The Kings of Scotland and Durham', in Gerald Bonner, David Rollason and Clare Stancliff (eds), *St Cuthbert, His Cult and His Community to AD 1200* (Woodbridge, 1989), 311–23.

Joseph Betty, 'Downlands', in Joan Thirsk (ed.), *The English Rural Landscape* (Oxford, 2000), 27–49.

John Bintliff, 'Settlement and Territory: A Socio-ecological Approach to the Evolution of Settlement Systems', in Geoff Bailey, Ruth Charles and Nick Winder (eds), *Human Ecodynamics* (Exeter, 2000).

Stein Bondevik, John Inge Svendsen, and Jan Mangerud, 'Distinction between the Storegga Tsunami and the Holocene Marine Transgression in Coastal Basin Deposits of Western Norway', *Journal of Quaternary Science*, 13:6, 1998, 529–37.

Nicholas Brooks, 'The Development of Military Obligations in Eighth- and Ninth-century England', in Peter Clemoes and Kathleen Hughes (eds), *England before the Conquest: Studies in Primary Sources Presented to Dorothy Whitelock* (Cambridge, 1971), 69–84.

Dauvit Broun, 'The Origin of Scottish Identity', in C. Bjorn, A. Grant and K. Stringer (eds), *Nations, Nationalism and Patriotism in the European Past* (Copenhagen, 1994), 35–55.

Dauvit Broun, 'The Origin of Scottish Identity in its European Context', in Barbara E. Crawford (ed.), *Scotland in Dark Age Europe* (St Andrews, 1994), 21–32.

Dauvit Broun, 'Defining Scotland and the Scots Before the Wars of Independence', in Dauvit Broun, R. J. Finlay and Michael Lynch (eds), *Image and Identity, The Making and Re-making of Scotland Through the Ages* Edinburgh, 1998), 4–17.

Dauvit Broun, 'A New Look at *Gesta Annalia* Attributed to John of Fordun', in Barbara E. Crawford (ed.), *Church, Chronicle and Learning in Medieval and Early Renaissance Scotland* (Edinburgh, 1999), 9–30.

Dauvit Broun, 'Dunkeld and the Origin of Scottish Identity', in Dauvit Broun and Thomas Owen Clancy (eds), *Spes Scotorum, Hope of Scots Saint Columba, Iona and Scotland* (Edinburgh, 1999), 95–114.

Dauvit Broun, 'The Seven Kingdoms in De situ Albanie: A Record of Pictish Political Geography or Imaginary Map of ancient Alba?', in Edward J. Cowan and R. Andrew McDonald (eds), *Alba* (East Linton, 2000), 24–42.

Dauvit Broun, 'The Church of St Andrews and its Foundation Legend in the Early Twelfth Century: Recovering the Full Text of Version A of the Foundation Legend', in Simon Taylor (ed.), *Kings, Clerics and Chronicles in Scotland, 500–1297* (Bodmin, 2000), 108–14.

Dauvit Broun, 'The Welsh Identity of the Kingdom of Strathclyde *c.*900–*c.*1200', *The Innes Review*, 55:2, 2004, 111–80.

Dauvit Broun, 'Alba: Pictish Homeland or Irish Offshoot?', in Pamela O'Neill (ed.), *Exile and Homecoming. Papers from the Fifth Australian Conference of Celtic Studies* (Sydney, 2005), 234–75.

Dauvit Broun, 'Contemporary Perspectives on Alexander II's Succession: The Evidence of King-lists', in R. D. Oram (ed.), *The Reign of Alexander II, 1214–49* (Leiden, 2005), 79–98.

Dauvit Broun, 'The Property Records in the Book of Deer as a Source for Early Scottish Society', in Katherine Forsyth (ed.), *Studies on the Book of Deer* (Bodmin, 2008), 313–62.

Michael Brown, 'Regional Lordship in North-east Scotland: The Badenoch Stewarts', *Northern Scotland*, 16, 1996, 31–53.

David H. Caldwell, 'The Monymusk Reliquary: the *Breccbennach* of St Columba?', *PSAS*, 131, 2001, 267–82.

N. Cameron, 'St Rule's Church, St Andrews, and Early Stone-built Churches in Scotland', *PSAS*, 124, 1994, 367–78.

S. Carter, R. Tipping, D. Davidson, D. Lang, and A. Tyler, 'A Multiproxy Approach to the Function of Postmedieval Ridge-and-Furrow Cultivation in Upland North Britain', *The Holocene*, 7, 1997, 447–56.

T. M. Charles-Edwards, 'Kinship, Status and the Origins of the Hide', *Past and Present*, 56, 1972, 3–33.

T. M. Charles-Edwards, 'Picts and Scots', *The Innes Review*, 59:2, Autumn 2008, 168–88.

Thomas O. Clancy, 'Annat in Scotland and the Origins of the Parish', *Innes Review*, 46, 1995, 91–115.

Thomas O. Clancy, 'Iona, Scotland, and the Céli Dé', in Barbara E. Crawford (ed.), *Scotland in Dark Age Britain* (St Andrews, 1996), 111–30.

Thomas O. Clancy, 'Columba, Adomnán and the Cult of Saints in Scotland', *Innes Review*, 48:1, 1997, 1–26.

Thomas O. Clancy, 'Scotland, the 'Nennian' recension of the *Historia Brittonum*, and the *Lebor Bretnach*', in Simon Taylor (ed.), *Kings, Clerics and Chronicles in Scotland, 500–1297* (Bodmin, 2000), 87–107.

Georges Comet, 'Technology and Agricultural Expansion in the Middle Ages: The Example of France North of the Loire', in Greville Astill and John Langdon (eds), *Medieval Farming and Technology: The Impact of Agricultural Change in Northwest Europe* (Leiden, 1997), 12–39.

Edward J. Cowan, 'The Scottish Chronicle in the Poppleton Manuscript', *The Innes Review*, 32, 1981, 3–21.

Edward J. Cowan, 'Myth and Identity in Early Medieval Scotland', *Scottish Historical Review*, 63, 1984, 111–35.

Edward J. Cowan, 'The Historical Macbeth', in W. D. H. Sellar (ed.), *Moray: Province and People* (Edinburgh, 1993), 117–42.

Richard Cox, 'Modern Scottish Gaelic Reflexes of Two Pictish Words: **pett* and **lannerc*', *Nomina*, 20, 1997, 47–58.

Barbara E. Crawford, 'The Earldom of Caithness and the Kingdom of Scotland, 1150–1266', *Northern Scotland*, 2, 1974–75, 97–118.

Barbara E. Crawford and Simon Taylor, 'The Southern Frontier of Norse Settlement in North Scotland', *Northern Scotland*, 23, 2003, 1–76.

Barbara E. Crawford, *The Govan Hogbacks and the Multi-Cultural Society of Tenth-Century Scotland* (Glasgow, 2005).

Althea Davies, 'Upland Agriculture and Environmental Risk: A New Model of Upland Land-use Based on High Spatial-Resolution Palynological Data from West Affric, NW Scotland', *The Journal of Archaeological Science*, 34, 2007, 2053–63.

Althea Davies and Fiona Watson, 'Understanding the Changing Value of Natural Resources: An Integrated Palaeoecological-Historical Investigation into Grazing-Woodland Interactions by Loch Awe, Western Highlands of Scotland', *Journal of Biogeography*, 34:10, 2007, 1777–91.

Wendy Davies, 'Celtic Kingships in the Early Middle Ages', in Anne J. Duggan (ed.), *Kings and Kingship in Medieval Europe* (London, 1993), 101–24.

A. G. Dawson, D. Long, D. E. Smith, 'The Storegga Slides: Evidence from Eastern Scotland for a Possible Tsunami', *Marine Geology*, 82, 1988, 271–76.

Alastair G. Dawson, Kieran Hickey, John McKenna and D. L. Fraser, 'A 200-Year Record of Gale Frequency, Edinburgh, Scotland: Possible Link with High-magnitude Volcanic Eruptions', *The Holocene*, 7, 1997, 337–41.

Alastair G. Dawson, Sue Dawson, and Stein Bondevik, 'A Late Holocene Tsunami at Basta Voe, Yell, Shetland Isles', *Scottish Geographical Journal*, 122:2, 2006, 100–8.

A. G. Dawson, K. Hickey, P. A. Mayewski and A. Nesje, 'Greenland (GISP2) Iice Core and Historical Indicators of Complex North Atlantic Climate Changes during the Fourteenth Century', *The Holocene*, 17, 2007, 427–34.

W. Croft Dickinson, 'The Toschederach', *Juridicial Review*, 53, 1941, 85–111.

Piers Dixon, 'The Medieval Peasant Building in Scotland: The Beginning and End of Crucks', in Jan Klápště (ed.), *The Rural House from the Migration Period to the Oldest Still Standing Buildings* (Prague: Tiskárna Zaplatílek, 2002), 187–200.

T. N. Dixon, 'A Survey of Crannogs in Loch Tay', *PSAS*, 112, 1982, 17–38.

S. T. Driscoll, 'The Archaeology of State Formation in Scotland', in W. S. Hanson and E. A. Slater (eds), *Scottish Archaeology: New Perceptions* (Aberdeen, 1991), 81–111.

Stephen T. Driscoll, 'Formalising the Mechanisms of State Power: Early Scottish Lordship from the Ninth to the Thirteenth Centuries', in Sally Foster, Allan Macinnes, and Ranald MacInnes (eds), *Scottish Power Centres from the Early Middle Ages to the Twentieth Century* (Glasgow, 1998), 1–31.

Stephen T. Driscoll, *Govan from Cradle to Grave* (Glasgow, 2004).

Andrew J. Dugmore, Douglas M. Borthwick, Mike J. Church, Alastair Dawson, Kevin J. Edwards, Christian Keller, Paul Mayewski, Thomas H. McGovern, Kerry-Anne Mairs, and Guðrún Sveinbjarnardóttir, 'The Role of Climate in Settlement and Landscape Change in the North Atlantic Islands: An Assessment of Cumulative Deviations in High-Resolution Proxy Climate Records', *Human Ecology*, 35, 2007, 169–78.

David N. Dumville, 'Kingship, Genealogies and Regnal Lists', in P. H. Sawyer and I. N. Wood (eds), *Early Medieval Kingship* (Leeds, 1977), 72–104.

David N. Dumville, 'Cethri Prímchenéla Dáil Riata', *Scottish Gaelic Studies*, 20, 2000, 170–91.

David N. Dumville, 'Ireland and North Britain in the Earlier Middle Ages: Contexts for *Míniugud Senchusa Fher nAlban*', in Colm Ó Baoill and Nancy R. McGuire (eds), *Rannsachadh na Gàidhlig 2000* (Aberdeen, 2002), 185–212.

David N. Dumville, 'The Chronicle of the Kings of Alba', in Simon Taylor (ed.), *Kings, Clerics and Chronicles in Scotland, 500–1297* (Cornwall, 2000), 73–86.

A. A. M. Duncan and A. L. Brown, 'Argyll and the Isles in the earlier Middle Ages', *PSAS*, 90, 1956–57, 192–220.

A. A. M. Duncan, 'The Laws of Malcolm MacKenneth', in A. Grant and K. Stringer (eds), *Medieval Scotland* (Cambridge, 1993), 239–73.

A. A. M. Duncan, 'Yes, the Earliest Scottish Charters', *SHR*, 78:1, April 1999, 1–38.

A. A. M. Duncan, 'The Foundation of St Andrews Cathedral Priory, 1140', *SHR*, 84:1, April 2005, 1–37.

Alexis Easson, 'Ouncelands and Pennylands in the West Highlands', in L. J. Macgregor and B. E. Crawford (eds), *Ouncelands and Pennylands* (St Andrews, 1987), 1–12.

William Elder-Levie, 'The Scottish Davach or Dauch', *SGS*, 3, part 2, April 1931, 99–110.

Eric Fernie, 'Early Church Architecture in Scotland', *PSAS*, 116, 1986, 393–411.

Katherine Forsyth, 'Evidence of a Lost Pictish Source in the *Historia Regum Anglorum* of Symeon of Durham', in Simon Taylor (ed.), *Kings, Clerics and Chronicles in Scotland, 500–1297* (Bodmin, 2000), 19–34.

Katherine Forsyth, Dauvit Broun and Thomas Clancy, 'The Property Records: Text and Translation', in Katherine Forsyth (ed.), *Studies on the Book of Deer* (Bodmin, 2008), 131–44.

Sinéad Ní Ghabhláin, 'The Origin of Medieval Parishes in Gaelic Ireland: The Evidence from Kilfenora', *The Journal of the Royal Society of Antiquaries of Ireland*, 126, 1996, 37–61.

W. Gillies, 'Some thoughts on the toschederach', *SGS*, 17, 1996, 128–42.

A. Grant, 'Thanes and Thanages, from the Eleventh to the Fourteenth Centuries', in A. Grant and K. Stringer (eds), *Medieval Scotland* (Cambridge, 1993), 39–81.

A. Grant, 'The Province of Ross and the Kingdom of Alba', in Edward J. Cowan and R. Andrew McDonald (eds), *Alba* (East Linton, 2000), 88–126.

Alexander Grant, 'The Construction of the Early Scottish State', in J. R. Maddicott and D. M. Palliser (eds), *The Medieval State: Essays Presented to James Campbell* (London, 2000), 47–72.

Alexander Grant, 'Service and Tenure in Late Medieval Scotland, 1314–1475', in Anne Curry and Elizabeth Matthew (eds), *Concepts and Patterns of Service in the Later Middle Ages* (Woodbridge, 2000), 145–79.

Judith Green, 'King Henry I and Northern England', *Transactions of the Royal Historical Society*, 17, 2007, 35–55.

Nicky Gregson, 'The Multiple Estate Model: Some Critical Questions', *Journal of Historical Geography*, 11:4, 1985, 339–51.

Colin A. Gresham, 'Medieval parish and township boundaries in Gwynedd', *Bulletin of the Board of Celtic Studies*, 34, 1987, 137–49.

Dawn M. Hadley, 'Multiple Estates and the Origins of the Manorial Structure of the Northern Danelaw', *Journal of Historical Geography*, 22:1, 1996, 3–15.

M. A. Hall, 'Of Holy Men and Heroes: The Cult of Saints in Medieval Perthshire', *The Innes Review*, 56:1, 2005, 61–88.

Matthew H. Hammond, 'Ethnicity and the Writing of Medieval Scottish History', *SHR*, 85, 2006, 1–27.

Máire Herbert, 'Rí Éirenn, Rí Alban: Kingship and Identity in the Ninth and Tenth Centuries', in Simon Taylor (ed.), *Kings, Clerics and Chronicles in Scotland, 500–1297* (Bodmin, 2000), 62–72.

D. Herlihy, 'The Carolingian Mansus', *The Economic History Review*, new ser. 13, 1, 1960, 79–89.

C. Warren Hollister, 'The Five-hide Unit and the Old English Military Obligation', *Speculum*, 36, i, 1961, 61–74.

Della Hooke, 'Pre-Conquest Woodland: Its Distribution and Usage', *Agricultural History Review*, 37.2, 1989, 113–29.

Benjamin T. Hudson, 'The Language of the Scottish Chronicle and its European Context', *Scottish Gaelic Studies*, 18, 1998, 57–73.

Benjamin T. Hudson, 'The Scottish chronicle', *SHR*, 77, 2: no. 204, 1998, 129–61.

K. H. Jackson, 'The Duan Albanach', *SHR*, 36, 1957, 125–37.

Andrew Jones, 'Land Measurement in England, 1150–1350', *Agricultural History Review*, 27:1, 1979, 10–18.

G. R. J. Jones, 'The Multiple Estate as a Model Framework for Tracing Early Stages in the Evolution of Rural Settlement', in F. Dussart (ed.), *L'Habitat et les Paysages Ruraux d'Europe* (Liège, 1971), 251–67.

G. R. J. Jones, 'Multiple Estates and Early Settlement', in P. H. Sawyer (ed.), *Medieval Settlement* (Norwich, 1976), 15–40.

G. R. J. Jones, 'The Models for Organisation in *Llyfr Iorwerth* and *Llyfr Cynferth*', *Bulletin of the Board of Celtic Studies*, 39, 1992, 95–118.

Rhys Jones, 'The Formation of the *Cantref* and the Commote in Medieval Gwynedd', *Studia Celtica*, 32, 1998, 169–77.

Rhys Jones, 'Problems with Medieval Welsh Local Administration – The Case of the *Maenor* and the *Maenol*', *Journal of Historical Geography*, 24, 2, 1998, 135–46.

Rhys Jones, 'Changing Ideologies of Medieval State Formation: The Growing Exploitation of Land in Gwynedd *c*.1100–*c*.1400', *Journal of Historical Geography*, 26, 4, 2000, 505–16.

Roy Loveday, 'Where Have all the Neolithic Houses Gone? Turf – An Invisible Component', *Scottish Archaeological Journal*, 28:2, 2006, 81–104.

Alan Macquarrie, 'The Kings of Strathclyde, *c*.400–1018', in Alexander Grant and Keith J. Stringer (eds), *Medieval Scotland: Crown, Lordship and Community* (Edinburgh, 1993), 1–19.

Alan Macquarrie, *Crosses and Upright Monuments in Strathclyde: Typology, Dating and Purpose* (Glasgow, 2006).

Gilbert Márkus, 'Dewars and Relics in Scotland: some clarifications and questions', *The Innes Review*, 60:2, 2009, 95–144.

D. P. Kirby, 'Strathclyde and Cumbria: A Survey of Historical Development to 1092', *Transactions of the Cumberland and Westmorland Antiquarian and Archaeological Society*, 62, 1962, 77–94.

Andrew McKerral, 'Ancient Denominations of Agricultural Land in Scotland: A Summary of Recorded Opinions, with Some Notes, Observations and References', *PSAS*, 78, 1943–44, 39–80.

Andrew McKerral, 'What was a Davach?', *PSAS*, 82, 1947–48, 49–52.

Andrew McKerral, 'The Lesser Land and Administrative Divisions in Celtic Scotland', *PSAS*, 85, 1950–51, 52–64.

John MacQueen, 'Pennyland and Davoch in South-western Scotland: A Preliminary Note', *Scottish Studies*, 23, 1979, 69–74.

Basil Megaw, 'Notes on "Pennyland and Davoch in South-western Scotland" ' *Scottish Studies*, 23, 1979, 75–77.

Edward Meldrum, 'Medieval Castles and Towerhouses', in Loraine MacLean (ed.), *The Hub of the Highlands* (Lerwick, 1975), 141–54.

Ralph Mentel, 'The Twelfth-Century Predecessors of Glasgow Cathedral and their Relationship with Jedburgh Abbey', in Richard Fawcett (ed.), *Medieval Art and Architecture in the Diocese of Glasgow* (Leeds, 1998), 42–49.

M. Morgan, 'The Organization of the Scottish Church in the Twelfth Century', *TRHS*, 4th ser., 24, 1947, 135–50.

Kenji Nishioka, 'Scots and Galwegians in the "Peoples Address" of Scottish Royal Charters', *SHR*, 87, 2008, 206–32.

Patrick Nugent, 'The Dynamics of Parish Formation in High Medieval and Late Medieval Clare', in Elizabeth FitzPatrick and Raymond Gillespie (eds), *The Parish in Medieval and Early Modern Ireland: Community, Territory and Building* (Bodmin, 2006), 186–210.

Donnchadh Ó Corráin, 'Irish Regnal Succession, A Reappraisal', *Studia Hibernica*, 11, 1971, 7–39.45

Donnchadh Ó Corráin, 'Creating the Past: The Early Irish Genealogical Tradition', *Peritia*, 12, 1998, 177–208.

Donnchadh Ó Corráin, 'The Vikings in Scotland and Ireland in the Ninth Century', *Peritia*, 12, 1998, 296–339.

Richard D. Oram, 'Davachs and Pennylands in South-west Scotland: A Review of the Evidence', in L. J. Macgregor and B. E. Crawford (eds), *Ouncelands and Pennylands* (St Andrews, 1987), 46–59.

Richard D. Oram, 'Gold into Lead? The State of Early Medieval Scottish History', in Terry Brotherstone and David Ditchburn (eds), *Freedom and Authority* (East Linton, 1999), 32–41.

Richard D. Oram, 'David I and the Scottish Conquest and Colonisation of Moray', *Northern Scotland*, 19, 1999, 1–19.

Richard D. Oram, 'Continuity, Adaptation and Integration: The Earls and Earldom of Mar, *c.*1150–*c.*1300', in Steve Boardman and Alasdair Ross (eds), *The Exercise of Power in Medieval Scotland c.1200–1500* (Chippenham, 2003), 46–66.

Richard D. Oram, 'A Fit and Ample Endowment? The Balmerino Estate, 1228–1603', in R. Oram, *Life on the Edge: The Cistercian Abbey of Balmerino, Fife (Scotland)* (Forges-Chimay, 2008), 61–80.

H. O'Regan, A. Turner, and R. Sabin, 'Medieval Big Cat Remains from the Royal Menagerie at the Tower of London', *International Journal of Osteoarchaeology*, 16, 2006, 385–94.

A. J. Piper, 'The First Generations of Durham Monks and the Cult of St Cuthbert', in Gerald Bonner, David Rollason and Clare Stancliff (eds), *St Cuthbert, His Cult and His Community to AD 1200* (Woodbridge, 1989), 437–46.

Anna Ritchie, *Hogback Gravestones at Govan and Beyond* (Glasgow, 2004).

M. J. H. Robson, 'Territorial Continuity and the Administrative Division of Lochtayside, 1769', *Scottish Geographical Magazine*, 106:3, 1990, 174–85.

John Rogers, 'The Formation of Parishes in Twelfth-century Perthshire', *Records of the Scottish Church History Society*, 27, 1997, 68–96.

Alasdair Ross, 'The Dabhach in Moray: A New Look at an Old Tub', in Alex Woolf (ed.), *Landscape and Environment* (St Andrews, 2006), 57–74.

Alasdair Ross, 'The Identity of the "Prisoner of Roxburgh": Malcolm Son of Alexander or Malcolm Macheth?' in S. Arbuthnot and K. Hollo (eds), *Fil súil nglais – A Grey Eye Looks Back: A Festschrift in Honour of Colm Ó Baoill* (Ceann Drochaid, 2007), 269–82.

Alasdair Ross, 'Moray, Ulster, and the MacWilliams', in Seán Duffy (ed.), *The World of the Galloglass: Kings, Warlords and Warriors in Ireland and Scotland, 1200–1600* (Bodmin, 2007), 24–44.

W. D. H. Sellar, 'Celtic Law and Scots Law: Survival and Integration', *Scottish Studies*, 29, 1989, 1–27.

Norman Shead, 'The Origins of the Medieval Diocese of Glasgow', *SHR*, 48, 1969, 220–25.

Grant G. Simpson and Bruce Webster, 'Charter Evidence and the Distribution of Mottes in Scotland', in K. J. Stringer (ed.), *Essays on the Nobility of Medieval Scotland* (Edinburgh, 1985), 1–24.

Christoph Sonnlechner, 'The Establishment of New Units of Production in Carolingian Times: Making Early Medieval Sources Relevant for Environmental History', *Viator*, 35, 2004, 21–37.

J. H. Stevenson, 'The Laws of the Throne – Tanistry and the Introduction of the Law of Primogeniture', *SHR*, 25, 1928, 1–12.

Keith Stringer and Alexander Grant, 'Scottish Foundations', in A. Grant and K. J. Stringer (eds), *Uniting the Kingdom* (London, 1995), 85–108.

'Supplement to the *Scottish Historical Review*, List of Abbreviated Titles of the Printed Sources of Scottish History to 1560', *SHR*, 1963.

Alice Taylor, '*Leges Scocie* and the Lawcodes of David I, William the Lion and Alexander II', *SHR*, 88, 2009, 207–88.

Simon Taylor, 'Place-names and the Early Church in Eastern Scotland', in Barbara E. Crawford (ed.), *Scotland in Dark Age Britain* (Aberdeen, 1996), 93–110.

Simon Taylor, 'Generic-Element Variation, with Special Reference to Eastern Scotland', *Nomina*, 20, 1997, 5–22.

Simon Taylor, 'The Coming of the Augustinians to St Andrews and Version B of the St Andrews Foundation Legend', in Simon Taylor (ed.), *King, Clerics and Chronicles in Scotland, 500–1297* (Bodmin, 2000), 115–123.

Simon Taylor, 'The Toponymic Landscape of the Gaelic Notes in the Book of Deer', in Katherine Forsyth (ed.), *Studies on the Book of Deer* (Bodmin, 2008), 275–308.

Alan Thacker, 'Lindisfarne and the Origins of the Cult of St Cuthbert', in Gerald Bonner, David Rollason and Clare Stancliff (eds), *St Cuthbert, His Cult and His Community to AD 1200* (Woodbridge, 1989), 103–22.

Alan Thacker, 'Dynastic Monasteries and Family Cults, Edward the Elder's Sainted Kindred', in N. J. Higham and D. H. Hill (eds), *Edward the Elder, 899–924* (Suffolk, 2001), 248–63.

F. W. L. Thomas, 'Ancient Valuation of Land in the West of Scotland: Continuation of "What is a Pennyland?" ', *PSAS*, 20, 1885–86, 200–13.

Amanda M. Thomson, Ian A. Simpson, and Jennifer L. Brown, 'Sustainable Rangeland Grazing in Norse Faroe', *Human Ecology*, 33, no. 5, 2005, 737–61.

William P. L. Thomson, 'Some Settlement Patterns in Medieval Orkney', in Colleen E. Batey, Judith Jesch and Christopher D. Morris (eds), *The Viking Age in Caithness, Orkney, and the North Atlantic* (Edinburgh, 1993), 340–48.

William P. L. Thomson, 'Ouncelands and Pennylands in the West Highlands and Islands', *Northern Scotland*, 22, 2002, 27–43.

Richard Tipping, 'The Form and Fate of Scotland's Woodlands', *PSAS*, 124, 1994, 1–54.

Richard Tipping, 'Climatic Variability and 'Marginal' Settlement in Upland British Landscapes: A Re-evaluation', *Landscapes*, 3(2), 2002, 10–29.

Richard Tipping, Althea Davies and Eileen Tisdall, 'Long-term Woodland Dynamics in West Glen Affric, Northern Scotland', *Forestry*, 79(3), 2006, 351–59.

Kenneth Veitch, ' 'Replanting Paradise': Alexander I and the Reform of Religious Life in Scotland', *Innes Review*, 52, no. 2, 2001, 136–66.

Kenneth Veitch, 'Kinloss Abbey, 1229', *Innes Review*, 55, no. 1, 2004, 10–33.

Valerie Wall, 'Malcolm III and the Foundation of Durham Cathedral', in Gerald Bonner, David Rollason and Clare Stancliff (eds), *St Cuthbert, His Cult and His Community to AD 1200* (Woodbridge, 1989), 325–37.

Björn Weiler, 'William of Malmesbury on Kingship' *History*, 10, 2005, 3–22.

G. Whittington, 'Placenames and the Settlement Pattern of Dark-age Scotland', *PSAS*, 106, 1974–75, 99–110.

Ian D. Whyte, 'Shielings and the Upland Pastoral Economy of the Lake District in Medieval and Early Modern Times', in John R. Baldwin and Ian D. Whyte (eds), *The Scandinavians in Cumbria* (Leeds, 1985), 103–18.

Angus J. L. Winchester, 'The Multiple Estate: A Framework for the Evolution of Settlement in Anglo-Saxon and Scandinavian Cumbria', in John R. Baldwin and Ian D. Whyte (eds), *The Scandinavians in Cumbria* (Leeds, 1985), 89–102.

Gareth Williams, 'Land Assessment and the Silver Economy of Norse Scotland', in Gareth Williams and Paul Bibire (eds), *Sagas, Saints and Settlements* (Leiden, 2004), 65–104.

Gareth Williams, 'The *Dabhach* Reconsidered: Pre-Norse or Post-Norse?', *Northern Studies*, 37, 2003, 17–31.

P. A. Wilson, ' 'On the Use of the Terms "Strathclyde" and "Cumbria" ', *Transactions of the Cumberland and Westmorland Antiquarian and Archaeological Society*, 66, 1966, 57–92.

Alex Woolf, 'The 'Moray Question' and the Kingship of Alba in the Tenth and Eleventh Centuries', *SHR*, 79, 2000, 145–64.

Alex Woolf, 'Dún Nechtain, Fortriu and the Geography of the Picts', *SHR*, 85, 2006, 182–201.

Alex Woolf, 'The Cult of Moluag, the See of Mortlach and Church Organisation in Northern Scotland in the Eleventh and Twelfth Centuries', in Sharon Arbuthnot and Kaarina Hollo (eds), *Fil súil nglais A Grey Eye Looks Back* (Ceann Drochaid, 2007), 299–310.

Alex Woolf, *Where was Govan in the Early Middle Ages?* (Glasgow, 2007).

Patrick Wormald, 'The Emergence of the *Regnum Scottorum*: a Carolingian hegemony?', in Barbara E. Crawford (ed.), *Scotland in Dark Age Britain* (St Andrews, 1996), 131–60.

Patrick Wormald, 'Anglo-Saxon Law and Scots Law', *SHR*, 88, 2009, 192–206.

Websites

http://www.trin.cam.ac.uk/chartwww/eSawyer.99/eSawyer2.html

http://www.ucc.ie/celt/published/G100002/index.html

http://ads.ahds.ac.uk/catalogue/adsdata/PSAS_2002/pdf/arch_scot_vol_002/02_480_489.pdf

http://stat-acc-scot.edina.ac.uk/link/1834-45/Kincardine/Fordoun/

http://canmore.rcahms.gov.uk/en/site/36385/details/court+stane/

http://pastscape.english-heritage.org.uk/

http://www.oxforddnb.com

http://www.isle-of-man.com/manxnotebook/manxsoc/msvol22/

Theses

A. R. Easson, 'Systems of Land Assessment in Scotland before 1400', unpublished PhD thesis, University of Edinburgh, 1986.

John M. Rogers, 'The Formation of the Parish Unit and Community in Perthshire', unpublished PhD thesis, University of Edinburgh, 1992.

Alasdair Ross, 'The Province of Moray, c.1000 to 1230', 2 vols, unpublished PhD thesis, University of Aberdeen, 2003.

D. E. G. Williams, 'Land Assessments and Military Organisation in the Norse Settlements in Scotland, c.900–1266 AD', unpublished PhD thesis, University of St Andrews, 1996.

Index